NO JUSTICE FOR AGNES

No Justice for Agnes

The Strange Death of Agnes Polreis and the Sensational South Dakota Murder Trials of Emma Kaufmann

Wayne Fanebust

THE CENTER FOR WESTERN STUDIES
Augustana University
2020

Publication made possible with funding by the Anne King Publications Endowment and Ronald R. Nelson Publications Endowment in the Center for Western Studies and by the National Endowment for the Humanities. The publisher wishes to acknowledge the assistance of Liz Cisar, Craig Johnson, and Hal Thompson.

ISBN: 978-0-931170-91-1

Library of Congress Control Number: 2020931827

Number 17 in the Prairie Plains Series, Second Printing 2023

The Center for Western Studies (CWS) at Augustana University seeks to improve the quality of social and cultural life in the Northern Plains, achieve a better understanding of the region, its heritage, and its resources, and stimulate interest in the solution to regional problems. The Center promotes understanding of the region through its archives, library, museum and art exhibitions, publications, courses, internships, and public affairs programming. It is committed, ultimately, to defining the contribution of the Northern Plains to American civilization.

In 2019 and 2020, the Center celebrates 55 years since its founding in 1964 by writer and English professor Herbert Krause and 50 years since its establishment in 1970 by the Augustana University board of trustees.

Visit the Fantle Building for The Center for Western Studies
Augustana University, 2121 S. Summit Avenue, Sioux Falls, South Dakota
605-274-4007 • cws@augie.edu • www.augie.edu/cws • Facebook • Twitter

Front cover: Agnes Polreis, *Sioux City Journal* (left); Emma Kaufmann, *Parkston Advance* (right); Kaufmann Mansion, *Center for Western Studies* (middle).

Back cover: (left to right) George W. Egan, *Library of Congress*; First Emma Kaufmann Trial Jury, *Moody County Historical Society*; George Rice, *Moody County Historical Society*

Printed in the United States of America by
Anundsen Publishing Company

Dedicated

to the memory of my friend

J. Bruce Blake

1931-2017

Contents

Preface and Acknowledgments

Many years ago, back in the 1970s when I was a "wannabe" writer, I met Cathy Joslyn. She was a history buff who had a keen interest in South Dakota history. She owned and operated a used bookstore in Sioux Falls called Prairie Winds. I was a frequent customer and we got to know each other. One day during the course of talking about local history, Cathy mentioned the Kaufmann murder trials, something that I knew nothing about. I soon learned that the trials were grand spectacles, the subject of outrage, scandal, and controversy in the early twentieth century—an out-of-control, wild spasm of sensationalism that erupted in South Dakota, but was not confined to that state.

It began in 1906, when Emma Kaufmann, a woman of wealth, was arrested and charged with murdering her live-in maid, sixteen-year-old Agnes Polreis, a recent immigrant whose family was living in Parkston, South Dakota. Cathy said that she and a friend, Freda Hosen, were researching the story with a view to writing a book about the most sensational murder mystery in South Dakota history.

I was immediately taken by the strange story. During the course of our discussion, Cathy said that she had gone to Flandreau, South Dakota, where both murder trials had occurred, for the purpose of interviewing Bessie Pettigrew, then a lady in her nineties. Bessie would have been a very young woman in 1906, with family connections to Flandreau, when the explosive news about the death of Agnes Polreis hit the presses of the state and nation. But when Cathy asked Miss Pettigrew a question about the infamous murder case, the old woman, with a stern face of disapproval, augmented by the pointing of her finger, responded with a warning. "Don't you dare meddle in that matter; you have no business researching or writing about that. Some things are better left alone. You leave it alone."

What was she so upset about? What was it that she believed should be kept secret—and why? What was it about the great Kaufmann scandal that riled an old woman long after all those who had played a role in the drama were dead? Bessie took her secrets to the grave, as did so many others. As a result, the answers to many questions will forever be a blank page, but from the time of my discussion of the Kaufmann case with Cathy, I was hooked. I was curious to know why the mere mention of the Kaufmann case angered Bessie Pettigrew. Why should the death of young Agnes Polreis remain a secret? Perhaps there was a story to tell here, before all interest and knowledge of the case disappeared into the mists of time.

Cathy and Freda never did write a book about the Kaufmann murder trials, but I thank them for their interest and effort. Other writers before them, some with first-hand knowledge of the case, failed to include the Kaufmann case in their histories. Their attitude—like that of Bessie Pettigrew—was to leave it alone.

The disappearance of the trial records from the Moody County Courthouse in Flandreau sharply hints that an effort was made to hide the truth. I went to Flandreau and spoke to the court clerk, asking her if the county retained records of old cases. "We keep everything," was her reply. Then I told her I wanted to see the files on the Kaufmann murder trials. She recognized the name and said that some time back a reporter inquired about those records. The clerk said that she spent an entire day digging through the archives—but found nothing. Maybe there was a cover-up.

But the lack of court records failed to deter me. I am an ardent advocate for the underdog and for exposing and writing about the dark side of history, so I most eagerly and happily took on the challenge. And what you are about to read is the result of my research and analysis. I am proud to say that I have gone where no writer has gone before.

This book is for and about Agnes Polreis. This is her voice, painfully silenced in 1906. She was a victim of a social system, a legal system, and a medical profession that cared little for people like her. Her tragic death touched off a major fight among newspapers in South Dakota, and she became entangled in a web of ugly class warfare. The death of this little peasant girl who could barely speak English was so strong that it generated a force powerful enough to cause a United States senator to lose his seat.

She was used as a pawn by a newspaper editor who hated the rich. She was disrespected and marginalized by newspapers that favored the rich and saw her—an uneducated immigrant from a poor family—as a lesser being, an undesirable. Agnes' voice in the narrative may seem overpowered by the noise arising from the towering personalities of other figures, but she *is* the central figure in my story, *her* story.

It is also the story about Parkston, a small, southeastern South Dakota town in Hutchinson County. It was the people of Parkston who courageously stood up against the powerful men in Sioux Falls who wanted the tragedy to have a short life. Had not the Parkston folks stepped up and demanded a thorough investigation, the horrible details of Agnes' suffering and death may never have come to light.

In researching and writing the story of Agnes' short life and tragic death, I made important contacts from among the historical community. I had several good visits with Freda Hosen at her Sioux Falls home. She was very knowledgeable, interested, and helpful, and I thank her very much. Thanks also to Lora Gerlach from Parkston, who invited me into her home so I could take notes from the old binder of Parkston newspapers that she picked up at a rummage sale. Father John S. Rader at the Sacred Heart Catholic Church in Parkston was willing to let me see the burial records of Agnes and her family, and I thank him.

Another very important contact was Trista Friman, the Library Director at the Parkston Public Library. She eagerly assisted me with newspaper microfilm of the *Parkston Advance*, and I thank her very much. And it is a pleasure to extend a very special thanks to Joe Kirby from Sioux Falls for giving me a picture of his great-grandfather, Joe Kirby, and for reading the chapters about his illustrious relative's role in the Kaufmann murder cases.

Newspapers far and away provided the greatest amount of the research material because the delicate and scandalous subject matter had been studiously avoided by historians. Their lack of attention to this important story has only inspired me. Fortunately, the newspapers that reported in vivid detail on the crime scandal have been preserved on microfilm and are available at many libraries in the state. The key South Dakota libraries were Siouxland Libraries in Sioux Falls and the public libraries in Parkston, Mitchell, Yankton, and Vermillion. The South Dakota, Iowa, and Minnesota state historical societies also contributed valuable newspaper microfilm. I thank them all.

The easy access to the vast newspaper archive at the Library of Congress provided invaluable information that would have otherwise gone undiscovered. This treasure trove of information enabled me to flesh out the narrative with factual and colorful detail. While historians from the past may have wanted this story to disappear, this writer has resurrected the ugly and shocking details about the mysterious demise of an innocent girl whose American experience ended abruptly in a hopeless and painful death many miles from her home and the loving arms of her parents, who were unaware of her suffering.

I want to thank my good friend, the late Bruce Blake, for his interest in the great mystery that resulted in the placement of a historical marker on the old Kaufmann property in Sioux Falls. Thanks also to my friend and fellow writer David Swan for researching and writing the marker script and for the many "Kaufmann discussions." Thanks very much to Harry Thompson and the Center for Western Studies for taking on the task of publishing the book, our second collaboration.

Others that I want to remember and thank are Tom Maldari, Dave Davis, Cindy McFadden, Steve Bointe, and Bill Waggoner, my friends and colleagues at the Minnehaha County Historical Society, the Center for Western Studies, the Sioux Falls branch of Westerners International, the South Dakota State Historical Society, the Siouxland Heritage Museums, and the San Diego Independent Scholars.

To my dear friend and fellow artist Paula Habbena, thank you so very much for the careful and thoughtful reading and editing of the manuscript. Without your assistance and expertise, the entire project would have failed.

I also want to extend special thanks to Nita Habbena for her helpful insights and constructive comments.

And as always, I owe a special measure of gratitude to my family. Thanks to my brothers, sisters, in-laws, and cousins, all of whom have been faithful cheerleaders and readers. And finally, to my daughter Danae and my precious grandchildren, Angelina and Hunter, thanks for your love, support, and affection; if you could only hear the thunderous and everlasting applause I send your way.

Wayne Fanebust
Sioux Falls, South Dakota

Chapter 1

Pity the Poor Immigrant

Under the shadow of what may prove to be a most brutal murder, the people of this city [Sioux Falls] are dazed by revelations that make their blood run cold.

The Soo Critic
June 14, 1906

In June 1906 America crossed an important medical and political threshold, and in so doing, left behind what one writer described as "The Golden Age of Quackery." It had been a long and colorful age, one that started during the colonial period and then rolled on unfettered through the decades, the unscientific patent medicine business going unchallenged. Valued at tens of millions of dollars annually, the great "Medicine Show" shamelessly pranced out in front of an inept and largely unregulated medical profession. Then in June 1906 President Theodore Roosevelt signed into law the Pure Food and Drug Act to become effective on January 1, 1907.[1]

The federal government—that had for so long been small and weak and under the influence of corporate America—was starting to flex some newfound muscle for the benefit of the people. The makers and sellers of phony cures were given notice that they would be put out of business, and the medical profession was warned that it too was under new scrutiny. Good news for Americans but for one South Dakota girl, Agnes Polreis, a victim of a mysterious and tragic death, the bold measure came too late. The sixteen-year-old girl died before the historic bill became law.

Agnes Polreis,
Sioux City Journal, June 16, 1907.

Agnes Polreis came to America in 1905 from Bodersdorf, Hungary,[2] with her family, thus joining the countless millions of Europeans who crossed the Atlantic Ocean with their apprehensions and expectations. Like other immigrants, she was apprehensive because she was leaving behind, perhaps forever, all the people and things that were familiar, but also hopeful because America was the land of promise and opportunity. Her destination was Parkston, Hutchinson County, South Dakota, where other members of the Polreis family had settled and were prospering.

Parkston was a small prairie town in central South Dakota, platted in 1886 along the line of the Chicago, Milwaukee, and St. Paul Railroad. The town received some ready-made assets from Dakota City, a village located two and a half miles from Parkston. The railroad ignored Dakota City, a dot that barely had time to make the maps, so rather than try to compete with a new town with a train, the pragmatic merchants and others, including a newspaper, the *Parkston Advance,* decided that the reasonable course was to move to the railroad. The businessmen and townspeople eagerly put their buildings and futures on wheels—and Parkston was born. The only reminder that Dakota City once existed was a small cemetery of the same name.

The Polreis family, headed by John and his wife, Theresa, from Austria-Hungary, formed a small ripple in the huge wave of immigration from Eastern Europe. Agnes was the youngest of fourteen children of whom only six were living when they said good-bye to the old country.[3] They were part of the mass of people that followed the Irish, Germans, Scandinavians, Russians, and Italians, all of whom came to America in great numbers. America: the place of open borders where people of talent and ambition could get rich and where the ordinary poor could at least shed the last vestiges of peasantry.

Having relatives waiting for them meant that they would not be total strangers in a strange land. And upon reaching their destination, on November 1, 1905, the Polreis family took up residence with relatives on a farm just west of Parkston. It was a humble beginning, which promised little or nothing, but the Polreis family could count itself lucky to live near a small town at a time when thousands of other immigrants in eastern cities were living in squalor, the victims of discrimination, graft, oppression, and grinding poverty.

The Polreises were hard-working people who understood that nothing would be given to them. Rather, they would have to earn their way, and in a community of other thrifty and sturdy folks, they quickly gained a reputation as worthy citizens. But they could not realistically expect to be regarded as anything else. Because the Polreis family was clinging to the lower rung of the mobility ladder, their children, including Agnes, had little potential for finding wealth and fame, and had it not been for her tragic and shocking death, Agnes would most likely have been lost to history.

Agnes could speak very little English, and there would be no time or opportunity for her to learn a new language. Parkston had a school but education was not in her future. Like many other immigrant girls of limited means, she had to go to work instead of school. In a poor family, it was expected that able-bodied teenagers would work to augment their father's meager income. And it was common for immigrant girls to work as live-in maids and servants for wealthy people in the bigger towns and cities.

A steady flow of immigrants coming into South Dakota meant there were plenty of applicants to do housework. The newspapers were teeming with advertisements asking for "A Good Girl" to work in a home. The problem facing the wealthy was that there were never enough "good girls to go around." It was revealed that in cities such as Sioux Falls, where third-story attics meant that servant girls would sweat in the summer and shiver in the winter, the flow of lowly immigrant girls was never enough to meet the demand. Hence, many a matron was deprived of servants and thereby the status she desired and felt she deserved.

In 1907 a journalist addressed the issue of domestic shortages, along with the challenges faced by girls who chose to cross the Atlantic Ocean for the possibility of a better life in America. The writer postulated that it took five years for an immigrant girl from Europe to evolve into one of "Uncle Sam's own daughters." In the interim, she had to accept employment wherever it was available and to the extent possible—considering her intellect—learn to speak English and accept the customs and habits of native-born girls. Overall, "she must work out her own salvation."[4] And if she failed there were countless acres of dirt to cover her misfortune.

~

In 1906 Sioux Falls, with a population of approximately 12,000 people, was the "big city" in South Dakota. Located about seventy miles east of Parkston, the city had two daily newspapers and upscale neighborhoods where a hard-working girl, with references, would have no trouble finding a job. But Agnes didn't have to rely on a newspaper; a Parkston man took the liberty to recommend her to a business acquaintance in Sioux Falls.

Agnes had no choice, but she was willing to work, and the "butcher's family" in Parkston was her first employer in America. She worked there for seven weeks but she was not entirely satisfied. She wanted to work in a bigger town where the wages would be higher. A girl in the town of Mitchell, twenty miles north of Parkston, found a position for Agnes, and she was preparing to make the move when she learned that Moses and Emma Kaufmann, in Sioux Falls, had an opening for a live-in maid. She would be paid good wages to work in a nice home in the big city, where she would be "treated as if she was their own child." The recommendation came from William Moeller.[5]

What he didn't tell her was that, because she was living at a time when a boss had nearly absolute power, workers had no rights except the right to work so long as the boss was satisfied. A worker, especially a domestic, could be kicked to the curb without notice and with no recourse but to hit the street and find another job. Built into the system was an incredible incentive to work extra hard and tolerate abuse.

William Moeller ran a saloon in Parkston called the Sioux Falls Saloon.[6] He was acquainted with Moses Kaufmann, a Jewish immigrant from Germany who had come to America in 1875 at age 24.[7] Kaufmann had talent and prospered, and in 1906 he was an officer and director in the Sioux Falls Brewing Company. On a visit to Parkston, Kaufmann informed Moeller that he was looking for a maid to serve his wife at their residence in Sioux Falls. Moeller recommended Agnes. Although her parents approved of the arrangement, the girl "cried bitterly when she left" on the train.[8] Moses Kaufmann met Agnes at the Salem Depot, about midway between Parkston and Sioux Falls, and accompanied her the rest of the way to their destination because he didn't want her to "fall into bad hands."[9]

In Sioux Falls he introduced her to his wife, Emma, at their stately mansion at the corner of Summit Avenue and 7th Street. The house was built in 1888 at a cost of $10,000. In its annual, year-end "brag" article, the *Daily Argus-Leader* proudly informed its readers that the Kaufmann house was one of many fine residences completed in 1888, at the peak of the Dakota Boom. Designed by architect Joseph Schwartz, the Kaufmann mansion was declared to be among "the finest yet built in Dakota,"[10] a part of an exclusive neighborhood that today is known as the Cathedral Historic District. The house that Schwartz built was indeed a gem among gems, but it was destined to become the subject of wonder and intense, morbid curiosity.

Moses and Emma Kaufmann had been living in Sioux Falls since 1882. Emma was born in Missouri and spent her younger years in St. Louis with her adoptive parents, Jacob and Rosa Blum. Little is known about Emma's early years. It was reported that she was living with a "tribe of gypsies" when she was adopted by the Blums, a Jewish couple. And although she later married a Jewish man, Emma Kaufmann never "embraced Judaism."[11]

Emma's adopted mother, Rosa Blum, was the aunt of Moses Kaufmann and at some point took up residence with the Blums in St. Louis. When and where the young couple got married is unknown, but it was reported that Moses "wooed and won" her in the Blum home.[12]

Jacob Blum was born in Württemburg, Germany, in 1824 and came to America in 1865 with his wife when he was twenty-four years old, settling in New Jersey. From there the couple lived in Philadelphia, Pittsburgh, St. Louis, and Nebraska City, Nebraska. Throughout the long sojourn, Blum was a dealer in hides and wool, a business that he had pursued in Germany.[13]

~

The Kaufmanns' daughter had died as a child, but their son, Charles, born in December of 1885, was a college student in 1906. When Dana R. Bailey was collecting information on Sioux Falls citizens for his book on Minnehaha County history, he was unable to pin down Moses Kaufmann for even a brief interview. Therefore, Bailey conceded that Kaufmann's "early life is a sealed book."[14] He would always be a secretive man, even when flushed out of hiding by the dramatic events following the death of Agnes Polreis.

It was known that the Kaufmanns and the Blums moved from St. Louis to Nebraska City, where they had jointly engaged in business, but after their general store went bankrupt, the two couples came to Sioux Falls.[15] Kaufmann was not the kind of man to give up, and in April of 1885, the *Sioux Falls Daily Press* announced that "Mose Kauffman" [sic] was the new proprietor of the beer bottling department of the Sioux Falls Brewing Company. The new owner was called "one of the best known and most energetic business men of the city." It was fully expected that "Mr. Kauffman[n] will work up a big business." Kaufmann had also been working as a "general agent" for the brewing company, and would continue dealing in furs, hides, tallow, and pelts, "at the old stand."[16]

On March 6, 1886, the lives of Moses Kaufmann and his wife took a significant turn toward a prosperous future, when Kaufmann and Moriz Levinger, a native of Bavaria, assumed ownership and control of the Sioux Falls Brewing Company.[17] The brewery was one of Sioux Falls' oldest businesses, having been started on October 7, 1873, when John McClellan sold four hillside lots on north Main Avenue to two Yankton men. But it wasn't until the summer of 1874 that construction of the brewery started, and thereafter North Main Avenue was frequently called "brewery hill." The brewery was first operated by S. S. Nelson and George A. Knott. In 1875 C. K. Howard replaced Nelson, and the business was named George A. Knott & Company. It was eventually incorporated as the Sioux Falls Brewing Company.[18]

On March 2, 1886, the *Sioux Falls Daily Press* reported that John McClellan had applied for a court-appointed receiver for the Sioux Falls Brewery Company. Judge C. S. Palmer scheduled a hearing and then issued an order prohibiting the management of the company from disposing of any assets. On March 6 the parties appeared with their attorneys, and an arrangement was made with Moses Kaufmann and Moriz Levinger assuming management and control over the brewery. The receivership was canceled and everyone walked away happy.[19]

Advertisement for *Blue Label* beer, Sioux Falls Brewing and Malting Company, *Sioux Falls Daily Press*, October 4, 1908.

Moriz Levinger came to Sioux Falls in 1884 and worked for the company as a brewer. His expertise, combined with Kaufmann's business acumen and lobbying ability, brought the brewery to new prominence. Their beer was popular locally and sold throughout Dakota, as well as parts of Iowa, Minnesota, and Nebraska. The product of the brewer's art was once described as "strictly pure and can harm no one." Moreover their beer was "recommended time and again for persons out of health as a most beneficial tonic."[20]

In 1897 they experienced beer nirvana when their Blue Label brand hit the marketplace. It was a project that began in secret. An ace brewer from Chicago was hired by Kaufmann and Levinger to create a new brew. Using the best Canadian barley and Bohemian hops, he created a beer that caused a sensation among beer drinkers and other brewers. Blue Label was declared to be "the richest, finest, best flavored" beer to come out of South Dakota or "anywhere else."[21]

By 1906 Kaufmann and Levinger were millionaires thanks to sales of their "beneficial tonic." But first they had to wade through a flood of litigation concerning the ownership of the brewery as well as the legal authority to make beer. The complicated series of court cases that started in 1886 was finally concluded on March 3, 1894, at the state supreme court. The last case against the brewery came up in September 1890, a year after South Dakota became a state. The Law and Order League had started an action in circuit court to shut down the brewery as a "liquor nuisance" under a recently passed state law.

At the conclusion of the trial, Judge Frank R. Aikens ruled that the brewery was a nuisance, and therefore had to be shut down. The case went to the South Dakota Supreme Court, and in a strangely reasoned decision, the ruling of the lower court was reversed. Beer, wrote Justice Howard G. Fuller, was not covered by the statute because it was not truly an intoxicating liquor. He went on to state that many varieties of beer did not contain malt and therefore could not intoxicate. "We hold that the term 'beer' in the absence of evidence as to its quality or effect, does not import an intoxicating liquor."[22]

Levinger and Kaufmann were, at long last, free to brew and sell beer, and they embarked on a long and very profitable venture. Throughout the 1890s, while America was wallowing in a depression of historic proportions, the Sioux Falls brewery made money. So much so that in 1899 the company launched the construction of a massive new facility, six stories high, made of quartzite stone from an East Sioux Falls quarry.[23] It was a spare-no-expense project that promised to be the crown jewel of the business community, an architectural wonder, and a monument to America's love of beer and the entrepreneurial success of Kaufmann and Levinger.

~

On February 15, 1906, Agnes Polreis began her employment as the live-in servant of Emma Kaufmann. At a healthy 138 pounds, Agnes was a strong, attractive, well-adjusted girl with no history of medical problems when she entered the luxurious Kaufmann household. By June 1 she was dead and her body was unceremoniously shipped back to Parkston in the company of her brother-in-law, Andrew Sailor, in a coffin paid for by Moses Kaufmann. They traveled by train to Mitchell and by wagon the rest of the way.

Agnes died at the Sioux Falls Hospital, a medical facility located "away from the noise and dirt of the city," at the corner of 19th Street and Minnesota Avenue.[24] Dr. William A. Germain sent Agnes to the modest, wooden, two-story facility that in 1894 had been incorporated to care for the sick and injured, "not for private gain but for public good."[25] A major improvement in hospital care came about with the death that same year of Helen McKennan, a wealthy Sioux Falls woman. In her will she bequeathed $25,000 to the city of Sioux Falls to build a "free public hospital."[26] This was too late, however, to provide for the desperately ill Agnes Polreis.

Railroad depot in Parkston, South Dakota.
Courtesy Ed Monson Collection.

The well-respected Dr. Germain was summoned to the Kaufmann residence by Emma Kaufmann early on the morning of June 1, 1906, thus drawing him into what became one of the greatest crime scandals to ever wrap its coils around the state of South Dakota. Without examining Agnes, Germain wrapped her in Moses Kaufmann's coat and sent her to the Sioux Falls Hospital, where she died a few hours after her arrival. Already semi-conscious when treated by the hospital nurses, she said very little. Germain officially listed the cause of her death as "chronic anemia," with "diabetes and gangrene" as contributing causes.[27] Dr. A. Zetlitz of Sioux Falls, who "was called in shortly before the girl died," agreed with Dr. Germain.[28]

Since she had lived in anonymity, her death and burial drew very little attention. The *Argus-Leader*, a popular daily newspaper in Sioux Falls, didn't so much as give her a small obituary. When her death finally made it into print, newspapers misspelled her name. Her funeral, before her grieving family, at the Sacred Heart Catholic Church in Parkston, was followed by burial in the church cemetery. It was a sad and tender ritual that honored the short life of a young woman and it was, quite likely, and unwittingly, part of a cover-up. For shocking events following the funeral of Agnes Polreis suggest—and many believed—that certain people wanted to get her body in the ground as quickly as possible.

Although she died on June 1, the story did not break until the 9th and it was a Yankton, not a Sioux Falls, newspaper that blasted the opening salvo in a terrible affair that would long occupy the press throughout the state and many parts of the nation. "**PARKSTON EXCITED**" was the headline in the *Yankton Press and Dakotan*, for although Agnes was allowed to be buried with quiet dignity, people who viewed the body of "Miss Colreis," [sic] could not help but notice "some marks about the head and neck that seemed unnatural." Still, nothing was said because some felt that bringing it up would be insensitive to the grieving mother. But enough had been seen to arouse the curiosity and suspicious anger of the Parkston people who attended the funeral.[29]

At the outset it was believed that the priest who conducted the funeral service, Father J. J. Reiland, was the first to notice the marks. Despite having been told not to open the casket, Reiland did so in order to anoint Agnes' forehead with oil and so properly perform the rites of the dead. Having noticed the suspicious marks, he conveyed his concern to others after the service.

The editor of the *Parkston Advance*, however, tried to set the record straight: "The facts are that the wounds on the body were first discovered by Andrew Rauscher, and by him communicated to Father Reiland."[30] Rauscher was the local undertaker in charge of the body at the funeral. While he was "working over the body," he accidently moved a wreath of flowers from Agnes' head and saw a wound near her hairline.[31] Although admonished not to open the casket because of decomposition, Rauscher noticed a "disarrangement of the lid that made it advisable to remove it," and in so doing, he saw "bruised features . . . almost hidden by flowers."[32]

William Moeller, the Parkston saloon man, got the last word on the subject. In an interview with the *Argus-Leader*, Moeller insisted that it was his daughter—an intimate friend of Agnes—who first noticed the marks. "My daughter was so persistent in the claim that there were wounds on her head" that others were alerted, stated Moeller.[33] Miss Moeller had carefully studied the body of her friend, noticing that "from one finger the bone projected and that her hair was cut away." Others at church took note of the "disfigurements."[34] Suspicions were fully aroused and the mystery quickly deepened. Angry excitement raced breathlessly through the town of Parkston and beyond. An innocent and worthy young girl had died a strange death in Sioux Falls and people wanted answers.

Hutchinson County authorities were informed of the condition of the body and were convinced that action was needed. By their order and authority, the body of Agnes Polreis was exhumed and an autopsy was performed by two local doctors, Dr. G. A. Landmann and Dr. H. B. Schofield, the Hutchinson County physician. The examination revealed cuts, bruises, and gashes all over her head and body. Very noticeably, there were cuts on each shoulder, each over two inches long. "The edges of one were very clear cut as if made by a knife." These wounds appeared to be older than the wound on her head. The left knee of the dead girl was "red and greatly swollen." There was a contusion to the back of her skull, the bones of several fingers were broken, and "in many ways the body showed marks of extreme violence."[35]

The state's attorney for Hutchinson County, J. L. Quinn, wanted straight answers so he went to Sioux Falls. There, he paid a visit to the undertaker who prepared the body for burial.[36] At this point, Quinn was considering a case for murder.

A body buried with last rites was expected to remain in the ground. And whenever a body was exhumed, especially under suspicious circumstances, the event ignited the anger and morbid curiosity of the entire community. So it was with the people of Parkston.

"**SUSPECT MURDER**" was the headline for the article in the *Sioux Falls Daily Press*, on June 10. A *Press* interview with Parkston police justice John Fish summed up the anger and suspicion from among a Parkston committee of citizens that came to Sioux Falls: "We are firmly convinced that this young lady did not die from disease or natural causes, but from foul play." He went on to explain that when Agnes left Parkston she was "a healthy, robust girl weighting 135 pounds." Fish told the *Press* reporter that the parents of Agnes, "for the last two months," had "heard no word from her," then they were abruptly told that "she was dead and the body was awaiting [sic] in Sioux Falls." When Andrew Sailor, a brother-in-law of Agnes, went to Sioux Falls to take custody of her body, he was "advised that the coffin not be opened, but to bury her without looking at her," because she was already badly decomposed.[37] The entire matter looked and smelled like trouble.

~

Overall, the reporting on the early stages of the Kaufmann case by the *Yankton Press and Dakotan* was superior to the journalistic output of the Sioux Falls newspapers. The Yankton newspaper's reports were better organized, more readable, and contained more details than its rivals. So it came as a surprise to the public that on the 11th, the *Yankton Press and Dakotan* pulled in the reins, having learned that the *Daily Argus-Leader* in Sioux Falls was reporting the death of "Miss Bolris [sic]" in dramatically different terms.

In an interview, Dr. Germain said that Agnes had suffered from vertigo while doing housework for Emma Kaufmann, causing her to "fall down while crossing the floor." Mrs. Kaufmann said that Agnes fell down the stairs one night cutting her head and that a "large abscess later developed on one shoulder." Although Mrs. Kaufmann dressed her wounds and "did everything possible to help the girl," her condition got so bad that Dr. Germain was called. Both the Yankton and Sioux Falls newspapers concluded that the demise of the Parkston girl was very unfortunate but all very natural, and nothing was thought to be wrong until, according to Dr. Germain, "at Parkston someone started the rumor of foul play."

Pumped for more details, Dr. Germain stated emphatically: "There is absolutely no foundation whatever for the rumors of foul play. This girl died last Friday evening at the Sioux Falls hospital of anemia . . . accompanied by vertigo." He went on to say that "I found the patient suffering from anemia, which had developed into diabetis [sic] with grangrene [sic]. The fingers and the toes of the girl had begun to rot and slough off." Germain, a well-respected physician, was holding court and sounding off like a man who wanted to put the matter to rest once and for all. And to remove all clouds of doubt, he insisted that "had I been disposed to cover it up do you suppose I would have taken the girl to the hospital where she would be under the inspection of nurses and others?" He concluded his remarks by saying Agnes' parents and other Parkston people had come to a false conclusion.[38]

But late in the afternoon of June 11, a reporter for the *Argus-Leader* called on the Minnehaha County state's attorney, Alpha F. Orr, who said the matter was under investigation. Orr had reviewed the reports of five doctors who had conducted a second postmortem on the body, and he indicated that it was highly probable that arrests would be made the next day. Hutchinson County had taken another bold step, and officials were actively negotiating with the high-powered Sioux Falls attorney Joe Kirby to assist State's Attorney Quinn in making out a criminal case in the death of Agnes Polreis.

The reporter learned that Quinn and a contingent of Parkston's leading citizens had been in consultation with Orr and a case was rapidly developing. Dr. Sydney Olney and Dr. Thomas J. Billion, state medical examiners from Sioux Falls, were part of the conversation. The two Sioux Falls doctors, along with Dr. W. M. Quinn from Menno, South Dakota, and Parkston's Dr. Schofield and Dr. Landmann, had conducted a second autopsy on the body of Agnes Polreis. Her body had been taken from the grave a second time and carried to Parkston to a vacant building on Main Street where a postmortem was performed, the doctors removing her heart and brain.[39] They had concluded that her death was not the result of diabetes or vertigo, notwithstanding the reputation and opinion of Dr. Germain. Nevertheless, Dr. Olney cautiously advised that it would be best for all to withhold judgment until a full investigation was completed. But when asked point blank if he found any evidence that would support Germain's opinion that diabetes was the cause of death, he was constrained to say that "we searched for signs of diabetes with negative results."[40] Olney was also quoted as saying, "the aggregation of physical injuries might have produced death."[41]

Germain must have felt he was cornered and needed a way out. When pressed, he admitted that there were many wounds on Agnes' body and that he ordered the nurses to bathe her so he could then conduct an examination. But this never came to pass, he explained, because she died.[42] This weak explanation doesn't get him off the hook. His attitude toward the girl was one of utter contempt and a violation of the Hippocratic Oath.

Born in Delafield, Wisconsin, in 1855, Dr. Germain had developed a thriving medical practice in Sioux Falls, following his arrival in 1882. Educated in public schools, he went on to graduate from the University of Wisconsin at Madison. After teaching for two years, he studied medicine and graduated from Butler Medical College, in Butler, Indiana. In Sioux Falls his medical skills earned him a term as the president of the state board of health, and he once served as the local surgeon for the Chicago, Milwaukee, and St. Paul Railroad. Dr. Germain did very well financially and over the years became the owner of a large amount of residential property in Sioux Falls.[43] He was well-respected and, prior to the death of Agnes Polreis, his life had been free from scandal or suspicion.

Both Germain and Olney once belonged to a short-lived organization called the Minnehaha County Medical Society. The group was organized on May 16, 1883, and was remembered years later because of a fistfight between Dr. John C. Morgan and Dr. Edward Watson, the latter not a member of the society because he was so disagreeable. The two doctors duked it out "over a patient," whom both had been called to treat "in an emergency." They fought until Morgan's wooden leg came off. Watson left the area, but Morgan, who came to Sioux Falls in 1873, stayed and practiced medicine in the city, achieving a high level of respectability.[44]

~

As new information accompanied by wild speculation rushed in, Sioux Falls found itself a city transfixed with the Kaufmann case, a place where ordinary belief was suspended in an atmosphere of shock and horror. "**SENSATION IN SIOUX FALLS**" was the headline on the *Omaha Daily Bee*. This newspaper, followed by reports from other states, raised the level of excitement and speculation by hinting that a "woman and a man" were suspected of murdering a servant girl.[45] The conversation everywhere in Sioux Falls was about the awful calamity that had not only resulted in the horrible death of Agnes Polreis but had also dealt a severe blow to the tranquility and reputation of the city. No other event in the history of Sioux Falls, founded in 1856, had ever caused so much confusion, anger, and outrage.

Emma Kaufmann, *Parkston Advance,* Parkston, South Dakota, December 7, 1906.

The anger and hate was focused on Emma Kaufmann, and odd stories of her alleged evil nature began to surface. It was said that she had once mistreated her own elderly parents, "turning them out when they were too old to work."[46] But that seems unlikely because her adoptive father, Jacob Blum, was a successful businessman in Sioux Falls and he had worked until a few weeks before his death at eighty years of age, on October 22, 1904. Emma and her two stepsisters were at his deathbed.[47] It was an act that at the very least expressed respect.

The obituary of the venerable Jacob Blum was soon forgotten, while bits and pieces of the personal life of his adopted daughter were the talk of the town in the summer of 1906. The questions on the lips of the people seemed to be the following: What could have motivated anyone to wreak such cruelty and torture on an innocent girl? Emma Kaufmann was believed to be mentally unbalanced, but was she capable of torture and murder? And what was the actual cause of the death of the girl?

Reasonable minds may differ, but was Dr. Germain being reasonable? Or was he motivated by other influences? A journalist, who had apparently talked to Dr. Germain, concluded that the doctor attempted to "shield her [Emma Kaufmann]" by covering up her "neglect to secure proper medical treatment for the suffering girl until it was too late."[48] The twists and turns in this story kept coming.

The nineteenth century was a time of great inventions and great leaps forward in technology, communication, and transportation. These were the areas where money was spent and money was made. Had medical science kept pace with the great inventors and innovators, diagnosing disease and rendering proper treatment would have been done with much more compassion and accuracy. Most doctors were devoted to healing, but they lacked the knowledge that more advanced training would have made available to them, had more money and effort been directed into medical science.

Advancements in transportation and technology pointed toward a better life for all, but it was still a "man's world." The chauvinistic attitude trumped the need for changes in the political and social status concerning the role of women in America. For example, in 1906 women still did not have the right to vote, nor could they serve on juries. Their role in society was subservient to that of men. In fact, they were almost invisible, lacking an identity separate from their husbands and fathers. Newspapers invariably referred to a married woman with her husband's name and the title "Mrs.," implying a form of control and ownership. Unless something scandalous, tragic, or terrible happened in their lives, their names were rarely found in print. In the case of Emma Kaufmann and Agnes Polreis, their names were blazoned across the pages of America's newspapers and would remain the subject of headlines, articles, arguments, and speculation for years to come.

CHAPTER 2

A TALE OF HORROR AND BRUTALITY

Mrs. Emma Kaufmann [was] placed under arrest accused of the murder of her servant, Agnes Polreis.

Sioux Falls Daily Press
June 13, 1906

Over the course of nine days following the death of Agnes Polreis, her body was exhumed twice for two separate examinations by doctors and other concerned citizens who examined the cuts and wounds "which appeared on the body at the time it fell into the hands of the undertaker."[1] She was taken from the grave a third time so that undertaker LeRoy D. Miller, from Sioux Falls, could identify, for the record, the remains as that of the body he sent from Sioux Falls to Parkston.[2] With no further indignities to endure, Agnes was buried for the last time and allowed to rest among her fellow dead in the cemetery north of Parkston,.

While talking to a reporter, Miller denied with emphasis that he or anyone from his mortuary firm suggested or ordered that the "coffin not be opened" at the funeral. Miller, who was also the Minnehaha County Coroner, insisted that he "did not say a word that could be construed in that manner."[3] But Sioux Falls and Parkston residents were angry, and it was time for all those involved in the case to stake out their positions carefully and thoughtfully.

Miller was an astute businessman and professional, having come to Dakota Territory in 1870 as a small boy, and he was unlikely to make a stupid mistake. The family settled on a homestead in Wayne Township, Minnehaha County. After an education in country schools, Miller moved to Sioux Falls in 1887 where he was engaged in the livery and hack business. He started his undertaking business in 1903, next door to his stable, and over time, Miller Funeral Home would thrive and grow in both reputation and prominence.[4]

If Miller and others were looking for the matter to subside, however, they were greatly mistaken, because throughout South Dakota, curiosity, tension, and anger were on the rise as the strange death of Agnes Polreis became a scandal. A young immigrant girl had died a mysterious and seemingly tortuous death while in the employ of a wealthy and prominent family. Although the Kaufmanns were Jewish, the local newspapers showed no tendency toward anti-Semitism. Nor was there any public outcry of religious discrimination in Sioux Falls in the spring of 1906, a time when Jews were being massacred by mobs in Russia.

Of course the story didn't need anti-Semitism to make it sizzle. Everyone knew that the likeable and popular Moses Kaufmann was a millionaire married to a brooding, eccentric woman with few friends. She was a good musician but seldom played her piano.[5] A visitor to the Kaufmann house expressed surprise at the apparent lack of books.[6] It was said that she almost never read a newspaper, had no interest outside of her home, and would sit for hours in her rocking chair "absolutely motionless and in a sort of daze."[7] Other accounts reported that she had "a kindly countenance" and was not possessed of a face that "would portray the least inclination to cruelty."[8]

But the majority of the Sioux Falls community thought she was a strange woman who had turned a hard face to the world, whose solitary habits made her the subject of mystery and speculation. Other Jewish women in Sioux Falls left her alone.[9] Who knew what went on behind the closed doors of the Kaufmann mansion? Historically, large houses were often the subject of wonderment and suspicion, giving rise to tales of mystery and suspense. With arrests imminent, the *Press and Dakotan* warned that "whatever the outcome, South Dakota seems assured of a gigantic sensation."[10]

Sensing the weight of the oppressive mystery, the *Parkston Advance* demanded answers without delay. While that newspaper was not unduly shrill or biased, it painfully noted that Agnes was healthy when she entered into service at the Kaufmann mansion. The *Advance* did not outright accuse the Kaufmanns of anything criminal, but as the girl's employers, the paper felt they owed all concerned a full and honest explanation "about her condition and the causes from which she received the wounds."[11]

The *Sioux Falls Daily Press* was of the same opinion. The evidence gathered thus far was deemed to favor some kind of criminal misconduct. Young Peter Erickson, a hired hand of Moses Kaufmann, was questioned by the authorities but he "would give up nothing." His refusal to talk, however, didn't mean he was off the hook. The pressure on Erickson was equal to that on State's Attorney Alpha F. Orr. The Parkston citizens committee demanded that a "searching investigation be made and that the guilty parties be brought to account." It was quickly shaping up to be one of the "most sensational murder cases ever known in Sioux Falls"[12]—and a chance for local newspapers to increase circulation.

This would prove to be an accurate prediction and it started with the arrest of Emma Kaufmann. She was arrested without incident at 2 P.M. on June 12, and charged with the murder of Agnes Polreis on a complaint drafted by State's Attorney Orr. She was immediately taken to the courtroom of Police Justice A. B. Wheelock for a preliminary hearing. Mrs. Kaufmann was represented by Frank R. Aikens, one of Sioux Falls' leading attorneys. Aikens had served as a circuit court judge in Minnehaha County, and for that reason he was usually referred to in the news media as "Judge" Aikens.

Born in New York City in 1855, Aikens immersed himself in the study of law at an early age and was admitted to the New York State Bar in 1877. After practicing law for a short time in Rome, New York, he succumbed to the lure of the West and traveled to Dakota Territory in 1880, stopping first in Sioux Falls and then in Canton, the county seat of Lincoln County, where he opened a law office. He did quite well in Canton in both law and politics, serving in the territorial legislature. In 1889 he was appointed to the Dakota Territory

Supreme Court as an associate justice, and when in that same year South Dakota became a state, he was elected judge of the second circuit. When his term on the bench expired, he returned to law practice in Canton until 1895, when he moved to Sioux Falls and joined a law firm. As a judge, Aikens was described as a good listener and was always thoroughly prepared for each case that came before him.[13]

He formed a law partnership with Harry E. Judge, and by 1906, Aikens was one of the state's leading attorneys, known for his arm-twisting tenacity. He made money and a good reputation from handling numerous divorce cases "under the easy law" in South Dakota. A Sioux Falls newspaper man called him "A Fixed Stare" because of his penetrating eyes, which reflected a determination to break witnesses and persuade juries.[14] In today's parlance he would be known among other lawyers as a "leg biter." Aikens would prove to be a very zealous advocate for Emma Kaufmann, and the case made him a local celebrity.

The prosecution team at the preliminary hearing was led by special prosecutor Joseph "Joe" Kirby, hired by the people of Hutchinson County. Kirby was a native Iowan, born in 1863 and raised on a farm. Early on, he showed an interest in the law and studied for a time in New Hampton, Iowa. On June 28, 1886, he arrived in Sioux Falls and within thirty minutes, he was reading law books in the office of a law firm. He was admitted to practice on November 12, 1886, and came out of the gate in high gear. It was said that no other lawyer in Sioux Falls was "more untiring, indefatigable and persistent" than Joe Kirby, who never seemed to lack for clients.[15]

Endowed with a keen intellect, and destined to make his mark in the West, the heady young lawyer rode his bicycle from town to town trying cases. From time to time, he careened into bouts of bad behavior. In October of 1888 he attended a performance at the Sioux Falls opera house. "Between the acts," he "put on his hat and placed his foot on the railing." Seeing this, a disapproving police officer approached Kirby from behind, "shook his frame violently," and ordered the barrister to "remove both his hat and feet." Kirby complied but later had the officer arrested for assault and battery.[16]

The opera house incident was a signal to all that Joe Kirby was not one to accede merely to a slight or an insult. He was headstrong and aggressive, and sometimes in the extreme. In 1904 Kirby filed suit against J. B. Martindale, an eastern firm that published a lawyers' directory, for failing to give him an accurate rating.[17] Having chosen the legal profession, he had a platform for picking and winning a fight, and the volatile lawyer was not afraid to use his fists to reinforce his point of view.

Prosecuting attorney Joe Kirby.
Courtesy Joe Kirby, Sioux Falls, South Dakota.

Kirby did stumble on his way to a successful legal profession. In 1896 he was arrested by a detective and charged with having received stolen property in the form of a large amount of postage stamps that had been taken by thieves from post offices in Waubay, Miller, and Highmore, South Dakota.[18] He was tried in the circuit court in Sioux Falls in June of 1897. The charge against him was "knowingly having stolen property [postage stamps] of the United States in his possession." The jury retired for deliberations and soon found itself mired in a series of "stormy sessions" in "the sweat box," during which time there was "considerable arguing." One juryman insisted that he "would stay in the jury room until his hair turned white as snow before he ever agreed to a verdict of guilty." But on the twenty-fourth ballot the jury finally agreed to a verdict of guilty. The verdict was a surprise to "almost everyone."[19]

Kirby—also shocked and in a state of disbelief—disputed the verdict and the judge heard him out. After his personal plea for leniency, the judge sentenced him to two years in prison.[20] About two weeks later, the judge ruled on the matter of disbarment. Claiming the ruling was not personal but rather a "matter of moral turpitude," he ordered Kirby's debarment for two years.[21]

Two days after being disbarred, Kirby was in the headlines again. He had represented an Ohio man, Emery Lattanner, in a divorce proceeding in the circuit court at Yankton. A divorce decree was issued and Lattanner fled to Canada. Soon after, it was discovered that Lattanner had submitted forged and false documents to the court. An angry judge set aside the divorce decree, and the *Argus-Leader* hinted that "Joe Kirby may have to explain."[22]

But Kirby apparently ignored the Lattanner matter and concentrated on his own, more serious, legal problems. As it turned out, the conviction at the first trial was but one step in a long process that ultimately resulted in a third trial. It was then that the "charm" intervened and the entire business screeched to a halt; a mistrial was declared after a juror "lost his senses." Eventually, the unstoppable Joe Kirby got back his license to practice and worked his way up to being one of the leading attorneys in Sioux Falls. He started the Western Surety Company in 1900, a bonding agency that to the present time is still one of the major businesses in Sioux Falls, having been managed by generations of Kirbys.[23]

~

When attorney Joe Kirby took on a case, he kept one goal in the forefront of his mind: beat the hell out of the other side. In all likelihood, it was this approach by Kirby that prompted the slow-moving State's Attorney Orr to take the matter seriously. For even after the second autopsy on the body of Agnes Polreis, and the resulting reports of five doctors, Orr—a friend of Moses Kaufmann—was reluctant to go forward with the case, and probably would not have done so had Joe Kirby not been added to the team.[24]

The polar opposite of Kirby, Orr was an empathetic man who could be moved to tears when others would turn away with no display of emotion. When he ran for state's attorney in 1904, a newspaper wag suggested that his supporters were backing him for two terms because Orr would not be ready for work until his second term commenced.[25] Orr was deliberate to be sure. But he was also sensitive, unpretentious, and intelligent, with no desire to shine, almost as if he would have preferred to slip through life anonymously. Nevertheless, he was dragged into the spotlight of history by the Kaufmann case, which erupted on his watch. Like it or not, he was forced to assert himself in a manner that belied his personality.

And on the serious charge of murder, the search for the truth moved forward. Slowly at first, but picking up speed, it was to become a powerful, raging storm that promised to leave a random and tragic trail of destruction in its wake. Knowledgeable observers understood that it would be a show not to be missed, made so by the personalities of Aikens and Kirby, two of the best trial attorneys in the state.

~

At the counsel table with Kirby and Orr sat Hutchinson County State's Attorney J. L. Quinn, who represented the people of Parkston. The number of people from Parkston and elsewhere who attended the hearing was not very large, as the arrest of Emma Kaufmann, at this point, was not widely known. The well-behaved spectators, mostly newspapermen and lawyers, listened as Aikens quietly read the charges to his client while she sat beside her husband. It had been almost two weeks since the death of Agnes, and the accused had "undergone a surprising metamorphosis," according to those who knew her, for they could clearly see on Emma and her husband "the marks of the terrible strain."[26] Was this evidence of guilt, many wondered?

The first witness to testify at the preliminary hearing was Arthur A. Snashall, a mortician employed by the L. D. Miller undertaking company. After being sworn in, with Kirby asking the questions,

Snashall testified that he had been called to the Kaufmann house on the morning of June 1, 1906, for the purpose of taking Agnes Polreis to the Sioux Falls Hospital, which he did. Later that day, when he was advised that Agnes had died, he returned to the hospital and took her body to the Miller undertaking facility. Snashall said he first learned of the wounds on the girl when he "took off the bandages to embalm the body." Kirby did not ask why the funeral home did not notify the authorities when there was evidence of the possibility of foul play.

Dr. Sydney Olney, who had practiced in Sioux Falls since 1877, was the next witness and he described in detail his findings from the second autopsy. He said the body of Agnes Polreis was "not excessively emaciated," but he found deep lacerations on the scalp and on the back of the head that he believed were "produced by external violence." He also described wounds to the shoulders that looked like they were made with a knife. The wounds were fresh and the tissue was healthy, not gangrenous. The skin on one hand was "loosened and one finger was gone." The left knee "was greatly swollen and the skin was separated from part of the legs and feet." Olney testified that he examined the heart and the brain and found a blood clot on the latter, "which had apparently been there for several days before death." Concluding his testimony, he said "the girl had no diabetes."[27]

When pressed by Aikens on cross-examination, the cautious Dr. Olney held his ground. Aikens asked him point-blank: "Were the wounds on the body of Miss Polreis self-inflicted?" Dr. Olney replied, "I have tried one hundred times to make myself think so, but I can't catch on to the idea. They are not."[28] It was a swing and a miss for the defense.

It was a complete rejection of Dr. Germain's hasty explanation of the cause of the death of Agnes Polreis. Germain had been made to look as though he were incompetent or a liar. People were suspicious of Germain because he was the personal physician for the Kaufmanns, and many suspected an attempted cover-up. It was beginning to look as though the wily doctor was involved in a nefarious plot to hide the truth, which was coming apart in court.

The third witness was Dr. H. B. Schofield, of Parkston, who had done the first autopsy and had assisted with the second. Questioned by Quinn, the country doctor reinforced the prior testimony of Olney. Schofield also said that the wounds "taken collectively could have caused the death of the girl" and further, that because she was in a malnourished condition when the wounds were inflicted, she was predisposed to die. After he stepped down from the witness stand, court adjourned for the day, with many more witnesses expected when the hearing resumed.[29] It was also suggested that "the supposed accessories to the crime will be made to answer to the offense charged against them."[30]

~

There were no further arrests, and when testimony resumed the next morning the courtroom was packed to "suffocation." People stood on the sidewalk outside "peering through the windows," trying to get a peek at the participants and hear the lurid details. As the excitement mounted, the restless gawkers grew angry and a strange foreboding filled the air. Mrs. Kaufmann—veiled and dressed in black from head to toe—who began the day "calm and cool," showed signs of unease and nervousness as the dramatic hearing ran its course. Her husband sat in front of her in an attempt to shield her from the curious gaze of the crowd. The cross-examination of the witnesses by her attorney, Judge Aikens, led court watchers to believe that he was trying to establish as a defense that Agnes Polreis "was the victim of vertigo and that the wounds" on her body were caused by frequent falls.[31]

John Polreis, father of the victim, testified through an interpreter. He was described as "a stolid, unemotional man," but "deadly earnest." Although unable to understand English, "his countenance showed that he was catching the drift of the testimony."[32] William Moeller and Mrs. N. T. Grosz were called as witnesses to confirm the identification of the girl's body and to establish that she was in good health when she left Parkston for Sioux Falls. Coroner L. D. Miller described the wounds and testified that he had "suggested that it was a case for the coroner but was dissuaded."[33] The suggestion to investigate was made to Dr. Germain, who said that he would furnish a death certificate and that ended the discussion about an inquest.[34] Strangely, the coroner whose duty it was to investigate a suspicious death was overruled by a doctor.

Sioux Falls Hospital, 19th Street and Minnesota Avenue.
Courtesy Siouxland Heritage Museums.

Jeannette E. Larson, the superintendent of nurses at Sioux Falls Hospital, was next to offer testimony. Larson recalled that Agnes was in the company of Dr. Germain and Snashall when she was admitted to the hospital. The patient was "suffering in great pain" and was therefore taken to a private ward.[35] Larson recalled that the patient was in a "desperate condition" and then went on to describe the wounds on her body, noting that only one had become gangrenous. Larson also said that Agnes' hair was "matted" and that her body was "blue" and "much emaciated." Her weight was 110 pounds. She recalled that the only audible words from Agnes were, "I ache all over," and that she complained about her stomach. On cross-examination, Larson said that Agnes was conscious until an hour before she died and that she was able to speak but simply repeated herself.

Dr. Thomas J. Billion was next to swear to tell the truth and nothing but the truth. He had been practicing medicine since 1891, after graduating from Clayton Medical College at Omaha.[36] His testimony was based on his examination of the exhumed body of Agnes Polreis. Dr. Billion reaffirmed the prior testimony of Dr. Olney, that there was no "evidence of heart disease or diabetes," that the "blood clot was close to the external injury on the head," and therefore could have been caused by a blow to the head. Under cross-examination, Billion actually strengthened his direct testimony by saying that it was his opinion the injuries to Agnes were not self-inflicted because it would be physically impossible to do so. "Considerable force was required to produce the wounds noted," he stated.[37]

The sum and substance of the testimony by the prosecution's medical experts was stated thusly: "the experts were unable to testify that any one of the wounds or that the blood clot caused death, but that they were all sufficient to have caused [the] same."[38] Barely concealed in the ambiguity was the sense that deadly force had been applied, more than once.

The prosecution was well on its way toward getting an indictment. Then to tie it all together, the person thought to be a key witness was sworn in. Peter Erickson, referred to as a Norwegian, but born in Illinois, had been in the employ of Moses Kaufmann for about two months prior to the hearing. He worked at the Kaufmann house doing everything from pulling dandelions to washing windows, but he resided elsewhere. Erickson was the man everyone was waiting to hear testify. The people of Parkston had, from the outset, believed that "this man Erickson knew more than he was willing to tell."[39] Talk on the streets of Sioux Falls was that Erickson had left town,[40] but that proved to be false, for he appeared in court, and from start to finish, he was a powerful and persuasive voice for the prosecution.

The instant that Peter Erickson took the oath, interest in the proceedings intensified. After three questions into his examination, Joe Kirby stood up, leaned over the desk, and looked directly into the eyes of the witness. The gesture added excitement to the scene and everyone remained deathly silent.[41]

Seemingly at ease and speaking freely, Erickson said that he was acquainted with Agnes and that he assisted in carrying her to the ambulance on June 1, 1906, in the presence of Dr. Germain. Erickson testified that on a prior occasion, he personally saw an "angry and harsh" Emma Kaufmann "poke the girl in the ribs with a broomstick," causing her to "whimper." When further questioned by Kirby, he went on to say that eight or nine days before she was sent to the hospital, "I found the girl lying on the kitchen floor in a pool of water. Mrs. Kaufmann said she had put hot water on her to get her up, and that the girl was the stubbornest mortal she ever saw." He said he was ordered to "shake the girl, which I did, though I felt sorry for her." He said that Mrs. Kaufmann shook her roughly too, dropped her to the floor, and struck her with a broomstick, after which he carried Agnes upstairs and placed her on her bed.

Erickson had scored major points for the prosecution but he wasn't finished. The young man testified that Emma Kaufmann "rolled" Agnes out of bed and onto the floor. He said that "several times I saw the girl plead with Mrs. Kaufmann." He recalled seeing Agnes on her knees with her hands held up, as if begging her tormentor to stop, saying "Frau Kaufmann" repeatedly. Erickson testified that on the afternoon of the day before Agnes was taken to the hospital, he was told to dress Agnes' wounds and that, while doing so he could smell turpentine on her feet. When questioned, Mrs. Kaufmann said the turpentine was needed to reduce the "inflammation." Erickson noticed the skin was missing from her feet.

Significantly, Erickson testified that he did not see head wounds on Agnes until "the day she was taken away" to the hospital.[42] This supported the prosecution's contention that the head wounds, which Kirby and his team believed were the cause of her death, were inflicted the night before she died.

The following is an excerpt from the direct examination of Peter Erickson by Joe Kirby:

> Q: Did she [Emma Kaufmann] tell you anything about the girl taking a foot bath or anything?
>
> A: She told me about having the girl bathe her feet in ashes soaked with water.
>
> Q: Did you notice the smell of anything around the room?
>
> A: I noticed the smell of turpentine.
>
> Q: Did you have a talk with Mrs. Kaufmann about that?
>
> A: Yes. I asked her if she had used turpentine and she said she did to remove the swellings.

> I told her I thought it was too strong and she said she did not think it was.[43]

The case was about to catch fire and Erickson's testimony was the spark that started the inferno. Several newspapers covered the preliminary hearing and their reports varied wildly in their characterization of Erickson's testimony. On the mild side, the *Argus-Leader* reported that a single poke with a broomstick "was the only evidence of ill-treatment that he [Erickson] saw."[44] On the wild side, a Mitchell newspaper reported that Agnes was "beaten with a club until she sank down to the floor," and when she got up she was "pummeled by Mrs. Kaufmann's fists into semi-consciousness."[45] The *Parkston Advance* reported that "Mrs. Kaufmann was in the habit of beating the girl with a club about the head and shoulders."[46] Perhaps somewhere in between the two extremes, one might find a kernel of truth.

The court took a break until 2 P.M. and the reporter for the *Argus-Leader* caught a quick interview with John Polreis, father of Agnes, who was the youngest of fourteen children, only five of whom were still living. Speaking through an interpreter, he said his family had been living in America for only seven months. His wife was in Sioux Falls but was unable to attend the court session.

When court resumed the spectators, mostly women, were seated. The crowd had grown larger, with groups of children standing outside at the windows behaving in a manner that was annoying to the sheriff and his deputies. Men who had found seats were asked by Justice Wheelock to give them up for some ladies who had arrived late.

The afternoon session was taken up by Aikens' cross-examination of Erickson. Erickson's prior testimony was brought up by Aikens but the witness said nothing that would impeach him or damage the prosecution's case. Very little new information was revealed during the hour-long cross-examination. He did say that the only incident of actual battery he witnessed was one poke with a broomstick by Emma Kaufmann while Agnes was on the floor. And when pressed by Aikens about seeing Agnes on her knees saying "Frau Kaufmann" repeatedly, Erickson could not say whether she was begging for her life or pleading not to be fired. Erickson also said that he came to the Kaufmann house after he learned that Ag-

"Star witness" for the prosecution, Peter Erickson, *Minneapolis Journal*, June 23, 1906.

nes was dead, and that in the presence of Henriette Levinger he noticed that Emma Kaufmann was not crying.[47]

When the graphic testimony of Peter Erickson ended, he emerged as the "star witness" for the prosecution. One report noted that his testimony was "straightforward," as if he was "anxious to tell the truth without flavoring it."[48] His testimony surprised and shocked all those present and was soon the talk of the town. It was a fitting climax to the dramatic case presented by the prosecution, and it came crashing down on Emma Kaufmann like an avalanche of ill-omen. The law presumes innocence, but an uninformed and biased public presumes guilt.

~

A confident State's Attorney Orr rested for the prosecution at 3:05 P.M. on June 13. Aikens asked for a transcript of the evidence, but did not put on a case nor call a witness for the defense. The curious fact that Aikens did not call Dr. Germain was something that probably did not escape the scrutiny of others. The court adjourned and a further hearing was scheduled for June 20, 1906. The prisoner, Emma Kaufmann, was turned over to the custody of the Minnehaha County sheriff, Nyrum E. Phillips.[49]

For the sheriff and others associated with the case, the restless volume of noise from all the newspapers would ensure that no one would get a good night's sleep any time soon. Newspapers from out of state were not slow in swooping in for a good story. Among them was the *Minneapolis Journal*, which put out a report immediately following the first phase of the preliminary hearing. This article, and other lurid accounts, would prove that the newspapers were not just telling the story—they were part of the story.

Calling it "one of the most damnable crimes ever committed in South Dakota," the *Journal* came out swinging with a report that read like a horror story written by Edgar Allan Poe. Describing the second exhumation, the reporter wrote, "about one hundred Parkston people stood over the grave." Then after the doctors completed their ghastly work, "the body was replaced in the grave, [and] the verdict was whispered thru the crowd . . . and the spectators dispersed." To add further mystification to an already bizarre article, the reporter wrote, "it is understood that Mrs. Kaufmann is a Jewish gipsy, who many years ago was adopted by a well-known family of Minnehaha County pioneers."[50] It was titillating to be sure, but not true, and in their haste to out-shock their rivals, the *Journal* printed a photograph labeled "Agnes Polreis," but it was clearly a picture of another, much older woman.[51]

But the events leading up to the hearing—and the hearing itself—were well-covered, and better covered, by area newspapers. Among them the *Parkston Advance*, John W. Peckham, publisher, had done so in a calm and deliberate manner, which respected both judicial due process and the anger coming from the people of Hutchinson County. That no undue emotion or bias is shown in the article of June 15 is a tribute to the publisher of the *Advance*. After summing up the testimony that most surely pointed to a crime, the *Advance* declared that "the matter should be cleared up and that the family should get the justice accorded to American citizens by our constitution."[52]

After listening to the testimony at the preliminary hearing, the Parkston people probably believed they would get justice for Agnes, and they must have felt that their investment of $15,000 to hire Joe Kirby was money well spent. The money was raised by donations from the Hungarian settlers and from an appropriation by the Hutchinson County Commission.[53] The Parkston people left Sioux Falls for their homes, "well pleased with the progress of the case."[54]

Emma Kaufmann (upper left) and woman erroneously identified as Agnes Polreis (lower left). *Minneapolis Journal*, June 23, 1906.

They left behind a city that was stunned and overwhelmed by all that had been revealed in the press and at the hearing. The Kaufmann case was *the* topic of conversation in the streets, saloons, and trains, and over dinner tables. Among the looming questions in the public mind was: Why are not more arrests made? Attention was focused on "several prominent people connected with covering up" the crime. Without naming anyone, the *Sioux Falls Daily Press* noted that "there are some badly frightened accessories to the Polreis supposed murder who slip about the city with hanging heads."[55] And Peter Erickson? He was slipping about the city looking for a new job.

Chapter 3

More Shocking Revelations

> *A small trunk of wet, worn and blood covered clothing belonging to Miss Polreis before her mysterious death . . . is considered strong evidence that the girl came to a violent death.*
>
> *The Daily Argus-Leader*
> June 18, 1906

The *Daily Argus-Leader* and the *Sioux Falls Journal* covered the Kaufmann case grudgingly because they had to, because the story wouldn't go away, but a weekly Sioux Falls newspaper, the *Soo Critic*, was an exception. Published in a building at the "foot of 9th Street,"[1] near the west bank of the Big Sioux River by a firebrand and partisan Democrat, John A. Ross, assisted by his able wife Maggie, the *Critic* charged into the tragic affair like a wounded buffalo chasing a terrified hunter. A self-described crank, Ross boasted that his newspaper represented the interests of the poor, the voiceless, the unions, the working man, and the under-privileged classes in general. But class warfare was just one of his causes.

In the manner of the late and famous Horace Greeley, the crusading editor of the *New York Tribune,* the quixotic Ross was in the habit of engaging in fights over moral issues. Like the popular Greeley, Ross had a variety of causes that he pursued with a passion. He criticized lax divorce laws. He disapproved of prostitution, saloons, and gambling and, like the gadfly he was, Ross wrote stinging editorials condemning booze and bars while needling the authorities to take action against them.

Most of all, Ross hated the rich for he believed that wealth and the power it engendered could and invariably would oppress and brutalize the rest of the people. He had his targets. In 1903 Andrew Carnegie donated $35,000 to build a new library in Sioux Falls—an act of generosity that Ross spurned, calling the stylish quartzite stone building a "monument to greed." Better had Carnegie built homes for the poor at a cost of $500 per house, for Ross believed it was the hard labor of the poor that made Carnegie a wealthy man.[2]

Ross insulted multi-millionaire Carnegie because he believed that exploitation and wealth were inseparable. He saw in the Kaufmann case the chance to vent his hatred of the wealthy and champion the cause of the downtrodden, including immigrants. The Kaufmann case gave the self-righteous Ross a platform to attack the privileged and powerful, and he carried on as if he had been commanded by God to act. Emma Kaufmann would soon learn that she was living in an unfair and unforgiving world.

The feisty Ross, who came to South Dakota from Marinette, Wisconsin, was in fact a decent and prolific writer, although he habitually abbreviated certain words. For example, "brought" became "brot," and "though" was spelled "tho," and of course, "Sioux Falls" was sometimes spelled "Soo Falls." Still for descriptive writing, the flowery Ross was in a class all by himself. He often wrote like a man on a holy mission, and at times more like a novelist than a journalist. Anyone who read his newspaper coverage of the tragic demise of Agnes Polreis was exposed to a graphic, sizzling, and proverbial description of "death by a thousand cuts."

There was nothing superficial or oblique about Ross' writing; he went straight for the jugular. If the coverage of the Kaufmann case by the better established newspapers weakened and failed to arouse or entertain, Ross could be counted on to provide some sizzle. From his first to his last article, he would not let his readers forget that the

Kaufmann family was rich and powerful and Agnes Polreis was poor and powerless. While some people believed that the *Critic*'s reporting was too severe and that it put Sioux Falls in a false light, Ross didn't give a fig about the exposure. It was more important to get justice for Agnes Polreis, for in doing so, Sioux Falls would be redeemed.

The *Critic* covered the preliminary hearing, and the resulting article was a rant against the rich, an essay about horror and evil that had the tone and content of a Gothic novel. Casting aside all pretense of even-handed journalism, Ross went on the attack, lashing out on those he opposed and casting bits of praise at those he favored. With his newspaper as his weapon, he was a man in hot pursuit of an outcome that he struggled hard to articulate.

It does appear that Ross managed to interview a member of the Polreis family. In the June 14 issue of the *Critic*, Ross reported that Agnes had faithfully written to her parents once a week until about a month before she died. Ross surmised that it was her weakened condition that explained the lack of further letters. What her parents did not know, according to Ross, was that Agnes was "enduring those weeks of silence, the tortures of the inquisition."

Ross quickly developed a cover-up theory based on his belief that certain people were in a hurry to get the body in the ground so that no one would notice the wounds. He stated that the body of Agnes Polreis was turned over to a relative with a warning not to open the casket. But once opened, the marks of violence were apparent and although Hutchinson County officials went to Sioux Falls to demand an investigation, they could "arouse no interest on the part of the proper officers . . . to whom they rightfully . . . appealed." Ross continued, noting that it was common knowledge that there had been "difficulty in keeping servants in the Kaufman[n] household." Next, he took a swipe at the *Argus-Leader* for informing its readers that the people from Parkston were satisfied that Agnes had died from natural causes, based on Dr. Germain's determination of death. To Ross and his readers, the remark suggested that the *Argus-Leader* was hiding something, or someone, or both.[3]

To those readers who might have wondered why Agnes didn't flee the Kaufmann house, a reporter for the *South Dakota State Forum*, a weekly Sioux Falls newspaper, noted that the girl was a virtual prisoner in the mansion, "in a little back room under the gable." He revealed that a "lady who was passing by the Kaufmann house a week before the death of Agnes saw the girl hanging clothes in the yard." The lady was drawn to her "piteous" appearance so she stopped, "thinking the girl wanted to speak to her." But Agnes, who could not speak English, and therefore could not say what she most certainly had on her mind, "said nothing . . . and the lady walked on."[4] And in doing so, she unknowingly passed up what might have been the last chance to save Agnes.

Ross also offered an explanation for Agnes' inability to escape. He also noted her recent arrival in America and inability to speak English and concluded that she was at a distinct disadvantage and was therefore vulnerable to domination. The unsophisticated Agnes was merely a domestic, bound to a state of servitude. She had no understanding of the law or her rights. She was a girl "cowed by the power of wealth."

After all, she was living in the last years of the Gilded Age, when vast fortunes and political power combined to dominate all aspects of American society. It was a time when the law was often administered in a harsh and domineering way, a time when merely being a "suspicious character" could get someone tossed into jail or run out of town. Ross could have further elaborated on the injustice and excesses of unfettered capitalism and its impact on the average person, but he did not. Rather he focused on the preliminary hearing.

Cartoon of Peter Erickson "witnessing" Emma Kaufmann beating Agnes Polreis, *American Republic*, January 22, 1909.

He found the testimony of Peter Erickson especially illuminating and damning, and therefore expanded upon it to reach what he believed to be its logical conclusion: "Mrs. Kaufman[n] is a woman of ungovernable temper; and when in a fit of anger, of a cruel disposition." The wife of a "well-known brewer" had shook Agnes, threw her out of bed, pounded her with a broomstick, and had "thrown hot water on her." These were examples of "the most fiendish acts, of diabolical cruelty." These "untold agonies endured for days by the poor helpless girl call to the heart of every man for justice," wrote Ross.

Unable, or unwilling, to control his indignation, Ross was on fire, fueled by journalistic outrage, his anger spilling out on the printed page, where he told a story of torment and slow death. Still he tempered his remarks slightly by saying that "no prejudice should be held against Mrs. Kaufman[n] because she is the wife of a rich brewer," but on the other hand, "no leniency should be shown her because she is the wife of a rich and influential man." Ross called on everyone to insist that all those "connected with this outrage on this innocent girl, and the crime against the laws of God and man, should meet with full and just punishment."[5]

This was his opening salvo—there would be much more to come. The drama unfolding in Sioux Falls promised to be supremely sensational, and Ross, with his *Critic*, was sure to be at the forefront of the story, probing, prodding, and revealing juicy details, true or false, that other local newspapers would not print.

The staff at the *Argus-Leader* must have felt the sting of Ross' accusatory article, and that of a similar piece in the *Mitchell Clarion.* The latter hinted that the Sioux Falls daily was among those newspapers attempting to make certain that the truth was dead and buried along with the girl. The Mitchell paper asserted that "the circumstances surrounding the death of Agnes Polreis were such that it looks as if there was a concerted and systematic effort" to cover up the truth and shield guilty parties from arrest. How could the girl's body be viewed by Dr. Germain, by the nurses and other hospital personnel, and finally by the coroner and the undertaker, without rousing some suspicion?[6]

The *Argus-Leader* printed the critical comments and then struck back, calling the report "wholly false." The only reason that the death of Agnes Polreis had not been reported sooner was because "the papers did not know of it." Further, the visit of Hutchinson County State's Attorney J. L. Quinn to Sioux Falls took place quietly, with him taking "every effort to keep it from the papers." To clear his paper from any accusation that it was part of a cover-up, the editor of the *Argus-Leader* wrote that once it had information of a crime, the paper threw itself into the story. Devoting "nearly three columns a day," argued the Sioux Falls editor, surely does not "look like suppressing the facts." He made it clear that his newspaper would not "shield or whitewash" local officials or people.[7]

The nasty fight between the *Argus-Leader* and a growing number of other newspapers caught the attention of the editor of the *Yankton Press and Dakotan*. That newspaper called on the warring elements to cease fire long enough for the authorities to investigate and establish the facts. Then, getting in a dig of its own, the *Press and Dakotan* conceded that it would be alright for the protagonists to resume "the practice of mudslinging."[8]

The *Weekly Cataract* was in the mood to sling some mud and its target was the *Argus-Leader* and its powerful political ally. The *Cataract* and its publisher, George W. Kingsbury, Jr., included U.S. Senator Alfred B. Kittredge in its accusatory article, warning that there would be political consequences for him unless the *Argus-Leader* stopped its soft-shoe approach to reporting on the Kaufmann case. The South Dakota senator was losing the support of the German people of Hutchinson County and elsewhere in the state because he was "keeping this unreliable paper [*Argus-Leader*] alive." Kingsbury offered a dire prediction: Sioux Falls and its merchants would find themselves isolated and abandoned by the other towns and cities in the state. The Parkston people, he declared, have already "placed the stamp of disapproval upon Sioux Falls beer because 'there is blood in it.'"[9]

Much damage had been done, the mud had hit its mark, and journalistic feathers were ruffled as they had rarely been ruffled before. Since the *Argus-Leader* was a Republican newspaper, and the *Critic* and the *Mitchell Clarion* were Democratic, they were fierce rivals on the political front. But taking on the *Weekly Cataract*, also a Republican newspaper, was especially poisonous, for it pointed to intra-party turmoil. Adding the politics of murder to the cauldron would only heat up the debate and drive all factions further apart, thus ensuring lasting enmity. As long as the Kaufmann case was in the news, there would be no peace within the Republican party or between parties.

Waiting for the June 20 resumption of the preliminary hearing, Sioux Falls and the rest of the state remained in suspense, aware that every question only raised more questions. Then it was learned that a trunk, containing "clothing belonging to the dead girl," had been received in Parkston. Turned over to State's Attorney Quinn, the trunk's contents were inspected in the presence of witnesses, where it was found that the garments were wet, stained with blood, and smelled of turpentine. Horror! Despite evidence that some of the items had been washed, "the bloodstains corresponded in position to the numerous cuts which marred the young body, and their condition is eloquent [sic] of the awful suffering which the girl passed through."[10]

Among those who viewed the gruesome contents of the small trunk was Mrs. N. T. Grosz, for whom Agnes had worked before leaving for Sioux Falls. She identified the trunk as having belonged to Agnes, but the condition of the clothing, "covered with blood and dirt," was such that she found it very difficult to locate the "girl's name on some of the garments." Agnes, she recalled, was "neat; never had a sore on her body or soiled clothes in her room for any length of time." The inspection of the trunk—opened by a key given to Quinn by Moses Kaufmann—was almost too much for some to bear. Men turned "their faces away from the terrible sight" while women wept.[11]

When Ross of the *Critic* got wind of the trunk's existence, his trumpets of outrage blasted symphonic and his anger soared to new heights. Since he put out a weekly paper, he was able to accumulate information from other news sources—and he was always eager to pounce. On June 21, 1906, the front page of the *Critic* read, "**TORTURE WAS UNPARALLELED**," with a sub-headline that compared the suffering of Agnes Polreis to "A Tale of Inquisition Horror." If Ross was upset before, he was in a blind uproar now, and in a slash-and-burn article he demanded that the city of Sioux Falls take action to "redeem her honor" and that witnesses be bound over. His bias against Emma Kaufmann now out of control, he reminded his readers that some of the forty-nine wounds "found on the head and body of the child seem almost beyond belief." Pounding away, Ross wrote that Snashall, the undertaker, had declared that "the girl's body was the worst he had seen in ten years."[12] In an interview with a Mitchell newspaper, Snashall confessed that "the body of Miss Polreis was the first one [that] he . . . was afraid to touch."[13]

As horror piled upon horror and the mystery surrounding the death became increasingly more macabre, Ross wanted nothing less than a quick conviction for murder followed by an immediate execution. Emma Kaufmann must hang, Ross demanded. Anything less would be a mockery of justice and would leave the city of Sioux Falls in a state of purgatory, beyond rescue and redemption.

Another newspaper, the *Sioux Falls Journal*, joined the fray and soon found itself the target of the *Critic*. After analyzing the evidence revealed by the prosecution and its witnesses, the *Journal* suggested that the case was weak and that "Mrs. Kaufmann would be a free woman today," had she lived in a large city and been faced with the same flimsy evidence. No one had actually seen anyone inflict wounds on Agnes' body, so how could anyone rightly accuse Emma Kaufmann or anyone else?

The *Journal* article openly and shamelessly mocked the sentiment of the people who believed that some unspeakable and horrible treatment resulted in the death of an innocent girl. "The Polreis girl must have suffered a thousand deaths before her spirit left the body. She in fact must have been on the rack for three weeks," was the sneering response to those who sympathized with the Polreis family. The attitude of the *Sioux Falls Journal*, under the editorship of Mark D. Scott, was condescending and mean-spirited in the extreme.

The reporter for the *Journal* seemed to have reached his own frenzy of bewilderment and disbelief. He speculated that the defense counsel for Emma Kaufmann would enter an insanity defense, which if successful, one could expect "the mightiest howl to go up that these western prairies ever heard." On the other hand, should she be convicted, he reminded his fellow citizens, there is no worse punishment than hanging. The reporter smelled blood but seemed more concerned about what the case was doing to the reputation of Sioux Falls than in what or who caused the death of Agnes Polreis.[14]

Over the past two years, Sioux Falls and the outlying areas had experienced disappearances, murders, shootings, and other acts of violence. The *Weekly Cataract* saw in the Kaufmann case yet another example of unchecked and unsolved crime, all a part of a "**RECORD OF HORRORS**." The ghastly, shameful record included a dead man found near a bridge, a farmer living near Baltic who had his brains blasted out, a man found dead on a sidewalk by a Sioux

Falls hotel, a dead baby found in a pile of rubbish, and the body of Chris Sven, found floating in the Big Sioux River. In every case, authorities remained baffled, the result of incompetence and lack of interest. Although the *Cataract* was playing second fiddle to the *Critic*, it pointed an angry finger at the former mayor, George Burnside, whose administration was connected to the "scandals."[15]

The extensive and lurid reporting on these incidents piled additional misery on the Polreis family. It was learned that Theresa Polreis, the grieving mother of the dead girl, had been living in a nightmarish state of helpless and hopeless sorrow, as though suffering the tortures of the damned. In her sorrow she would go to the rural cemetery late at night, alone, and three times she had to be taken away from Agnes' grave by concerned and sympathetic people. She told them that she was so hurt that "she wished to die." Losing Agnes was especially tragic, she indicated, since she had lost an older daughter, who had been shot and killed "by a jealous lover" in Vienna, Austria. Those who witnessed Theresa's agonies believed that her mind was failing, and that she, too, would soon be carried away by death.[16]

The *Minneapolis Journal* covered the Kaufmann case very closely. With a reporter in Sioux Falls, this newspaper was able to feature a series of articles, each one graphic, shocking, and lurid, as though intentionally competing with Ross. Writing about the clothing found in the trunk, the Minnesota reporter expanded on the accounts in South Dakota newspapers. He claimed that a "long galvanized iron stirring spoon, weighing seventeen ounces," was among the items discovered in the dreadful trunk. This spoon, declared the *Journal*, was the "weapon of death," which the prosecuting attorneys believed had caused Agnes' head wounds.

The article went on to assert that other domestics who formerly worked for Emma Kaufmann would be asked to testify that the defendant, "the wealthy Jewess," heaped cruelty on Agnes because she could not accept the loss of her own daughter.[17] The *Evening Star*, in Washington, DC, further revealed that two of her former maids, Anna Jenson and Mrs. Oscar Larson, both said that "they have fled from her wrath," running from the garret to the cellar, and that they were terrified by her appearance in their rooms at night, "her features working in hideous fashion as she glared at them."[18] Only one of her servants had the courage to stand up against her wrath, an

Irish girl who fought back. Not identified by name, the girl said she was there to work, not to be beaten, and when "attacked by this woman in her rage," she "administered a beating" to the lady of the house, after which she packed up her trunk and left, reported the Mitchell *Daily Republican*.[19]

Anna Jenson, an experienced housekeeper, provided a vivid description of her former employer, whom she called "penurious and a hard drinker."[20] At first, all went well in the mistress-servant relationship, but Mrs. Kaufmann's manner and attitude changed. She would unexpectedly go into a rage, chasing Jenson throughout the house "when the notion would strike her." She forbade Jenson from locking her door at night. "I was simply a slave while working for Mrs. Kaufmann. It was necessary for me to do everything that she told me to do or she would get angry." Jenson claimed that she had to work extra hard to escape the "blows" that "other girls claimed they received." Further, Jenson was forced to sit up late at night with her employer and "drink beer by the hour." Yet she felt sorry for the woman who, when she wasn't playing the role of an autocrat, spent so much time looking at "a fine painting of her daughter."[21]

According to Anna Jensen, the tormented Emma Kaufmann was obsessed with memories of her late daughter. "She used to make me tired bragging about that daughter of hers. She told me how much people admired her, and what a fine girl she was," the Parkston paper reported.[22]

Jenson's story was corroborated by information the newspapers received from other women acquainted with Emma Kaufmann. According to the Grand Forks, North Dakota, *Evening Times*, Jenson said that she "would sit brooding, in silence, for hours at a time before a life-size portrait of her deceased daughter," until she would scream "wild, demonical blasphemies against God for depriving her of her loved one."[23]

Unfortunately, the many newspapers that covered the story revealed very little about the Kaufmanns' deceased daughter. None mentioned her name, age, or cause of death. The *Evening Star* did state that their "only daughter" would have been about the same age as Agnes, "had she lived."[24] Another newspaper, in South Carolina, hinted at the date of her death, saying only that she died "several years ago."[25]

Losing her daughter was clearly a factor in her alleged unhinged mental state, but there was more. The Kaufmanns nearly lost their son, Charles Kaufmann, too. In March 1900 Charles was lying near death in a Milwaukee hospital, suffering from "complications" following foot surgery. With worried family members at his bedside, Charles was expected to die but the lad did recover.[26] The close call with Charles and the death of her daughter were hard blows from which Emma Kaufmann struggled to recover, making her life one of constant sorrow.

The Kaufmann Mansion, 632 West 7th Street. *Courtesy Center for Western Studies, Augustana University, Sioux Falls, South Dakota.*

The sad, tormented woman was caught in a downward spiral of perpetual grief, newspapers speculated, and she could not forgive "the Providence that left her alone in her declining years." Because of her sadness, she was "determined that no young girl about her should enjoy health and happiness." Therefore, "on the authority of every girl in Sioux Falls who had worked for the woman," Agnes Polreis was "kept a prisoner" and slowly tortured to death. The *Minneapolis Journal* claimed to know that four Sioux Falls girls who had worked at the Kaufmann home were prepared to testify that the wicked lady of the house was "cruel to them." They claimed that she locked their doors at night, refusing to let them out, and that during the night, she would go to their rooms and "stand over them with a fixed gaze," as though she "yearned to grab and strangle them."[27]

For these reasons, editors speculated, her attorneys would base their case on insanity, a defense that was rarely successful and wildly unpopular. The editor of the *Mitchell Clarion* saw this coming and flatly objected to it, insisting that "no insanity dodge or other subterfuge will be tolerated" by South Dakota people.[28]

Emma Kaufmann was by rumor, reputation, and some factual reporting a woman with serious character flaws. She lived in a time when the study of unusual behavior, often characterized as mental illness, was in its infancy, and most contemporaries probably concluded that the only remedy for her and others like her was institutionalization in an asylum. Ignorant people blamed her behavior on what they perceived to be "abnormal conditions of low mentality," characterized by a "large jaw and a receding forehead."[29] Decades later, psychiatrists might have concluded that she was suffering from an anti-social personality disorder (APD). A person with an APD is commonly referred to as a psychopath or a sociopath.[30]

A person with an APD leads a life of deception and manipulation, sometimes marked by a pattern of aggression or violence against others for whom the psychopath feels no empathy. Empathy is the ability to identify with and understand the feelings and needs of others. People who lack empathy are unable to make that connection and instead may commit harmful acts without remorse. Their victims are merely objects in human form.[31]

The constant disregard for the rights of others persists even though the perpetrator knows that it is wrong and that the threat of arrest is likely. The pleasure derived from cruelty is stronger than the fear of exposure and arrest. The hunger to dominate and inflict pain is overpowering, causing negative energy to flow. The psychopath may be a spouse- or child-beater, or he or she may simply neglect, deny food to, or fail to care for someone who is wholly dependent on the cruel, domineering individual. The loss of a loved one can increase the psychopath's cruelty.[32]

Their victim's pain and suffering may actually inspire a person with APD to commit further acts of brutality. The psychopath may use frightening facial expressions and gestures to create heart-thumping fear. Such deviant people are also inveterate liars. It has been said that "the heart of a psychopath's coldness seems to lie in the inability to make anything more than the shallowest of emotional connections."[33] Although her contemporaries lacked the clinical knowledge of a latter-day mental health professional, they undoubtedly saw, in the facts and fiction presented by the press, a hard road ahead for Emma Kaufmann

Chapter 4

A Prison in Disguise

The feeling here, especially among the women, is very bitter against Mrs. Kauffman[n] and many of them are telling stories.

Mitchell Daily Republic
June 15, 1906

While she probably did not read the damaging and damning newspaper reports, Emma Kaufmann remained within the confines of her fine home, as a prisoner, in the custody of Sheriff Nyrum E. Phillips, awaiting further proceedings by the justice court. She had hired other help, including a woman who acted as a nurse because the pressure-cooker legal mess had caused her to weaken. Still it was reported that she "exhibits not the slightest emotion." Her husband spent most of his time cloistered inside with her. The feeling among the public was that Moses Kaufmann, widely known as a decent man, had no knowledge of the alleged crimes committed by his wife, but that his "offense, if any, is said to be his attempt to shield his wife."[1]

One person missing from the household was Peter Erickson, fired on the day that he testified against Emma Kaufmann.[2] Even though he was not an immigrant, there was some fear that the "star witness" might disappear and possibly go to Norway. But the *Argus-Leader* believed otherwise. That paper noted that Erickson had signed his testimony—a large portion of the 106 typewritten pages of the hearing—and had his photograph taken. The attorneys for the prosecution were satisfied that sufficient precautions had been taken to ensure his appearance at the trial.[3]

A reporter for the *Yankton Press and Dakotan* went to Sioux Falls to ask questions and gauge the level of anger as a result of the startling revelations. One of the first people he spoke to was Arthur A. Snashall, the undertaker with the L. D. Miller firm. Snashall, who embalmed the body of Agnes Polreis, insisted that he did not in any way order anyone to leave her casket closed. He did not instruct the dead girl's relatives to bury her without viewing her body. And yet Agnes' brother-in-law, Andrew Sailor, who had come to Sioux Falls to take custody of the body, had a different story based on another source. Andrew had gone to the Kaufmann house and also met with Dr. Germain. The Parkston man insisted "that he [Sailor] had been told by someone not to open the casket."

The Yankton correspondent actually got a short interview with Dr. Germain, who it seems had altered his original opinion as to the death of Agnes Polreis. He confessed that he did not examine the girl at all, for he could not understand the "mixture of German and Austrian which the girl called language." So he blindly accepted Emma Kaufmann's explanation, and because he was a respected physician, his signature on the death certificate would mean that no inquest would be necessary.

The correspondent asked Dr. Germain point blank, "Will you claim before a court that her wounds were ulcers or the cuts gangrenous?" He responded, "Most certainly not. I am convinced now they were cuts, made with some blunt instrument, I know not what, and I believe I was deceived at the Kauffman[n] home." Having pinned him down for the record, it remained to be seen just what Dr. Germain would say in a court of law, under oath.[4] The doctor was also quoted as saying that he "jumped to a conclusion" when he declared that Agnes had succumbed to diabetes[5] and that he accepted as truthful "the story told by Mrs. Kauffman[n] that the girl was injured by falling down stairs."[6]

The Yankton reporter also learned that Sheriff Phillips was under fire for the perceived lenient treatment of his prisoner, Emma Kaufmann. The concern was why she wasn't in jail. Although presumed innocent, she had been formally accused of a horrible homicide, and yet she was allowed to remain in her home. Phillips responded to the criticism by saying that the Minnehaha County jail was no fit place for a woman prisoner, no matter what crime she was accused of committing.

The reporter agreed with this reasoning because he understood the jail to be nothing more than an "unsanitary hospital." Two years before, a grand jury had exposed and condemned the deplorable condition of the jail, and yet nothing had been done to correct the deficiencies. The first floor of the building contained the cells for men, and the upper floor, consisting of "four iron cages," was set aside for women. No women were housed in the cells because they were occupied by two Indian men, both of whom were "consumptive" and had been left to die. There was one other room that could be used to incarcerate Emma Kaufmann, but it was occupied by an "insane woman." For these reasons, the rat-infested jail was deemed off-limits to sane, female prisoners.[7]

Minnehaha County Sheriff Nyrum E. Phillips. Courtesy Dana R. Bailey, *History of Minnehaha County, South Dakota (Sioux Falls, SD: Brown & Saenger, 1899).*

The reporter took the side of Sheriff Phillips. People usually did. He was a Civil War veteran and a man of good character and proven integrity. "Nye" Phillips was a likeable and well-respected old-timer, a Sioux Falls original, a man who arrived at the Falls of the Big Sioux River in 1869 when the scenic spot was the site of Fort Dakota. It was said that "Uncle" Nye Phillips "has been a resident of Sioux Falls since the hills began to grow."[8]

Because of his hard work and loyalty to political operatives, Phillips always had a government job of some kind.[9] In the past he had served as county register of deeds and as warden for the state prison. In 1906 he was the sheriff of Minnehaha County. Through it all, his ties to the Republican Party were strong and he had recently been named to the party central committee. As such, it is very likely that Phillips was well acquainted with the politically influential Moses Kaufmann, whose wife the sheriff now had in his custody and control inside her handsome home.

Apparently, the hard-working sheriff was not all that concerned about his client escaping, for it was reported that a visitor caught Phillips sound asleep in "a large Turkish rocker." This individual recalled seeing "a small man with a gray mustache and beard" snoring rather loudly, indicating that the keeper of the prisoner was "asleep at the switch." The sheriff was suddenly awakened when Moses Kaufmann explained to his guest that he was in the presence of Sheriff Phillips, the man in charge of "guarding my wife."[10]

Although Moses Kaufmann remained at home as much as possible to comfort his wife and to avoid public contact, he was not without company. On June 18 a reporter from the *Yankton Press and Dakotan* called on Moses Kaufmann. In an article headlined "**SCENE OF CRIME**," the reporter began by stating that Mr. Kaufmann was in full support of his wife, whom he had loved for more than twenty-five years, and for whom he had "built . . . a beautiful home in Sioux Falls and satisfied her every wish."

The correspondent was quite won over by Moses Kaufmann. He saw the pain on Kaufmann's "usually jovial" face and as he spoke, "he could not, strong man that he is, prevent tears from starting from his eyes." His voice became almost inaudible, and he broke down. While grasping the visitor's hand, he said, "I believe my wife to be one of the best women in the world." The words came from "the bottom of his big heart, for Moses Kauffman[n] is one of the biggest hearted men in all South Dakota."

The reporter brought up the matter of the trunk that contained Agnes' wet, torn, and bloody clothing. Kaufmann "manifested the utmost surprise," saying he "knew nothing of what was in the trunk.

I merely gave the keys to her friends and had the trunk forwarded to them."

Kaufmann gave the Yankton reporter a tour of his home, which he described for his readers as a beautiful house immaculately furnished and bearing evidence of having been well maintained. "The floors glisten; the carpets have lost none of their delicacy of coloring; the draperies contain no dust; the curtains are snow white . . . and the cut glass sparkles like icicles in the sunlight." Kaufmann escorted the reporter to the kitchen, also a showplace. "The range looks like a mirror; the hard maple floor would do credit to the top of a kitchen table," the reporter remarked, because it was so clean.

Next he was taken to a steep stairway with an elevation of about ten feet. "It is down this stairway that it is claimed Agnes Polreis fell and received some of her worst wounds," explained the reporter. Kaufmann explained that it was necessary to build it steep, even though it was a challenge to negotiate. He said that his son, Charles, "fell down the stairway a year ago and received serious injuries."

Then, in what seems very strange under the circumstances, Kaufmann led the reporter to "the girl's room," a small room "under the northwest gable of the house" where Agnes Polreis suffered from "the terrible wounds found on her body only after death." The reporter was dumbfounded at what he saw: "Not a vestage [sic] of dirt, not a blood stain, not a bit of cloth or wisp of anything." The room looked as if it were brand new. It was "as white and vacant as the day when it was finished by the plasterer." The only furnishings were a washstand and bureau, a small bed, no more than three-feet wide with "nothing on it but a spring." While the reporter may have experienced an eerie, ghost-like shiver, he saw "no sign of life or death." He could see nothing that even hinted that "a human being had ever suffered in the room or that the life blood of Agnes Polreis was poured out on the clothing found in the trunk without leaving a trace in the room." Moses Kaufmann broke the silence. "Yes," said the brewer, "when I was a boy I would have been glad to have a room half this comfortable."[11]

Kaufmann had received another visitor at the great house, a reporter from the *Minneapolis Journal*, who came to call perhaps the same day as the Yankton man. When the Minneapolis journalist entered the elegant house, "Sheriff Phillips occupied a chair on one corner of the parlor." The reporter noticed that Kaufmann's face clearly showed signs of suffering and stress. When he tried to talk, his voice trembled and broke into "audible sobs and finally gave away to tears like a schoolboy."

The suffering man said that he had been away from home a "great deal." And with his son far away at school, Emma was left by herself. He was quoted as saying, "My wife always locked the door leading from the hallway to the girl's room, thus cutting the girl off from any other part of the house." Realizing he had just inadvertently incriminated his wife, he revised his statement, noting that Agnes "used the back stairs altogether, and I am inclined to believe she received some of the wounds from falling on the stairway, which is very steep."

At the time of the interview, the number of wounds on Agnes' body totaled forty-nine. But Moses Kaufmann was in no mood to talk about Agnes and told the reporter, "I would rather you not ask me about it, for this horrible affair will come out in court." In the meantime, he said he would stand by his wife, believing her to be "one of the best women in the world." He admitted that his wife was still grieving over the loss of their daughter, and insisted that they were being "persecuted by the people of Parkston."[12]

The "persecuted" Emma Kaufmann was in her mansion, confined to her room, when the reporters were given their tour. She made no appearance, which should not have surprised either reporter because she was ill and had recently been visited by Dr. Thomas J. Billion and Dr. Sydney Olney. They came at the request of Sheriff Phillips, who wanted his prisoner examined to determine whether she could be transferred to jail. Billion, speaking for himself and Olney, found that "her nervous system was quite seriously affected." They found her "ailing in other ways" and endorsed the action of Sheriff Phillips in leaving her at home. Being aware of the filthy condition of the county jail, the esteemed doctors concluded that they "would not recommend locking up a well woman . . . let alone one in the condition of Mrs. Kaufmann," reported the *Daily Argus-Leader*.[13]

The Minneapolis reporter was also taken to the room once occupied by Agnes Polreis and he, too, was amazed at how clean and new everything looked. It seemed impossible that anyone, so badly injured, with so many cuts and sores, could have spent any time in the room with its "white walls and scrubbed floors."[14] Today, of course, the room would have been part of a crime-scene investigation, under the custody and control of the police, but in 1906 the authorities allowed it to be cleaned to perfection, thus destroying all evidence, including violent acts that may have occurred there.

Some evidence was put on public display. On June 18, two days before the preliminary hearing was scheduled to resume, Hutchinson County State's Attorney J. L. Quinn, in the company of Parkston's leading businessmen, came to Sioux Falls with the trunk of tattered and blood-stained clothes belonging to Agnes. They were in town to attend the hearing but also to show off the clothing. A display was set up in "Parlor E" at the Cataract Hotel, which drew a large number of curious people.

"Throngs of women" showed up at the Cataract to view the "blotched garments," in response to the advertised exhibition. Tears flowed freely as the public looked at the bloody items, all of which bore testimony to the suffering of Agnes Polreis. Many women were heard "heaping curses on the head of the woman accused of the crime."[15]

The exhibit of the "trunk of gruesome clothing" was met with considerable criticism by some lawyers and a Sioux Falls newspaper, the *Argus-Leader.* It was seen as a shabby and disrespectful display that could only further inflame passions among the already angry public. Although Quinn disavowed having anything to do with the exhibit, the side show, barked the *Argus-Leader*, "has started street talk in connection with this case and a person can find as many rumors as he meets different people."[16]

John Emmke was one of the proprietors of the Cataract Hotel, a place that over time had become one of the leading hotels in the West. It was the brainchild of Harry Corson, who came to Sioux Falls in 1870 for the purpose of building a hotel. He purchased lots from Dr. Josiah L. Phillips at the corner of 9th Street and Phillips Avenue.[17] The original Cataract was a modest frame building, but over the years Corson improved upon and expanded his hotel, making it a destination for businessmen and society ladies. In 1900 it succumbed to fire, but the Cataract was rebuilt and reclaimed its reputation for excellence and grandeur.

According to court documents, Emmke claimed that Quinn was in charge of the clothing exhibit that began on the evening of June 18. On the 20th Sioux Falls Mayor Frank W. Pillsbury sent Chief

Cataract Hotel, Sioux Falls, South Dakota.
Author's Collection.

of Police Frank Wade to the hotel.[18] Wade ordered Quinn and his people to pack up and get out because the mayor believed that the ghastly exhibit tended to "inflame the public mind and might lead to a riot if continued."[19] Quinn was also upbraided by other lawyers working on the case for exhibiting "the bloody undergarments" of the dead girl."[20] Clearly, Quinn had acted in a manner unbecoming of a state's attorney.

An editorial in the *South Dakota State Forum*, a Sioux Falls weekly, roundly criticized the gruesome exhibition of wet and bloody items from the trunk brought from Parkston. The editor scolded the Parkston people, who "seem to be afraid that Sioux Falls will not give them justice." They are mistaken, declared the editorial, and furthermore the display damages their cause while it "attempts further sensationalism." Mayor Pillsbury was applauded for putting an end to the lurid exhibition.[21]

~

Unfortunately, the sensational and explicit newspaper reporting, along with the gruesome exhibit of clothing had sufficiently poisoned the public mind, and on the morning of June 20, 1906, when the Kaufmanns arrived at the Sioux Falls City Auditorium, a large crowd, the largest yet, was waiting, ready to unload. One reporter who was present said the crowd reminded him of a "big political rally."[22] But this was the politics of anger and hate, a wild carnival atmosphere, that meant no one would witness a quiet, dignified court proceeding.

In a carriage driven by the coroner, L. D. Miller, Sheriff Phillips and the Kaufmanns were delivered to their dreaded destination.[23] A "dense mass of humanity" lined the sidewalk and pressed forward so that police officers had to push the crowd back to allow the pale and nervous Emma Kaufmann and her small party to get through. While they squeezed their way into the auditorium, angry women hissed and spit to express their hatred of the veiled and terrified defendant.[24]

Justice A. B. Wheelock had arrived at 8 A.M. for the hearing expected to start at 10 o'clock. Already anxious and curious people were waiting to get inside and take a seat, and by 9 o'clock the hearing room was filled. A reporter for the *Argus-Leader* said the crowd "was so dense that he got through with the assistance of an officer." One eager observer had gone to an adjacent room and tried to "peer through an opening made for a stove pipe." Out in the street on the west side of the building, faces were pressed against the windows,

Sioux Falls City Auditorium. *Courtesy Center for Western Studies, Augustana University, Sioux Falls, South Dakota.*

and there were those sitting on the shoulders of others struggling to get a glimpse inside.[25] As the crowd was unruly and some were making threatening remarks, Mayor Pillsbury ordered the entire police force to be ready in the event that there was an outbreak of violence.[26]

Once inside, the Kaufmanns made their way to the counsel table. The room was full, with "every inch of space in the courtroom and adjacent hallways packed to suffocation." Spectators, mostly well-dressed women, "stood on chairs, on boxes, craning their necks" so they could hear the judge and the attorneys.[27] Among the anxious crowd was a sizable group from Parkston, "who had come in a vain fear that unless they were present, the court would let Mrs. Kaufmann off."[28] The eager spectators were expecting to see the trunk and its bloody contents be admitted into evidence. There was also a report that the "long galvanized iron kitchen spoon," which was allegedly used to inflict the head wounds, would also be introduced as evidence.[29]

The hearing itself was very brief because attorney Frank R. Aikens called no witnesses and made no defense whatsoever, although there was the expectation that he might make a motion to dismiss for lack of evidence. But he made no such motion, and after State's Attorney Alpha F. Orr requested that the defendant be "committed to the custody of the sheriff," pending trial, Justice Wheelock quietly ordered Emma Kaufmann to be held without bail on a charge of murder.[30] No trunk, no spoon, no motion.

The only thing Aikens wanted was that his client and her husband be allowed to leave in peace, and toward that end, Wheelock ordered the crowd to clear out.[31] But getting out proved to be just as hard as getting in, for there was virtually no law enforcement presence to protect the defendant's party, although protection had been promised. As the Kaufmanns, their lawyer, and the sheriff made their way out, the vicious crowd, populated by hissing and spitting women, pressed around them. One woman was seen with her "fingers set like claws," as if she were about to attack the terrified defendant. She screamed "String her up!"[32] It was noted that "young Billy West, one of the most notorious lads of the city," was "leading the women in the hissing game."[33]

To their shock and dismay, the carriage was not waiting for them, so the Kaufmanns and their escort hurriedly walked across the street to the A. T. Korthof livery stable. The crowd—having already made its decision as to the guilt of the accused—moved with them, exclaiming "Lynch her!" For a moment it was feared that the human swarm, now a mob, might break the perimeter and trample or take hold of Emma Kaufmann.[34] While the Kaufmanns were picking their way through the mass of snapping and snarling people, "representatives of the outside newspapers" tried to "get a kodak picture of Mrs. Kauffman[n]," but were denied by the efforts of the sheriff.[35] One "ill-mannered fellow," an "attaché" of a local newspaper, shoved a camera in the defendant's face. Thinking it was a gun, she was sure she was about to be shot.[36]

Once inside the livery stable, the terrified party boarded a carriage and, with the mob at one door, the rig suddenly bolted out of another door, taking the people by surprise. Then "the vehicle dashed up the street." With the fist-shaking, jeering, wild-eyed mob trailing for a short distance, "giving vent to shouts and derisive cries," the carriage pulled further away to safety. Denied their chance to capture or at least hurt Emma Kaufmann, the sullen crowd milled around until about noon, then dispersed.[37] Truly, the city of Sioux Falls was not on its best behavior that 20th of June 1906.

Emma Kaufmann was taken up the 7th Street hill to her home in the company of the sheriff, a move that did not sit well with the people. Soon another noisy group had gathered in front of the auditorium and demanded that the defendant be taken to jail forthwith. The group finally agreed to disperse after attorney Joe Kirby offered his "guarantee [that] the woman would be in jail before night."[38]

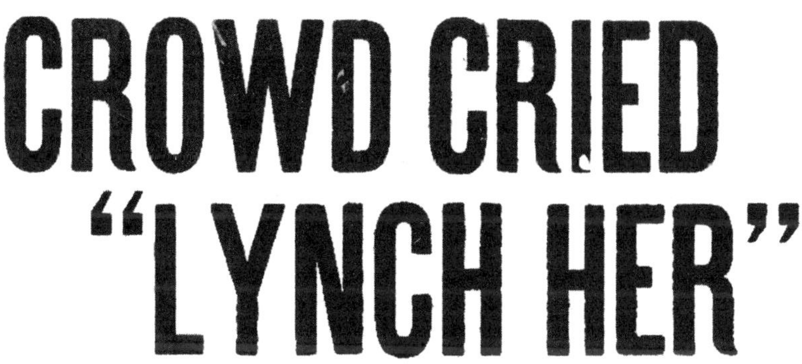
CROWD CRIED
"LYNCH HER"

Spokane Press headline, Spokane, Washington, June 20, 1906.

Kirby telephoned Aikens and warned him that "dire results" were in the offing due to the excitement in the city, and it would be better if the accused woman was sent to jail.[39] After a short conference between the attorneys, it was decided that Sheriff Phillips would escort Emma Kaufmann to jail, pending a bail hearing. Shortly before noon, she was behind the bars of a dingy jail cell in the company of her distraught husband, who could not bear to leave her side.[40]

The *Sioux Falls Daily Press* came out with a different version of the story. The decision to jail the accused was made after she, her husband, and the sheriff were safely inside the Kaufmann mansion. After a short while, a deputy sheriff driving a closed carriage pulled up at the house; he ran across the lawn and "when admitted to the house he explained hurriedly" that for the sake of safety Emma Kaufmann should be put in jail. She seemed unmoved by the idea, but an emotionally drained Moses Kaufmann "wrung his hands" and cried out, "Oh God, my God, what have I done, what have I done." But he, too, was convinced that it was the wise course of action.[41]

While Sheriff Phillips was escorting Mrs. Kaufmann to the county jail, a group of skeptical Parkston men followed along. They entered the sheriff's office and demanded that they be allowed to personally see that she was behind bars. This Phillips refused to do, telling them to take his word for it. The Parkston men pressed the issue, and after an angry exchange a compromise was reached. One man from the group would be allowed inside. At first, Agnes' brother, Paul Polreis, was chosen. Then they decided that John Fish, the Parkston justice of the peace, represent the group. Fish went inside and saw Emma Kaufmann lying on a cot. Satisfied, he offered an apology to the sheriff and left the office.[42]

An Illinois newspaper, the *Rock Island Argus*, offered yet another take on the jailing of Emma Kaufmann. Under the headline "**WOMEN SEND MRS. KAUFMANN TO JAIL**," the paper reported that the "city's socially elect" took "justice in their own hands" and jailed Mrs. Kaufmann. It was either that or "dynamite" the Kaufmann mansion.[43] The fine home had become a "house of horrors," and the object of public ridicule and wrath.

The editor of the *Parkston Advance* was worked up into a froth, and yet he managed to report on the events of June 20 with some clarity and in a manner that reflected the pain of an entire community. It was harshly critical of Dr. Germain, calling him "either a knave or a fool" for making out a death certificate based on natural causes without ever examining the body of Agnes Polreis. The feeling against him in Parkston was "very strong," and because he dishonored the medical profession, "he should be severely dealt with."

Then the editor addressed the trunk and its ghastly contents, which he felt told a tale of "torture and murder." Having seen the soiled and bloody garments, he stated that "it has conveyed an impression that all the hired witnesses, money and sympathy for the accused woman" will not be enough to save her. The article heaped praise on State's Attorney Quinn for his handling of the evidence in the trunk and for championing the cause of all the citizens of Hutchinson County—and that of poor Agnes, whose "only offense was the ignorance of the hell on earth she was getting into when she accepted employment with the Kaufmann woman."[44]

When the Hutchinson County people departed Sioux Falls, they did so with some satisfaction. Due process and fundamental fairness should have satisfied the citizens of Sioux Falls, too, but a few toughs remained discontented and wanted a lynching. Lynchings in South Dakota were rare, but in 1895 an unidentified man, "a tramp," was strung up on a telephone pole in Watertown by "a quiet and orderly mob."[45] The incident that brought shame to Watertown was not widely publicized.

The lynch mob would have made national news had they been successful. They gathered at the "Cataract Corner," at 9th Street and Phillips Avenue in downtown Sioux Falls, to discuss strategy. One of the hotheads, who identified himself as John Magoon from Sioux City, Iowa, was heard to say that if someone would find a rope, he would take charge and hang Emma Kaufmann. Overhearing this, police officer Jack Tracey collared Magoon and hauled him off to jail, the only arrest of the day.[46]

As the hours passed, the mob-inspired anger and hostility cooled. Men and women walked away muttering their displeasure as darkness deepened, having missed their chance to hang a woman without granting her the benefit of due process. But of course everyone knew that in order to get at Emma Kaufmann, they would first have to kill Sheriff Phillips. There was not a man who would dare to challenge him and therefore there would be no lynching in Sioux Falls.

Joe Kirby, although a part of the prosecution team, defended Sheriff Phillips' handling of the custody of Emma Kaufmann. A man of means, Kirby unflinchingly acknowledged that the rich had "natural advantages" and in all likelihood a poor person would have been jailed immediately. And yet from what he knew of Sheriff Phillips, he said, "I hardly believe it."

To some it may have seemed as if Kirby was being sympathetic to the woman he was prosecuting, but he was merely trying to quell suspicions when he explained state law as it applied to the custody of a person formally accused of a crime. In South Dakota it was the sheriff's duty to maintain custody and control over a suspect, but that responsibility did not require him to put the accused person in jail. If, for example, the person could be kept elsewhere, under vigilant guard, such an arrangement is within the law and coincides with the principle of presumption of innocence.[47]

Legal principles didn't seem to matter in the Kaufmann case. Reason, caution, and compassion were cast aside like worn-out slogans and replaced by a simplistic desire to define sin, assign guilt, and administer punishment. It was as if the rough justice of the Wild West had returned for an encore. The past, however, can never overtake the present, even though it can influence the future. So it was with the explosive and vulnerable Kaufmann case with its poisonous secrets, bizarre twists and turns, and enough dead ends to exhaust the clearest thinker.

Chapter 5

The Long, Slow Judicial Grind Continues

Public opinion has convicted Mrs. Moses Kauffman[n] of the crime of murder.

Daily Press and Dakotan
June 20, 1906

At last Emma Kaufmann was behind bars in the Minnehaha County jail, locked in a cell near a noisy, wretched female prisoner whose bizarre behavior was almost too much to bear. Charles A. Smith, author of *A Comprehensive History of Minnehaha County* (1949), paid a visit to the jail in his younger days. He left with a very negative impression, and when he was busy compiling his county history years later, he wrote, “we will not go into the details as to the conditions within the building,” preferring simply to “leave the rest of the story to the reader’s imagination.” He did mention, however, that “conditions were deplorable.” The filthy and vermin-infested facility was situated directly north of the county courthouse with only “a narrow boardwalk between the two buildings.”

Although the building was fit to be condemned as a fire hazard, the accused murderess was locked inside to suffer in the company of her sorrow-stricken husband and a nurse. On June 23 her twenty-year-old son, Charles, arrived from college in Ohio to join them.[1] It was a cozy arrangement that would not have been granted to the town drunk. But no one really expected her to remain in the miserable jail for very long. There was the expectation that, as a woman of wealth, she would soon be set free.

Then a story surfaced that she was not actually behind bars, but "was confined in a room on the top floor of the courthouse." Before she set foot inside the attic room, the *Weekly Cataract* reported, her husband had it "luxuriously furnished" and "papered with wall paper which cost not less than two dollars per roll."[2]

That such bizarre stories circulated attests to the fascination that had seized hold of the public's mind since the story broke. And as the days passed, morbid curiosity increased, spawning new rumors and speculation. People wanted to believe everything and anything. For instance, it was whispered around town that Emma Kaufmann was in the habit of indulging in "stimulants,"[3] thus adding to the catalog of her questionable character traits, all of which heightened the approach of her trial. With so much at stake and so much money invested in the outcome, the trial would be a show not to be missed.

There were trials in the court of public opinion that followed, and sometimes mocked, trials in a court of law, and on the whole many people believed that money and power influenced the outcome. It was easy to believe that when a poor man was hauled into court and charged with a crime, his case was rushed through the system—and he landed in jail. This double-standard and perceived injustice tended to grind away at the moral conscience of the less privileged, so that when a rich person was arrested for a serious crime, the poor shook their collective fist and shouted out in anger and glee. And so it was with the Kaufmann case.

One of those angry voices was, of course, that of John Ross of the *Soo Critic*. Always ready to jab the rich and attack the newspapers that supported people of wealth, Ross would not let go of the Kaufmann case, and he could not resist taking swipes at the *Argus-Leader* from time to time. When that newspaper reported that Mrs. Kaufmann rested better after the "crazy woman" was taken away to the state mental hospital in Yankton, Ross reminded his readers that the *Argus* was "solicitious" [sic] because she was "the wife of a rich and influential man."[4]

When there was a slight lull in the reporting, an outside newspaper came out with the headline "**DEAD GIRL'S MOTHER HAD A GRUESOME PREMONITION.**" According to a report in the *Minneapolis Journal*, Agnes' mother, worried sick because she had not heard from her daughter in several weeks, had a nervous breakdown just three days before the girl's death. Theresa Polreis woke up in the night screaming, "'Why doesn't my daughter write? . . . I know something awful is going to happen to her.'" Three days later, just minutes before Moses Kaufmann telephoned Parkston to tell the family of the death of Agnes, Mrs. Polreis "was pleading with a store keeper to telephone the wealthy brewer's residence . . . that she might hear her daughter's voice." When the storekeeper relayed the message that Agnes had died of "heart disease," Theresa Polreis "fell in a faint to the floor."[5] The public could count on the Minneapolis paper to keep the Kaufmann case in the news like a serialized horror story.

The premonition story originated with the Parkston delegation and was picked up by the *Sioux Falls Daily Press*, which deemed it worthy of a "place in the records of the London society for psychological research." The phenomenon was seen as an example of mental telepathy between a mother and child, where the "soul of one responds with visions to the anguish of the other." Spiritualism—the belief that souls in the astral plane could communicate directly with the living—was popular in the nineteenth century but was largely replaced by the science of psychology in the twentieth century. Nevertheless, according to the newspaper, for three days and nights, Theresa Polreis was haunted by a vague but persistent sense that something terrible was happening to her daughter. Her awful fears were confirmed by the "tremulous voice of the wealthy brewer."[6]

Such sensationalism added to the public's response to the larger narrative, but Theresa Polreis' premonition would have no impact on the course of the Kaufmann case. After so many emotional accounts, voices of clarity and reason were badly needed in the summer of 1906, and some were trying hard to be heard. One such advocate, the editor of the daily *Yankton Press and Dakotan*, tried to take on the role of spokesperson for fairness and calm.

A *Yankton Press* editorial on June 20, 1906, sharply criticized the blatant prejudice toward Emma Kaufmann, whose surname the paper habitually misspelled. Those who would rush to judgment were reminded that the presumption of innocence applies to all, rich and poor. Prejudice was leveled at the defendant because she was the wife of a rich brewer, a business that many looked upon as evil. Ignore that bias, the editor asserted, and look at the known facts. After all, the investigation was in its early stages and Mrs. Kaufmann might be innocent. Declaring "everything is in a state of chaos" so that it is "impossible to sift the evidence from wild rumors," the even-handed editorial reached out to those who believed in fair play, asking all people to rely on the judicial system and show respect for the rights of the defendant. Applying an appropriate coda to the loud, discordant public melody, the editor wrote: "those who can still think calmly and await the administration of justice are to be commended."[7]

Aware of the explosive tension in Sioux Falls, prosecutor Joe Kirby decided to call for calm. In a letter to the editor of the *Argus-Leader*, he berated the angry women who had demonstrated against Emma Kaufmann at the preliminary hearing. "Such females," he said, "came to the hearing with the appetite of a buzzard seeking carrion." These women had gathered at the Cataract to view the bloodied clothing of the victim, to satiate their "foul appetite." Pouring on the invective, he said they were a class of women "who infest morgues" and send "bouquets to wife murderers." To someone unacquainted with Sioux Falls, these women were "veritable viragoes." But Kirby was quick to point out that they were in the minority and that most Sioux Falls women acted in an appropriate manner and were a credit to their city and state.[8]

A return to order began to settle upon the residents of the city, and many women, in fact, came forward to denounce the lynch-mob mentality, making it clear that the "better class" of females wanted no part of the disgraceful behavior. Further, the Kaufmann attorneys threatened to file criminal charges against these women, who now, frightened, began to look for ways to keep their names out of the public eye lest they too fall victim to the dark storm of disgrace hovering above Sioux Falls.[9]

Still all eyes, including those with fire in them, remained on the Kaufmann case and its next appearance before the South Dakota

Supreme Court in Pierre, the capital city. Very little time expired between the indictment and the bail hearing. On June 21 the lawyers, including Frank Aikens and Alpha Orr, packed up and headed for Pierre because the state supreme court had original jurisdiction over the matter of bail.[10] Suddenly, the show was on the road and court watchers were expecting more delicious revelations.

Before he left Sioux Falls, Aikens spoke with a group of reporters at the Cataract Hotel, the site of many informal gatherings where the Kaufmann matter was discussed. He scoffed at those who believed bail would be denied: "I believe the court will have no hesitancy in releasing Mrs. Kaufmann on bail." Aikens called this incident nothing more than a "simple case of assault and battery." But he quickly added, as he turned to walk away, "I have never tried my cases in the newspapers and I do not intend to begin now."[11]

Emma Kaufmann had been resting in jail while her husband passed the time reading newspapers. He knew that should his wife be denied bail he would not be allowed to stay with her behind bars indefinitely.[12] Enforced separation was something the Kaufmanns did not want. However, where Emma would be kept over the next several months would be determined by the South Dakota Supreme Court.

Moses Kaufmann protected his wife with all his might and money because he loved her. He hired the best legal and medical talent and saw to her comfort, holding her hand as if the simple gesture would give her strength. He also took extraordinary measures to keep her picture out of the newspapers. Reporters worked diligently to get a photograph, but they were denied at every turn. Sioux Falls photographers were besieged and offered large sums of money for their negatives, but "without exception they refused to sell even a single photograph" of the accused woman. This suggests that Kaufmann money got there ahead of the reporters.

Finally, however, a reporter from the *Sioux City Journal* was able to get his hands on a photograph "from an acquaintance," who obtained one from an album owned by a friend of the Kaufmann family. Getting the scoop on the Sioux Falls newspapers, the *Journal* published a picture of Emma Kaufmann on June 25, 1906.[13]

Emma Kaufmann,
Sioux City Journal, June 20, 1906.

At the bail hearing before the Supreme Court in Pierre, Orr did the talking for the prosecution. Curiously, special prosecutor Joe Kirby did not attend. Frank R. Aikens spoke for the defense. His central argument was that the evidence presented at the preliminary hearing only supported a charge of manslaughter. Therefore, Emma Kaufmann should be allowed bail as a matter of law because manslaughter was a "bailable" offense.[14]

After listening to the arguments of the attorneys, Justice Richard Haney of the South Dakota Supreme Court stated in his written decision that "the Constitution of this state secures the right to everyone accused of a crime the right to bail in all cases," except in a capital case, and even then bail might be allowed as a matter of discretion if certain tests are met. Haney noted that in this case the "accused is charged with murder. If the proof is evident, or the presumption great her admission to bail is forbidden." After writing a detailed analysis of the evidence against Emma Kaufmann, Haney and the court decided that the proof "is not so plain and palpable as to warrant us in denying the defendant's application." Bail was granted in a sum that was reasonable and just under the circumstances.[15]

That sum was $25,000. On June 23, at about 5 o'clock in the afternoon, the decision of the court was wired to Sioux Falls. With great speed the bond was drafted and issued by the American Surety Company represented by C. L. McKinney. A number of other leading men of Sioux Falls signed it including Kaufmann's partner Moriz Levinger, along with Porter Peck, Charles Fantle, William Doolittle, and Harry Parmley, twenty-nine signatures in all. That these men, and so many others, were willing to sign gladdened the heavy heart of Moses Kaufmann; his friends had come to his rescue. Shortly before midnight the bond was presented to Judge Joseph Jones of the circuit court for Minnehaha County. He pronounced it a "most excellent bond" and signed his approval.

The county clerk had to be awakened so the bond could be filed and turned over to the sheriff. Since the hour was late, there was no attempt to release Mrs. Kaufmann, who, in the constant company of her husband and son, was looking forward to returning to her home, a stark contrast to the Spartan jailhouse accommodations. While she was confined to a cell, guards assigned by the chief of police patrolled the area around her house to protect it from vandals.[16] The public remained in a state of high anxiety, while demands were made concerning the arrest of all accessories to the crime.

A reporter for the *Yankton Press and Dakotan* tried to examine the bond that freed Emma Kaufmann, a document he believed to be a matter of public record. But he was repeatedly denied access and was told bluntly that "the public should have no interest in it whatever, and the public is not going to see it." He was also told that many of the men whose signatures were on the bond wanted secrecy. The bond was "buried by the sheriff or some other county official," so the correspondent left disappointed.[17]

At about 10 o'clock on the evening of June 26, the Kaufmanns departed the gloomy confines of the jail. It was reported that they went directly to the railroad depot because someone there mistook another woman for Kaufmann. The report proved to be a canard, for the Kaufmanns went to their home at the corner of Summit Avenue and 7th Street.[18] It was later learned that the woman thought to be Emma, boarding a train at the Great Northern depot, was actually the female prisoner whose wild antics in the jail caused Emma so much misery.[19]

News of the bail and bond was received in Parkston with great disappointment, many feeling it was a concession to wealth. It was the "feeling among the citizens" at Parkston that the release of the defendant meant that there would be no trial come November. The Parkston people believed that Emma would leave and never return, rather than face "certain conviction for the killing of Miss Polreis."

The *Parkston Advance* all but pronounced the case closed, and it was with sadness that, "even though the ends of justice should be defeated," the people could feel proud of their strong efforts and their interest in the case. In seeking justice for Agnes, they had done the right thing. They had freely and with great passion poured their time, energy, and money into the case but had nothing to show for it except the honor of having rallied around the Polreis family.[20] For a time, things quieted down in Parkston.

But not in Sioux Falls. The granting of bail did not sit well with the *Soo Critic.* Editor Ross absorbed the bad news and then launched an article that sharply attacked the South Dakota Supreme Court for its ruling. Before he criticized the law, Ross reiterated his dislike of the rich by declaring that in appearance, at least, there was "one law for the rich and quite another for the poor." This double-standard, this "disregard for the law," he believed, might cause mob violence. Having issued a warning, Ross tempered his remarks by saying the *Critic* "stands for justice, not vengeance."

Unfortunately for Ross, his article proceeded in a bumbling manner that probably frustrated readers. A careful reading of the article reveals that his main point seemed to be that the court did not thoroughly analyze the facts nor did it correctly apply the law. He further declared that State's Attorney Alpha Orr presented a weak, half-hearted argument against bail.

The Constitution of the State of South Dakota, under Section 8 of Article VI stated the following: "All persons shall be bailable [sic] by sufficient sureties, except for capital offenses, when the proof is evident *or* presumption great [emphasis added]." Ross conceded that proof was not evident but he believed that presumption was great. To support this point he asserted that "a large majority of people will say presumption is great" because it was clear "that the girl came to her death as a result of blows, and scaldings received at the hands of Mrs. Kaufman[n]." And since presumption, as he and others saw it, was great, no bail should have been allowed. He was also unwilling to let Orr off the hook, doubting that the state's attorney even presented an argument based on presumption.

To bolster his position, Ross brought up "a rule of common law" that stated a "person intends the consequences of his acts." He tied this principle to the case by pointing to the repetition of "brutal acts that might cause death." These acts, he believed, showed that the defendant intended to kill her victim or at least gave rise to the presumption great enough to overcome the right to bail. Clearly, he was struggling to make his point, a task made more difficult due to the phraseology of the South Dakota Constitution.

Ignoring the perceived vagaries of the Constitution, Ross questioned the thought process of Justice Haney. The justice, Ross said, placed all his focus on the first prong (proof is evident) of Section 8, Article VI, while ignoring the second prong. Ross insisted, incorrectly, that the use of the conjunctive "or" in Article VI meant that both prongs had to be considered. And because the court did not do so, it was in error. Actually, had the Constitution used the conjunctive "and" instead of "or," the court would have been required to consider both prongs.

Ross believed that the second prong, "presumption," drawn from all the known facts—the forty-nine wounds on the body of Agnes Polreis—was great enough to convict and certainly enough to deny bail, had the court taken all this into consideration. It was "well known," Ross insisted, "that Mrs. Kaufman[n] has mistreated hired girls. It is said by those who have worked for her that she dictated their acts beyond her right; fought them, pulled their hair, would not allow their rooms locked, [and] was brutal to them." That may have been true, but such evidence was not before the court.

Then he surveyed all the actual evidence presented at the preliminary hearing as if he wanted his readers to relive the horror of the crime. On the whole, his article is a rambling discourse by someone lacking legal training, a critique of the court's reasoning and ruling, and another public airing of the cruelty suffered by Agnes Polreis.[21]

Ross was unwilling to relent. The court's decision to allow bail only added to his indignation. He kept pressure on the *Argus-Leader* and its "misrepresentations," which not only showed sympathy for the accused but brought shame and humiliation on Sioux Falls and its people. He quoted a local property owner who sarcastically said, "The *Argus-Leader* writes about the bond question as if the people of Sioux Falls had to be kept away from signing with pike poles." The Kaufmann case was creating a sharp division of opinion in Sioux Falls and Ross was in the breach, hacking away. He believed, and so stated, that it was necessary for Sioux Falls and the state of South Dakota to censor the *Argus-Leader* so that it would stop printing misrepresentations.

Not satisfied with slamming the *Argus-Leader*, Ross gathered editorials and articles from other South Dakota newspapers and added their views to the weapons he was aiming at the accused wife of a "rich brewer." Among them, the *Mitchell Clarion* postulated that had the poor immigrant girl been accused of killing Emma Kaufmann "in the same diabolical manner," she would not have been given "every possible comfort" in jail and would have been denied bail. The *Sanborn County Herald* compared the foul murder of Agnes Polreis to the heinous massacres "committed . . . in the days of Indian raids and is far worse than murder." The *Watertown Times* was in accord with the *Critic*, calling the release of Emma Kaufmann an example of "giving the wealthy individual favors which the poor are refused." The *Parker Press* attacked Dr. Germain in a hard-hitting article, accusing him of engaging in a cover-up for the "accused Jewess" to clear her "skirts of all blame."[22]

The Kaufmann case was causing freedom of the press to run wild, its wheels careening perilously close to a libelous ditch. Reports on the case from newspapers throughout the country were, for the most part, inaccurate, but the prize for the most outrageous and inflammatory article goes to the *San Francisco Call*. On June 14, 1906, it stated that Agnes was "beaten with a poker until she sank to the floor, with water to make her rise, lifted to her feet only to be pummeled into a condition of semi-consciousness by the fists of her mistress."[23]

The *Sioux Falls Journal*, a conservative newspaper, maintained a cautious, but angry, approach to the case. Acknowledging that prospect of bail was about to be met with "a great howl," the *Journal* was of the belief that, if the court explained its decision carefully, the public might understand and accept it. Still the temperature of the "people in the common walks of life" was high due to the belief that the principle of "equality under the law" was ignored. The farmers were expressing their discontent and were now reluctant to allow their daughters to work as live-in maids, for fear that their girls' fate might be that of Agnes Polreis. Widespread distrust, the *Journal* predicted, would impact the fall election of 1906 and unpopular officials would lose their jobs.[24]

The *Minneapolis Journal* announced that the Kaufmanns were going to stay in Sioux Falls and "face the music."[25] But after only a few days in their commodious mansion, with a policeman standing guard outside, the Kaufmanns left town in a manner that can best be described as clandestine. On June 26, 1906, the *Press and Dakotan* broke the story, saying that the Kaufmanns decided "to take no further chances with the populace." Since the trains in and out of Sioux Falls were probably being watched, the paper speculated that the Kaufmanns, including son Charles, most likely traveled by carriage to a nearby train station where they boarded the cars for parts unknown.

This assumption turned out to be accurate. On July 4, the day that people normally gathered in town to noisily celebrate independence, the Kaufmanns quietly departed Sioux Falls. One paper presumed that the rich, but badly demoralized, couple would seek treatment at a sanitarium in an effort to recover from the effects of recent events.[26]

Several days after the Kaufmanns stole away from town, the *Argus-Leader* came out with an article on the subject. The Kaufmanns, said the daily newspaper, probably went to some "small and remote place, in seclusion," where Mrs. Kaufmann could find relief from the stress and strain. She needed rest and time to prepare for her trial. But the timing of the report suggested that the *Argus-Leader* was delaying the news so as to make sure the Kaufmanns were able to get safely out of town.[27]

The paper also reported that the people of Hutchinson County had hired a detective from the famed Pinkerton Detective Agency in Chicago to "shadow" the couple and make sure they did not leave the country.[28] "Every move the accused woman makes between now and the November trial . . . will be watched" to make certain that the beleaguered Kaufmanns do not attempt to "reach some foreign shore." Should she flee and forfeit her bond, the Parkston people were prepared to follow her to the "ends of the earth." Meanwhile, back at the Kaufmann mansion, ex-Deputy Sheriff Millard was on duty as the night watchman, although his employers had quietly slipped away without saying goodbye.[29]

There was speculation that they were bound for Europe, but anyone who may have known their actual destination was not talking. Moses and Emma Kaufmann, along with their son, had simply vanished. Later in July, it was reported that they were spending their free time at a Wisconsin resort, near Milwaukee, and that Moses Kaufmann was "negotiating for the sale of his interest in the Sioux Falls brewery." This information came from Charles L. Klewert, a distiller from Milwaukee and a personal friend of the Kaufmanns. Klewert also revealed that the Kaufmann family would leave Sioux Falls after the trial concluded and settle in another city.[30]

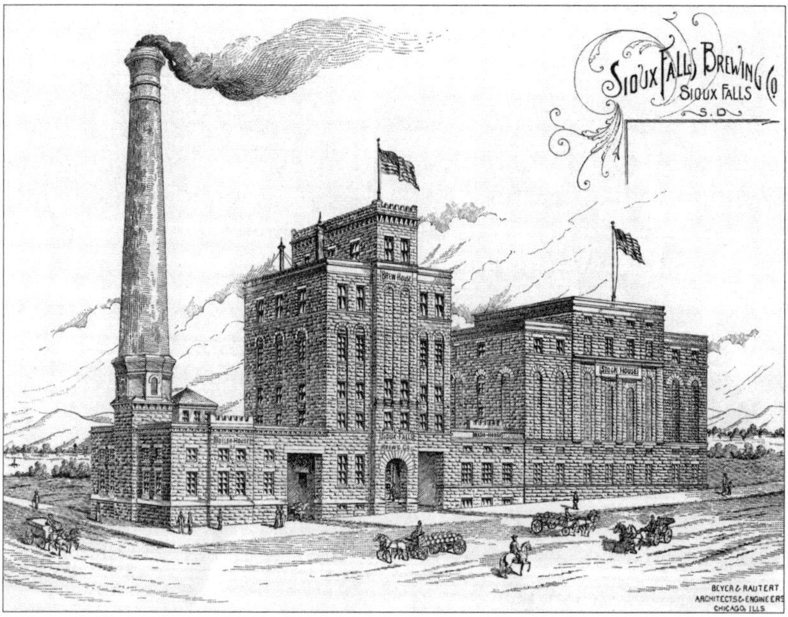

Sioux Falls Brewing Company on "Brewery Hill," Main Avenue.
Courtesy Siouxland Heritage Museums.

The *Argus-Leader* revealed that Mr. and Mrs. John Polreis had also left their home near Parkston and were staying at the farm of Joseph Schwartz, at Webster, in northeastern South Dakota. They had moved because Mrs. Polreis was suffering terribly over the death of her daughter and it was thought that the change of scenery would help her recover.[31]

In Parkston, people were busy raising funds to buy a grave marker for Agnes. A Sioux Falls monument dealer took note of their generosity and thoughtfulness and promised to erect "a handsome and costly" stone on the grave as soon as the engraving was finished.[32] In early July the F. H. Gillette Marble Works presented the gravestone to the Polreis family.[33]

It was a gracious act of generosity and sympathy, and no doubt was very much appreciated, but the Polreis family was still mired in grief. John and Theresa wrote an open letter to "Our Friends and To Whom It May Concern." Here, the grief-stricken mother held nothing back, condemning Mrs. Kaufmann in the harshest terms: "You, Mrs. Kaufmann, took Satan as your assistant when you tortured my loving daughter." She went on to say, "I can find no comfort in this world."[34]

~

The search for additional evidence continued. The *Sioux Falls Journal* reported that it was "known that many visits have been made to the east side dumping ground," searching for "bedding from the Kaufmann house." The prosecution claimed to know the "exact time" it was taken to the dump and the team "used for that purpose."[35] Indeed, the case had taken on the appearance of a Sherlock Holmes story.

In his role as sleuth-reporter, Ross of the *Critic* got a look at a letter allegedly written and sent by John and Theresa Polreis from Webster to Haus Demuth, editor of a German-language newspaper. The letter discussed the reasons that the Polreis family came to America in 1905, "land of the free." It also disgorged the horrible details of the death of their daughter in a manner that seemed calculated to outdo all other descriptions of the crime. In stark language that one might think came from Ross himself, the forty-nine wounds, the scalded feet, the skin falling from her legs, and the image of a starved, tortured girl were thrust into the face of the reading public. Then, reaching a crescendo, the letter concluded, "O, my God, think of the torture my poor child had to suffer. Since the crucifixion of Christ, never did anything so cruel happen."

Having condemned and vilified Emma Kaufmann in a series of articles, and now printing the letter word for word, editor Ross could hardly contain himself—he called for the arrest of Moses Kaufmann. "Who told Wm. Moeller that Agnes would have a good home, and be treated as one of the family?" he asked. That man was none other than Moses Kaufmann, the one person in the position to know how horribly his wife treated their hired girls. "He knew better. He knew something of the treatment his wife gave to domestics."

In calling for the arrest of Moses Kaufmann, Ross accused Moses of being "one of the main wheels of the republican machine lobby," who was "neither morally nor legally guiltless . . . in the judgment of a majority of the people of this state." But Ross did not believe for a minute that Kaufmann would be arrested because he was "a rich, influential politician."[36] The Kaufmanns were gone, but Ross wanted to make certain they were not forgotten.

Ross was a side show unto himself, a hero to his followers, all those who believed that wealth unduly influenced politics, justice, and the court system. To those who suffered from his incessant, egotistical ranting and editorial lashes, he was a noisy, mean-spirited, caustic crank. When he was the center of attention, he seemed to love every moment. He was a three-ring circus in one ring. In writing about the Kaufmann case, Ross created an army of demons that he sent out to attack the rich repeatedly. A fierce believer in the righteousness of his cause, he had his enemy by the throat and was not about to let go.

The dissenting newspapers, the small towns that were jealous of Sioux Falls, the farmers who were angry for having to work so hard for so little—all rallied to the standard of John A. Ross. The Kaufmann case was their chance to strike a blow at the rich, those they believed were responsible for their misery. Ross was their leader. His newspaper was "fearless in exposing wrong in high and low places." A Lennox, South Dakota, businessman wrote to Ross commending his "fearless paper," which he called the "voice . . . of the people." The *Critic*'s message was indeed influencing public opinion throughout southeastern South Dakota. Farmers in Lincoln and Turner County had decided to impose an economic boycott on the merchants of Sioux Falls as a punishment for electing corrupt or incompetent officials and for being weak-kneed in the pursuit of justice for Agnes Polreis. Truly, the Kaufmann case had created a firestorm without precedent. And it was raining threats, fear, and anger over South Dakota with cyclonic fury.[37]

The *Daily Argus-Leader* dropped the story after the Kaufmanns departed Sioux Falls and undoubtedly felt relieved. It did rise, however, to defend Moses Kaufmann and the Sioux Falls Brewing Company when both came under attack by a Sioux City, Iowa, newspaper. The *Sioux City Tribune* claimed that people were boycotting the brewery, it was losing money because of the Kaufmann case, and "president Kaufmann" would have to sell his interest in the company to save the business. Not true, was the retort from the Sioux Falls daily newspaper, for the brewery was "actually behind with its orders." And to further respond to the "yellow yarn," the *Argus-Leader*, under the editorship of Charles M. Day, declared that "Mr. Kaufmann is not and never has been the president," but is merely one of forty shareholders in the company.[38] This was a false claim because Moses Kaufmann, who held a management position, was far from being "merely" a stockholder.

A few days later, an interview with Kaufmann's friend, Charles L. Klewert, published in the *Milwaukee Sentinel*, revealed a case of deteriorating relationships between the brewer and other Sioux Falls businessmen. Allegedly speaking for his friend, Klewert said the Sioux Falls businessmen and the city's newspapers were shamefully abusing the man who had for years worked hard to increase the monetary value and reputation of his city. The paper reported that because of this undeserved treatment, the Kaufmanns were planning to leave Sioux Falls for good.

Klewert defended Emma Kaufmann, too. In his opinion, "She is the last person to be guilty of the crime charged against her." He decried the sympathy being poured out for Agnes, the "Hungarian servant girl" whose death was the result of "epileptic fits" that caused her to fall repeatedly and injure herself. Klewert pointed out that "[t]he Hungarian girl" was a Catholic and the Kaufmanns were Jews and that "some of the newspapers in Sioux Falls" were anti-Semitic. The Milwaukee reporter quoted Moses Kaufman as saying that there is "no doubt that racial prejudice had played a strong part in the stories spread about the case."[39] The interview caused some angst in Sioux Falls but added little of substance to the crime drama.

While the *Argus-Leader* preferred to maintain a respectful silence concerning the Kaufmann case, the *Critic* kept up the drumbeat. Ross went to visit the people of Parkston in August to gauge their interest in the case. Finding it still intense, Ross tried to reassure the friends and neighbors of the Polreis family that in the next election, the Minnehaha County voters would clean house, and the "angle-worm county attorney," along with Sheriff "Not I. Phillips," would not be celebrating re-election.[40]

Ross' antics most certainly rubbed many people the wrong way, including prosecutor Joe Kirby. Kirby politely asked Ross to stop reporting on the Kaufmann case because doing so might give the defense grounds for asking for a continuance or a change of venue. This Ross refused to do because he felt it was his duty to press his beliefs about guilt, his support of the Polreis family, and besides, a change of venue would be "the very best thing that could happen." Ross claimed that "the people of this county have no idea what an intense feeling exists throughout the state against this city and county" because of the lackluster prosecution by Alpha Orr, which appears to favor the defendant. Further, observed Ross, "it is well known that Minnehaha County has a bad reputation in the prosecution of criminals."

Ross used the occasion to pick on saloons, saying that the men nominated for sheriff and state's attorney "carry the saloon and brewery vote." He vowed to continue his attack on the saloon lobby because it "brought disgrace on the county." In response to Kirby's request to leave off on the Kaufmann case, he moved on to "stacked juries" and called out Moses Kaufmann for being the kind of rich man who would "buy jurors . . . if they can be purchased" in his rambling article.

No, Mr. Kirby, Mr. Ross will not keep quiet. "We may die poor, and even discredited, but Joe Kirby and the brewery together" cannot silence *The Soo Critic*, exclaimed Ross, "nor buy a line of our opinion," as it concerned the Kaufmann case. "We believe in the guilt of Mrs. Kaufmann" and other persons not named, for their part in the "revolting, heinous crime."[41]

It was a solid and cold rebuke of Joe Kirby, one of the state's leading attorneys and—like Ross—a prominent member of the Democratic Party. But it was classic John A. Ross, sticking to his guns. Unfortunately, the incident planted a seed of discord in Kirby, who was not a man to snub. If Ross knew Kirby well, he knew that the proud attorney would not simply forget about it.

Ross' nasty and unrelenting attacks against Kirby and others did more than create a sense of weariness and anger. From the racket emerged a rumor that the "Soo Falls Brewery and Mr. [Alfred B.] Kittredge" wanted to suppress the *Critic.* In other words, turn off the noise machine and silence Ross, thereby stopping "all alussions [sic] to the Kaufman[n] trouble."[42] But Ross had a high-minded opinion of himself. Anyone trying to silence him, including U.S. Senator Kittredge, would find out that the price of his silence was very high.

The year 1906 meant that South Dakotans would be treated to primaries, political conventions, and an election. The noisy, arm-swinging, in-your-face campaign season would soon be upon the people. The parade to the ballot box meant that men would vote and then wait to see how, if at all, the Kaufmann case influenced the election. The local election would be especially interesting and closely followed because the Kaufmann case had brought so much criticism on officials, especially the sheriff, Nye Phillips, the state's attorney, Alpha Orr, and to a lesser extent, the coroner, L. D. Miller. Would they be re-nominated? And if they were, would they win re-election come November? These were questions asked by many Sioux Falls voters.

The *Weekly Cataract* was opposed to having Miller continue as coroner. "It is firmly believed that if the coroner of this county had been a physician there would have been less of the sensational in the Kaufman[n] case."[43] Miller was re-elected, but only by a four-vote majority. Still he faithfully attended his coroner duties while concentrating on developing his undertaking business.

The *Soo* Critic—in a lengthy article that was vintage Ross—unloaded on Orr, running as a Republican for re-election as the Minnehaha County state's attorney. Orr, Ross said, did not enforce the law nor did he follow the law. Ross had a bone to pick with Orr, which had gotten stuck in his craw long before the Kaufmann case came up. It was all about Orr's refusal to issue a warrant for an arrest, at Ross' request, against someone who had "obtained money [from Ross] under false pretenses." Not satisfied with one incident, he charged that Orr was consistently unwilling to enforce liquor laws. He pointed out that a citizen living near one of the "road houses" on the west side of town complained about the booze and "bedlam at these places" and asked Orr to intervene, but he had declined.

Orr was in fact popular and was re-elected, though by a narrow margin. Ross failed to do him harm. The position of sheriff, however, was an easy target. Ross wildly disliked Nye Phillips for Phillips' perceived favoritism toward Emma Kaufmann. About a month before the election, Ross had a "fistic encounter" with Sheriff Phillips on a Sioux Falls street. They apparently came to blows because the editor had been hounding the sheriff about Peter Erickson, the key prosecution witness. Ross believed Erickson had been "spirited away" and demanded to know his whereabouts.[44] As it turned out, Phillips failed to win re-nomination at the Republican County convention because of the anti-Kaufmann "political capital" arrayed against him by his opponents. The erstwhile popular sheriff was deemed to have been "too considerate" of Emma Kaufmann.[45]

To replace Phillips, Ross supported Charles Nelson, a "poor man" with "a lot of boodle to buck."[46] Charles Nelson, a Democrat, was born in Minnehaha County to a pioneer Brandon family. His father, Andrew Nelson, claimed the distinction of losing two horses, stolen by Frank and Jesse James in 1876, when the infamous outlaws were on the run through Dakota following the Northfield, Minnesota, bank robbery.[47] Well educated in Sioux Falls, Nelson taught school, engaged in the implement business in Brandon, and served as deputy sheriff for three years.[48] He was elected by a wide margin, one of the few crumbs of victory that Ross was able to savor. The Republicans won, as usual, the major races.

Chapter 6

A Colorful Side Show

. . . and thereby to expose the said Joe Kirby to ridicule, hatred and contempt.

The Soo Critic
December 20, 1906

As 1906 was drawing to a close, Sioux Falls was becoming a prosperous and modern city with a population of about 12,000. Called the Queen City by town boosters, it was steadily pulling away from its pioneer past. Automobiles could be seen on the streets. These "horseless carriages" often spooked the horse-drawn carriages causing accidents and injuries, all reported in the newspapers. Future president Woodrow Wilson in 1906 called automobiles symbols of "arrogance and wealth" that would "spread socialistic feeling" throughout the country.[1] The public looked upon these "go-devils" as an expensive novelty for the rich, yet most realized they were here to stay. The great transition from horse to horseless was underway.

In 1906 the Bijou Theater opened its doors at 132 North Phillips Avenue, featuring "automatic vaudeville." The cost of admission was just a dime, and people flocked there every night to enjoy a new form of entertainment that was "in every sense, strictly moral and highly amusing."[2] The New Theater, actually older than the Bijou, was showing "moving pictures," advertised as the "best show of its kind ever seen in Sioux Falls."[3]

Movies were becoming increasingly popular. Over time, complaints surfaced about "the presentation of murder scenes" and other depictions of Wild West characters, claiming they had a "demoralizing" effect on the youth. They were "silent movies" so no one actually heard any actor say naughty words. Still, what people saw was enough to inspire angry protests against the showing of "blood and thunder dime novel stories," which caused the city council to consider some type of censorship.[4]

Other citizens, labeled "temperance cranks," pressed the local authorities to clamp down on saloons, the proliferation of which competed with the creation of churches. Drinking and gambling teamed up to give Sioux Falls a bad reputation. Worse yet was the long-standing problem of prostitution, which had galvanized an angry and organized opposition. The leading offending "business" was the notorious "Willowdale," a resort on West 12th Street, on the outskirts of town. But despite pressure on the authorities, little was done to stop the noisy, boisterous wagon loads of men who made their way out there, night after night, for a dip in the pool of sinful pleasures.

Other, more acceptable signs of progress were in the works, including a street car line and more manufacturing. The brewery was in high gear as orders for beer never seemed to diminish. And of course, Sioux Falls still had the Kaufmann case, the legal battle that seemed to have attached itself to the city like a strange disease that could only be cured by radical surgery.

John Ross of the *Soo Critic*—seen by some as a curse on the city—was looking forward to the next phase of the case. Having written himself into the role of a community moralist, he insisted that the entire city of Sioux Falls was on trial, its very reputation hanging in the balance. The people of Parkston and Hutchinson County had worked hard to raise money to prosecute the case; they had not given up nor had they lost interest. Rather they demanded that "justice be done in this case."[5] They respectfully asked that Minnehaha County pay a fourth of the cost, but no official offered to help. Ross asked whether Sioux Falls would redeem itself or go to the devil.

In Hutchinson County, folks had decided in favor of redemption, not just for Sioux Falls but for the entire state. The county commissioners met in October and voted to stand behind State's Attorney J. L. Quinn in his tireless effort to "push the prosecution" toward a successful result. Backed by the citizens of Parkston, the commissioners resolved to fight the "case to the bitter end."[6]

But to what end, people were wondering? Although clairvoyants, psychics, and fortunetellers filtered in and out of Sioux Falls, no one claimed to know what the future held. Still some speculated on the trial's outcome. The future is darker than yesterday, and this always gives way to some delicious expectation of what might happen next.

And the fighting was about to be renewed. The case that had created a national sensation was on the circuit court calendar for trial on November 26, 1906. State's Attorney Quinn was waxing confident about the future, telling a reporter for the *Yankton Press and Dakotan* that the prosecution had gathered more evidence since the preliminary hearing, "too much, in fact." Also, Peter Erickson was available and ready to testify in the trial that people believed was about to begin. He had not disappeared, as some had speculated.[7]

Nor had the celebrity defendant, for on the 26th, at the appointed time, the Kaufmanns and attorney Frank Aikens came quietly into the Minnehaha County Courthouse for an arraignment before Judge Joseph W. Jones. Having just returned to Sioux Falls, Emma Kaufmann was heavily veiled as she stood up to enter a plea of "not guilty," in a voice so soft that it was barely audible. "It was not generally known" that she was to be arraigned, so the audience was small and orderly; a total of eight women were present, along with a few men—a sharp contrast to the noisy, boisterous audience at the preliminary hearing.[8] The only odd feature of the proceeding was the physical appearance of Emma Kaufmann, in her dark, black veil, so dark that it obscured her facial features. Judge Jones, himself, was unsure of the identity of the woman facing him, for he asked whether she was the woman named in the state's information. From within the dark costume a voice was heard to reply, "It is."[9]

Aikens gave notice that he would ask for a continuance and requested that arguments be scheduled within the next few days. It was also reported that in the event the case would not be continued, there would be a motion by the defense to have the case tried before another judge. Although Jones was a very capable and well-liked judge, it was believed that, due to his "long and intimate acquaintance with all the parties to the case," both sides would prefer a more neutral judge. "There were no sensational features during the brief hearing," reported the *Daily Argus-Leader*, and Mr. and Mrs. Kaufmann sat quietly until their hack pulled up in front of the courthouse and carried them away.[10]

Two days later it was learned that Judge Jones had asked Judge E. G. Smith, circuit court judge for Yankton County, to try the Kaufmann case. Aikens filed an affidavit of prejudice and Judge Jones immediately contacted Judge Smith, who "accepted the invitation to preside at the trial." Smith would have control over the case going forward, including the task of ruling on Aikens' motion for a continuance. It was generally believed that Smith would rule in favor of the motion.[11]

The *Soo Critic* also reported on the hearing, in a matter-of-fact manner, except when it came to the request for a continuance. Ross clearly disliked the idea. To him it looked as though this was a stall tactic, disfavored by the public, since the defense "had since last June to prepare." Then Ross inserted a bombshell in his otherwise sedate article. "The *Critic*," he wrote, "is in possession of some facts that will startle the public, and create a sensation when the time comes to publish them." He hinted that the revelation would come sooner rather than later.

Ross accused the *Argus-Leader* of shielding Mrs. Kaufmann by "refusing to tell the truth concerning the trial." By this he meant that the *Argus-Leader* had misled the public when it reported that Judge Jones would "call another judge" because of his "long acquaintance with the family." Mincing no words, Ross called it a "lie, and the *Argus* knew it was." More than that it was calculated to "deceive and mislead its readers" and "put a favorable and false light on Mrs. Kaufmann's side of the case." Sticking the barb in a little further, Ross wrote that "Charley" Day and his newspaper "is full of corruption" and "is a minion of plutocracy." Along with his insults, Ross urged that anyone interested in getting the truth about the case should read the *Critic*.[12]

His rival, Charles Manley Day, was a veteran newspaper man who believed his product was superior. Born in Sidney, Iowa, Day came to Sioux Falls in 1886, immediately after graduating from Tabor College. He quickly found a job with the *Sioux Falls Daily Ar-*

gus, a newspaper published by the Goddard brothers. In April 1887 the *Daily Argus* merged with the *Sioux Falls Leader* and became the *Daily Argus-Leader.* Along with Jay Tomlinson, Day purchased the *Argus-Leader* and, under the leadership of the two men, it became one of the dominant newspapers in South Dakota.[13]

A contemporary described Day as a fearless man "of strong convictions" who never backed away from a fight. He was a "prolific writer, a good public speaker . . . whose ready wit never deserts him." Although he arrived in town dead broke, Day had the skill to turn his newspaper into a staunch cheerleader and supporter of South Dakota in general and Sioux Falls in particular.[14]

The tension between the *Critic* and the *Argus-Leader* was a microcosm of the class warfare playing out on the American cultural stage. Class warfare was nothing new or unusual; it was merely a product of social interaction and economic and cultural development. The rich asserted their high status, while the middle-class, caught between the rich and the poor, had to defend against both groups. The poor, of course, worked the hardest for least. In a trickle-down economy, that which trickled down was very little compared to that which stayed up. But because there was upward mobility in American society, there was always hope and even greater motivation to engage in the struggle. Cultural warrior John Ross, the self-proclaimed champion of the "have-nots," leveled his bugle blasts at the "haves." The Kaufmann case was a discordant melody in a popular early twentieth-century symphony.

Overall, the reporting on the Kaufmann case by the *Argus-Leader* was far less emotional than that by the *Critic.* Editor Day knew most of the important people in Sioux Falls, and he definitely did not want to step on any toes, as sore feet can inspire long and bitter memories, not to mention subscription cancellations. On the other hand, he didn't want to appear to be kowtowing to the big shots. His cautious approach to the case led to criticism by those who thought the *Argus-Leader* was trying to protect people connected with the case, including Dr. W. A. Germain.

A key defense witness in the case, Dr. Germain was apparently very confident that the case would be continued. On November 20 the *Argus-Leader* noted that he was preparing to leave town for his villa in Mexico, where he normally spent the winter months with his family.[15] His warm-weather getaway was more than just a fancy house. He owned three-hundred acres along Lake Chapala.[16] As it turned out, Dr. Germain could look forward to rusticating in comfort at his villa. But could he really get away from the cold shadows of a Dakota winter and the endless grind of the Kaufmann case?

~

On Saturday, December 1, 1906, a new chapter opened in the case now described as the "famous Kaufmann case." The defendant's motion for a continuance was argued before Judge Smith. Aikens presented a number of affidavits to support his request, all of which spoke to the mental and physical condition of Emma Kaufmann, who did not attend the hearing. He spent two hours reading the affidavits and arguing his case. He argued that, should the trial proceed on schedule, it was very likely that his client would suffer a complete physical and nervous breakdown. In her present state of mind, Aikens insisted that she was unable to "tell a connected story." To take the case to trial would be like trying it in her absence. A defendant in a criminal case has to be able to understand and participate in the proceedings, and Aikens strongly argued that his client was unable to do so in her present condition.[17] He also urged the court's indulgence because "he wanted her to be given a fair chance because she was a Jewess."[18]

Affidavits, signed under penalty of perjury, were submitted by Moses Kaufmann, Charles Kaufmann, Dr. W. A. Germain, Dr. Edwin L. Perkins, and Dr. S. A. Brown, all from Sioux Falls. Dr. Barnett of Neenah, Wisconsin, Emma's treating physician during the summer, submitted an affidavit. Mabel Phillips, from Ohio, the personal maid who attended her during her summer of exile at Lake Winnebago, Wisconsin, also swore out an affidavit.[19] The *Sioux Falls Journal* seemed to be in lock-step with the defense, noting in an article that "Mrs. Kaufmann has lost greatly in flesh since the preliminary examination last spring."[20]

Aside from the health of his client, Aikens said he needed a continuance because public opinion had turned strongly against her as a result of something that the Hutchinson County state's attorney, J. L Quinn, did. He was, of course, referring to the public display of the wet and bloody clothing from the trunk of Agnes Polreis at the Cataract Hotel. Aikens was furious in his condemnation of Quinn and the *Sioux Falls Daily Press*, blaming them for "inciting a riot at the preliminary examination last June."[21]

Although the *Parkston Advance* reported that Quinn would be leading the charge for the state, he was relegated to the back bench when the hearing opened.[22] Representing the prosecution, Joe Kirby addressed the court very briefly. In response to Aikens' plea for a fair chance for his client because she was a Jew, Kirby said that religion and nationality played no part in the matter and "at the same time paid the Jewish race a glowing tribute."[23]

Kirby asked that three physicians, one from Yankton, be appointed to examine Mrs. Kaufmann before any ruling was made on the motion for a continuance. The judge said he had no power to make such an appointment. He closed the session, postponing his decision for one week. The attorneys for the prosecution were thus given time to study carefully all the affidavits submitted by the defense.[24]

Not long after the session closed, a Jewish newspaper reported that Kirby had said he would be "proud to trace his descent from the race that had given the world the Ten Commandments." That same newspaper apparently felt there was more to the matter than Kirby's flippant remark. Since Aikens had expressed his concern over possible religious bias against his client, this did not "speak well for the Sioux Falls community."[25]

~

What the *Argus-Leader* and the *Journal* left out of their reports, the *Critic* was only too happy to add to the record. Ross said that Aikens became very agitated at the hearing and "denounced every paper in the city except one." The sensational and shocking reports, the angry attorney insisted, were the cause of his client's anxiety. Aikens—while strutting like a "turkey gobbler in spring time"—singled out the *Soo Critic* for special condemnation, saying it should be "suppressed" because it was the local equivalent of a William Randolph Hearst newspaper, of yellow journalism fame. Then, piling insult upon insult, Ross put Aikens in a class of low-life attorneys who "have cheated justice" and put the "law and lawyers in contempt of the masses of the people."

Ross wanted no leniency for Emma Kaufmann, pointing out that even if she had suffered mental anguish at the preliminary hearing when people yelled "Lynch her!" she had five months in seclusion with an abundance of medical help. She had plenty of time to get back on her feet. Besides, she looked to all appearances to be strong and healthy and in no way appeared as if she were suffering, physically or mentally. Was she nervous? Of course she was, and so would any other person on trial and facing the death penalty. As for his newspaper, the *Critic*, Ross said that if telling the truth makes his paper "yellow," then "yellow" reporting was something he would embrace. "There is a class of people," Ross wrote, "very much afraid of the truth." Ross, on the other hand, acted and wrote as if he feared no one.[26]

Ross felt that it was up to him to report boldly and fearlessly, if for nothing else, to make up for the lack of guts shown by other Sioux Falls newspapers. He had support from John W. Peckham and his Parkston newspaper. The *Advance* scolded the weak-kneed newspapers in Sioux Falls that had been treating the Kaufmann case "lightly," while "standing as dispensers of the news in the interest of courtesy to an old citizen." The *Advance* slammed Aikens' "star chamber" tactics and the "pettifogging plea" he made at the hearing for a continuance. "This seeking to delay the operation of justice . . . is a dodge invariably employed by the guilty to escape punishment."[27]

And yet, to no one's surprise, Judge Smith ruled in favor of granting the continuance; Aikens and his law partner, attorney Harry E. Judge, had once again scored a major victory. The case went over to the May 1907 term of court. It was a relatively easy decision for Judge Smith to make, based on the weight of the four doctors who submitted affidavits for the defense and, coupled with affidavits from Dr. Stephen Olney and Dr. Thomas J. Billion, submitted by the prosecution. All of them concluded, and the judge agreed, that the defendant would be "absolutely unable to be present in court without danger of a nervous collapse."[28]

The judge reminded both sides of the case and the public at large that the prosecution offered no evidence to refute expert opinions of the doctors. He also stated, with great eloquence, that "the law provides that justice shall be speedily done, [but] it does not provide [that] injustice shall be done. What the defense asks is not unjust."[29]

The *Critic* tore into the court's decision. Ross found no fault in the court's reasoning because the state put on an inexcusably weak argument against the continuance. Upset at Orr and Kirby, he let them have it. Aside from submitting two worthless affidavits from Olney and Billion, the prosecution was curiously passive, almost silent by comparison to the dramatic, "somewhat stilted," speech by Aikens, who completely dominated the court session. Kirby and Orr failed to mention or argue that the state was ready for trial. They said nothing about inconvenience to the state and nothing about another long delay that might cause them to lose key witnesses such as Peter Erickson.

Ross had long believed that Orr was weak, bland, or incompetent, but clearly he expected more from Kirby, the attorney hired by Hutchinson County as a special prosecutor. For a hired gun, Kirby had showed little fight and that bothered and intrigued Ross. He decided to take Kirby apart and expose him through the medium of the *Critic*, whom all knew was a perpetually angry newspaper.

Going back in time, Ross wrote, "the public is quite anxious to know why Mr. Kirby did not go to Pierre and resist the bond of Mrs. Kaufmann." People would be interested to know if Kirby was a principal of Western Surety Company, which "is reputed to be the bond for the Brewing Co., of many local and out-of-town saloon keepers." Then moving even closer to an accusation, Ross asked about "the visit of one of the leading financial men of the city to Mr. Kirby on the day he was to go to Pierre."

Ross all but said that Kirby had violated his oath as a lawyer, as to all appearances he had sympathized and sided with the defense. His last point, however, really must have stung: "If the efforts to convict Mrs. Kaufman[n] are to be measured by the efforts in opposing a continuance of the case, the state might as well save its money and enter a nolle at once."[30] After huffing and puffing against Kirby, Ross hit the nail right on the head when he wrote that Judge Smith most certainly had reached his decision based on "the showing made." And since there was very little effort put into the "showing," the judge must not be criticized for his ruling, and in fact would have been culpable had he ruled otherwise.[31]

Ross flayed Kirby in print on December 14, and on the same day he saw an opportunity to strike at State's Attorney Orr, one of his favorite punching bags. Ross believed Orr was a lazy prosecutor, who more than once had failed to do his duty. He urged the bar association to take up disbarment proceedings against Orr and asked his readers to support the action.[32]

Orr did nothing to retaliate against Ross, but Joe Kirby was not a man to give an insult a free pass. He struck back hard and fast. On the morning of December 18, he brought charges of criminal libel against John Ross, editor and publisher, for damaging Kirby's good name, character, and professional reputation. At the heart of the matter was Kirby's failure to go to Pierre for the Kaufmann bond hearing. A warrant was issued and Ross was promptly arrested and jailed. It happened with a speed that must have amazed all observers.[33]

Ross recovered quickly from the shock and roared back after being released, "**CRITIC EDITOR THROWN INTO JAIL**." He started his scalding article by calling the charge and arrest "one of the most infamous outrages ever perpetuated in a civilized community." Whereas the *Argus-Leader* merely laid out the basic facts of the Ross-Kirby feud, the recipient of the attorney's wrath provided much detail, with color and verve that reflected his anger, personality, and outrage.

It all started about 11:30 A.M., when Ross was arrested by Deputy Sheriff Hirsh. Although greatly surprised, Ross promised to appear in the office of the justice of the peace at 2 o'clock that afternoon, apparently satisfying Hirsh. Ross came in early, and not long after Kirby appeared, followed by two reporters. After Justice Dickey read the libel charge, Ross asked for a continuance until the next afternoon. It was granted and his bail was set at $300.

Ross expected that he would then be able to find someone to put up the bond money, but he was surprised to learn that he was headed for jail. A "nervous and uneasy" Deputy Hirsh said, "They gave me hell for not taking you down this morning and you'll have to go down now." On the way toward the jail, Hirsh said that ex-Senator R. F. Pettigrew, who was waiting at the county courthouse, would provide a bond. Then it dawned on Ross that he would be locked up and that there was a "fixed determination to railroad me to prison." He had aggravated Sheriff Nye Phillips so many times in the columns of the *Critic* that Phillips wanted his pound of flesh—and maybe a little more.

South Dakota U.S. Senator R. F. Pettigrew.
Courtesy Library of Congress.

Before Hirsh and Ross arrived at the jailhouse, they stopped at the courthouse and spoke to Pettigrew, who expressed the belief that Phillips, his longtime friend, would not toss the editor in jail. Pettigrew said, "Nye won't do that." Then an angry Phillips, who had arrived on the scene, spoke with Pettigrew. The former senator from South Dakota insisted that he would be responsible for Ross and "have the bond ready in an hour." Despite this, Ross was placed behind bars, a mere twenty minutes after leaving the office of the justice of the peace. In his own words: "I was in the common county jail," a place that was "condemned years ago."[34]

When Ross' rival, Mark Scott of the *Sioux Falls Journal*, learned of the dilemma, he gleefully went into attack mode. The *Critic*, he wrote, was "a weekly monstrosity calling itself a newspaper." Then Scott rubbed a generous portion of sodium in Ross' wounded ego. Ross, he said, was so unpopular and "discredited" in Sioux Falls that he would be hard pressed to find anyone who would post a bond. Far from calling the sheriff heavy handed, Scott wrote rather tartly: "Had the sheriff done his duty Ross would have been thrown into jail in the morning and thereby put into effect what Ross has been howling all along in the Kaufmann case, that the arrested party be put in jail at once." Scott most certainly believed that Ross had received his just desserts, and that he could expect little sympathy from the city or its people because his newspaper had for too long "blackened" everyone and everything it touched.[35]

The *South Dakota State Forum*, a community newspaper that reported stories of importance and relevance in a calm, non-partisan manner, came down in favor of Joe Kirby. The *Forum* editor took Kirby's side because he was merely defending his reputation as a lawyer from an unwarranted attack. "A newspaper has no right to impugn or challenge the character of any citizen, upon suspicion." Ross had merely engaged in a slash-and-burn attack on Kirby, in a blind and reckless pounding that was not fact-based. The people of Sioux Falls deserved better, according to the *Forum*. The editorial closed by predicting that after "Mr. Kirby got through with him [Ross] he will be more careful of putting his false ideas into print."[36]

But the sound advice was ignored by Ross. Two days after being tossed into a jail cell, confined in the same horrible place that held Emma Kaufmann for a short period of time, Ross decided it was the right time to re-hash all the ugly details of the case, with emphasis on the double-standard in the law, as he saw it, that treats the rich better than the poor. He was out on a bond supplied by R. F. Pettigrew and John McKee, and with his anger meter running high, Ross let Kirby, Phillips, and everyone else who hated him know that he would not be intimidated or silenced. Clearly, the criminal libel charge and the harsh treatment from Sheriff Phillips came about because of his incessant, high-pitched, accusatory articles on the Kaufmann case. He had become insufferable and his enemies wanted him punished even though the punishment would only embolden him, giving him reason to unleash more shot and shell. Ross drew a new line in the sand when he declared, "From behind prison bars if I must, I shall stand for truth."

As if there was still one person who had not read the gory details of the crime, Ross resurrected the specter of a helpless, tortured immigrant girl who had suffered at the hands of a fiendish, cruel woman, the wife of a "rich brewer" and a "legislative lobbyist." He reminded everyone of the cuts, the gashes, of feet bathed in "lye from wood ashes until the flesh was pulled off with her stockings." He praised the "justice-loving people of Parkston"—who offered to post bond for him—for having "unearthed the crime" that others intended to cover up for all time to come.

After the arrest, Ross criticized Sheriff Phillips for allowing Emma Kaufmann to stay in her "palatial" home when a dutiful public servant would have hauled her off to jail. "We said at that time that a poor person would have been shown no mercy, but would have been put right into jail." Pointing an accusatory editorial finger at Phillips, whose term in office was about to expire, Ross wrote, "Nye Phillips has proved the truth of our contention" that there is "partiality of those that execute the law."

Nye Phillips was indeed a very disgruntled man. He would soon be replaced as sheriff by Charley Nelson, the Democrat. Phillips had not been re-nominated for sheriff by the Republican Party. It seems that he angered even those from his own party for his perceived lenient treatment of Emma Kaufmann and was kicked to the curb rather ingloriously. Phillips could count himself a political casualty of the Kaufmann case.[37]

Ross, however, had other options. For a clever, determined man, there is always opportunity in adversity. Ross took the occasion of his humiliation at the hands of Kirby and Phillips to reach out to the people for support. There was $1,000 on the books, and if the good people who owed money to the *Critic* would pay in full, Ross could continue the good work. If readers want a "journal conducted in the interest of the whole people, and that does not fear wealth nor fawn to it, they can have it by simply paying their past dues." Going further, he sought to increase his subscriptions by 3,000 from the people of Minnehaha County. Ross put it on the back of the public, saying bluntly that "there is a scheme to crush us and wipe the *Soo Critic*," and if people want a newspaper that "is free and independent, bound to no man and to no interests," then step up and give it a chance to do the work for the average person. "Shall the paper live or die? It is with you to say, and to say soon."[38]

Support from other South Dakota newspapers was swift and strong and Ross proudly printed excerpts. Because of the petty and abrupt arrest and jailing of a fellow editor, his "brothers of the quill" scorched Joe Kirby and, for the most part, were generous in their praise of his victim. Ross had stood up to a powerful, rich man and other editors and publishers admired him for it. The *Jerauld County Review* crowed, "Mr. Ross is the only man in Sioux Falls who has courage enough to denounce the special consideration shown to Mrs. Kaufman[n] simply because she is the wife of a rich man." The *Tribune* from Dell Rapids noted that since Ross was not "a wealthy brewer," he "was bundled off to jail." The *Aberdeen Democrat* bellowed boldly, "Editor Ross . . . has paid the penalty for telling the truth by being despitefully cast into a dungeon."[39]

The *Parkston Advance*—a newspaper with a keen interest in everything Kaufmann—came down hard on Kirby, "who is supposed to be one of the attorneys for the prosecution." The editor further declared that "the average person who has kept track of this case" would likely conclude that "there is an effort . . . to intimidate the newspapers which have been instrumental in stirring up this investigation." The editorial continued, "It looks to us like a threat to the newspapers to keep out of the case" or face a charge of libel.[40]

Despite criticism from the press, Joe Kirby's attitude toward Ross went unchanged, and in fact, he upped the ante. He charged Ross' wife, Maggie, with criminal libel, arising from an article in the *Critic* entitled "Who is Joe Kirby?"[41] Angered over the critique, he swore out a warrant and had her jailed. Then after her husband returned from a business trip to Mitchell, he found Deputy Sheriff Hirsh waiting for him. It was New Year's Eve but Hirsh wasn't there to drink a toast to the New Year; he had a warrant for Ross' arrest based on yet another charge of criminal libel. Joe Kirby had struck again.[42]

But husband and wife were not dismayed in the least, for they had good work to do. After she was released on bail, provided by Pettigrew and L. C. Campbell, an insurance agent, Maggie proved to be as gutsy and resilient as her husband. She went on the road in eastern South Dakota, talking to people, taking new subscriptions, "meeting with splendid success at every place she visits," while adding hundreds of new subscribers.[43]

As the New Year was just getting started, Joe Kirby, the tormentor of Mr. and Mrs. Ross, experienced a sudden reversal of fortune. The citizens committee at Parkston fired him; he was off the Kaufmann case.[44] Word came to Sioux Falls by way of a telephone call to Maggie Ross, advising her that Kirby had been paid for services rendered in the case and that he was "discharged from further connection with it." When the news was announced in the *Argus-Leader*, it was said that the "revelation from Parkston was the feature of the Ross-Kirby libel affair." No doubt that it was. But when questioned about the matter by a reporter, Kirby merely said that for his part, he was still a member of the prosecution team and would not step aside until and unless State's Attorney Orr made it clear that he was off the case.[45]

Like any man of strength and determination, Kirby was not ready to slink away in silence. But it was true, he was off the case, and on January 24 it was announced that Joe Kirby was leaving Sioux Falls for an extended winter vacation in Cuba.[46]

It was revealed in the *Critic* that the Parkston citizens committee lost faith and trust in Kirby when he explained how he went about trying cases. In one instance, Kirby allegedly said that he had a "threshing machine run over the foot of the principal witness," thereby ensuring that he would not be available to testify against his client. In another case where defeat was imminent, Kirby allegedly said that he had a "whisky bottle smuggled into the jury room," and then he filed an affidavit with the court claiming the jury had been compromised and got a new trial and an acquittal for his client.[47]

The Parkston citizens committee was also disappointed with Kirby's rather tepid argument at the Kaufmann continuance hearing. So, all things considered, they were looking in another direction, having hired an outsider, George W. Egan, from the Logan, Iowa, firm of Cochran and Egan. No one knew at the time, but the Kaufmann case was about to take another strange twist. The new special prosecutor was no ordinary lawyer. Things were about to get very interesting and very messy. The proverbial bull had entered the china shop.

Chapter 7

Ride the Whirlwind

Mr. Egan is in the prime of life. He is a born orator and mentally and physically is a man of remarkable development.

The Soo Critic
March 7, 1907

George W. Egan, from Logan, Iowa, was a partner in the law firm of Cochran and Egan. The firm was deemed to be one of the most successful in the state of Iowa, with Egan as its rising star. This impressed the Parkston Citizens Committee, and they retained the firm to assist State's Attorney Alpha Orr in trying the murder case against Emma Kaufmann. John A. Ross, publisher of the *Soo Critic*, had a hand in the hiring. Ross claimed in an article in the *Critic* that in September 1906, while traveling through Iowa, he stopped off at the home of Sanford H. Cochran, "one of the strong lawyers of Iowa." Cochran was a "boyhood chum" of Ross' older brothers, hence the reason for the visit.

While talking about old times, the Kaufmann case came up and Cochran mentioned that some parties in Omaha wanted to engage his firm in the defense of Emma Kaufmann. This Cochran refused to do, but he mentioned that, if offered, his firm would join the prosecution. Ross recalled that he immediately wrote to the Parkston people and suggested that they investigate the Cochran and Egan firm, "recommending them as men of ability and fidelity." In October, two Parkston men came to Ross' Sioux Falls office and asked him to send a telegram to Cochran to set up a meeting in Sioux City. They met and the Cochran firm was retained.[1] The attorney/client relationship began on or about October 7, 1906.

All this transpired at the time the Parkston committee was growing weary of Joe Kirby, whom they were looking to replace. But Kirby, feeling that he was being squeezed out, didn't want the Iowa lawyers anywhere near the Kaufmann case, so he wrote a letter to Cochran and Egan, advising them that their services were not needed. "Mr. Orr, Mr. Quinn and myself . . . have concluded that we are entirely capable of trying the case without any outside help." He added that "too many lawyers" make the case look like a "persecution rather than a prosecution." Kirby concluded his letter by saying, "you may consider yourselves dismissed." The Kirby letter set all concerned parties in motion and soon there was a "lively" meeting at Parkston that included Cochran, John A. Ross, Orr, Quinn, and Kirby. When it was over, Kirby was officially off the case.[2]

Special prosecuting attorney George W. Egan. *Courtesy Library of Congress.*

Cochran dispatched his young partner, George W. Egan, to South Dakota to join the prosecution and, according to the *Critic*, he was highly qualified for the job. Born in 1873 in Bartlett, Iowa, to an impoverished Irish-American family,[3] Egan came to Sioux Falls flush with praiseworthy descriptions of his legal abilities, especially in delivering a convincing closing argument. In an Iowa criminal case four years prior, Egan's closing argument was "one of the most celebrated jury addresses ever heard in that state."[4]

Egan's life as a boy had been one of hardship and struggle. His father was a disabled Civil War veteran who left much of the farm work to young George. As such he was not able to attend school until the age of twenty-two, and yet he eventually graduated from the University of Iowa, where he excelled both academically and as a football player. That said, it was his skills as a debater that came to the fore; he was a natural.[5]

Young Egan also loved books, especially the classics and the Bible. He took Vernice Cochran, the daughter of his law partner, to be his bride.[6] The future looked promising for the young couple. George was a serious student of the law who, with "scholarly delight," traced modern laws back to "codes of the Romans." In hiring George W. Egan, the Parkstonites were getting more than a lawyer. They had acquired a man of high intellect fueled by a hard-driving personality, a man who was described by an Iowa congressman as "an orator who interests and charms an audience."[7]

But Egan left Iowa under a cloud of suspicion. He had been accused of rape by two women, one only seventeen years of age. The criminal charges were dismissed but an investigating committee of lawyers wanted him held in contempt of court and disbarred. Cochran, a former judge, intervened and managed to stop the disbarment proceedings on the condition that Egan would leave Iowa.[8] Egan did just that, and in South Dakota, the ambitious and loquacious lawyer found a new and fertile field of opportunity, much to his liking. Included in the package was the Kaufmann case, the ideal stage upon which Egan was about to showcase his talents.

John Ross was more than satisfied with the decision to hire Egan and stated confidently that the trial "will be the most famous ever heard in the west." Ross was looking for a hero, someone who could tilt lances with the forces of wealth and privilege in order to find justice for a poor, innocent girl, and in his eyes, George W. Egan was that man.[9]

Anticipating a hard fight for a conviction, Ross wrote, "Mr. Orr's future and that of Mr. Egan are bound up in the success of this cause."[10] Would they emerge triumphantly to the cheers of those who wanted Emma Kaufmann convicted and punished, or would they fail and be forced to wear the case like a yoke of defeat and humiliation? John Ross was anxious to know the answer to the looming question.

The passing of time would force an answer to that and many other weighty questions. For example, two years after the Iowa firm was retained, Maggie Ross revealed that the people interested in prosecuting Emma Kaufmann intentionally looked for legal help outside of Sioux Falls. It was widely believed that the "political and financial relations in Sioux Falls" were such that there would be no prosecution of Kaufmann.[11] In other words the power, politics, and social standing of the Kaufmanns outweighed the official desire to pursue justice for Agnes, a mere servant girl.

The outsider selected to pound away at the bastions of wealth and power—the thirty-four-year-old George Egan—was an excellent lawyer by reputation, and much was expected of him once he entered the local legal arena. The Kaufmann case seemed made to order for Egan, whose magnetic physical presence and brilliant diction promised to make him a star among South Dakota lawyers. His style was extremely combative and his presentation was one of flamboyance and passion, in some respects good qualities in a lawyer.

But there was another side of Egan's personality that no one in Sioux Falls knew anything about. People were about to learn that Egan was arrogant, self-centered, egotistical, and undisciplined. He had a way with words. He loved to talk, to engage in flights of oratory as though he felt that the very sound of his voice was pleasing to his listeners. Public adulation and praise went to his head. Had he used his gifts in an unselfish way, the rewards would have come easily and naturally. But it was not to be, and while he entered Sioux Falls rather quietly, he would stir up a storm of controversy the likes of which no one in the legal profession had done before. No one was prepared for George Egan.

In March 1907, when Egan stepped up to take charge of the Kaufmann case, Joe Kirby had returned from Cuba, and the South Dakota legislature, dominated by Republicans, was in session. Among the laws it passed was one that prohibited the playing of baseball on Sunday. The law signaled a radical change that some believed would kill the game because a professional team needed the Sabbath day revenue in order to survive.[12]

Another new law threatened to break the back of the "divorce industry," which had existed since statehood. The new law, backed by the churches, and especially Episcopal Bishop William Hare, upped the residence requirement from six months to a year. For many years Sioux Falls had been treated to a parade of rich and famous men and women who established "residence," usually in the Cataract Hotel, until their divorce was final.[13] The "quickie" divorce business made a lot of lawyers and merchants rich, but no one realistically expected the bonanza to last forever.

To those, including Ross, who considered this a dirty business, the closing of the "Divorce Colony" was good news and a victory for morality. Sioux Falls was thriving without the divorce business, for other enterprises were doing well. This included the automobile, which promised to revolutionize travel and stimulate the building of roads, bridges, and highways. The *Argus-Leader* proudly announced that Sioux Falls would soon have five new cars on its streets, noting that "there is nothing that adds more style and metropolitan air to the streets of a city than a good sprinkling of up to date automobiles." The Sioux Falls Auto Supply Company happily reported that "sales have never been better."[14] Located at 112-114 North Main Avenue, the dealer sold Ford, Jackson, and Rambler autos.[15]

The flashy, new automobiles shared the spotlight with the Kaufmann murder case, which was scheduled for trial in the May 1907 term of court. Moses Kaufmann, the long-suffering husband of the accused, certainly was focused on that date. He had resigned as an officer and director of the Sioux Falls Brewing Company. He announced that he was closing out all his interest in the company so he could "give his time to other business matters."[16] Translation: he was thoroughly caught up in his wife's murder case and had no choice but to give up the brewery business that he loved dearly. Indeed, his life had been turned upside down by the loss of prestige and power.

On May 9, as the clock was ticking toward the time of the trial, the ever-vigilant *Critic* announced that Frank R. Aikens would seek a change of venue. Ross insisted that Aikens' strategy was simply to stall the proceedings, hoping that the key witness, Peter Erickson, would go to Norway,[17] which seemed unlikely since he was a native of Illinois.[18] But Ross was suspicious of a plan to cheat justice.

The *Argus-Leader*, with obvious respect for the Kaufmann family, including the defendant's presumption of innocence, calmly noted that the "famous case" would be called up on May 20 for trial. At that time the defense would make a motion before Judge Smith for a change of venue based on prejudice in Minnehaha County, which made it impossible for Emma Kaufmann to get a fair trial. The daily newspaper also mentioned that George Egan and Sanford H. Cochran would be arriving on the train to assist State's Attorney Orr in resisting the motion.[19]

The *Critic* followed the *Argus-Leader* with a hand-wringing article about the change of venue. First, Ross castigated Aikens for breaking a promise. Aikens had made it clear at the motion for a continuance before the court in December 1906 that he would be ready for trial and would not seek any further delay. But a request for a change of venue, Ross insisted, would result in another continuance, and the public would have to wait until November 1907 for the trial. He went on to suggest that there was no realistic need for a change of venue because Minnehaha County prosecutors had a reputation for "very lax prosecution for a number of years."

Everywhere he looked, Ross saw gloom. Erickson was still in South Dakota, living at his parents' farm near Alpena, but there was always the chance that he might disappear. There was the possibility that someone might die, which also might favor the accused. And of course the longer the delay, the more likely it was that the public would lose interest. "It is our opinion that the accused in this case will not be tried."[20]

The interest in the case among outside newspapers remained unabated. Among them, the *Evening Times* from Grand Forks, North Dakota, reprised the sordid details of the death of Agnes Polreis, the thrice-exhumed victim, who "died in terrible agony." The rumor that reached Grand Forks was that the attorneys for "the woman will enter a plea of insanity." But then what other strategy could one expect from a defendant whose violent temper and "almost fiendish brutality" resulted in a murder case that promised to be "among the most notable in the history of the judiciary of South Dakota?"[21]

It was a murder case that the people of Parkston were eager to see come to trial. They wanted no further delays in their quest to get justice for Agnes. The dead girl's mother, above all others, needed peace, which could only come from closure. So great was her grief that she wrote a letter "To All Friends in Parkston Who Sympathize with Us in Our Misfortune." The poignant letter was published in the *Parkston Advance* under the byline "A Mother's Appeal":

> The grief for my poor unfortunate child, Agnes, gives me no rest, neither day nor night. It seems too great to bear much longer; I would welcome death as a great relief: Yet I desire to see those who so cruelly maltreated my innocent child be brought to justice as soon as possible.
>
> To see that this [trial] may be postponed again breaks my heart; which cries out unceasingly, Agnes, Agnes, my poor child Agnes, until it is relived in a torrent of tears.
>
> I often desire that I could visit the house where my child was so cruelly tortured, to lay down and die. Yet I trust in the mercy and justice of God and pray for help and strength to bear the Cross until the end.
>
> We the unhappy parents also desire that the cities and towns should help us poor people who have not the means to do anything.
>
> We also desire to extend our sincere thanks for the help, encouragement and consolation of our benefactors and sympathizing friends.
>
> Theresia Polreis[22]

A cynic might doubt the authenticity of the letter and insist that an unsophisticated peasant woman would lack the command of the language contained therein. But a sympathetic person could, with equal zeal, be convinced that it expressed genuine sorrow and be moved by its palpable sincerity, even if the grieving mother had some help writing it.

On Monday, May 20, 1907, Emma Kaufmann, her husband, and son entered the Minnehaha County Courthouse and took their seats beside their legal counsel, Frank R. Aikens and Harry Judge. Although she was well-represented by counsel and given comfort and support by her husband and son, Emma had reason to be uneasy, not because of any unfair treatment by the court but because of the intense public anger directed at her. Could it, would it, turn into mob violence? Only a few months before, a wealthy man in Charles City, Iowa, was taken from the jail by a mob and hanged on a bridge over the Cedar Rapids River. He had been accused of murdering his wife and, since he was rich, the people believed he would beat the rap.[23]

Fear and anxiety, like foreboding dark clouds, hovered over Sioux Falls as Aikens rose to challenge the presence of Egan and W. J. Hooper, another outside attorney, asking "what authority" permitted them to be in the courtroom. State's Attorney Orr explained that the two lawyers were "engaged to assist in the prosecution of the case without expense to Minnehaha County." Egan stood up and confirmed this.

Apparently satisfied, Aikens applied for a change of venue based on a number of affidavits that would prove a fair trial in Minnehaha County would be impossible "owing to the state of the public mind." One affidavit was from the defendant who declared that she was "yet in a very nervous condition" as a result of the demonstration made at her preliminary hearing. Mr. Kaufmann presented a sworn statement of the same substance. Other affidavits were from John Emmke, manager of the Cataract Hotel, D. C. Ricker, L. S. Tyler, J. A. Walker, and C. E. Hill, all testifying to the "feeling in the county against the defendant."[24]

In total, the defense team unloaded affidavits signed by 222 residents of Minnehaha County, all of which attested to the belief that Emma Kaufmann could not get a fair trial in the county because an unbiased jury could not be found. Among the signatories were prominent men of the county, including doctors, lawyers, businessmen, and political figures. Harry E. Judge, whose task it was to round up the affidavits, submitted one of his own, explaining that some men who did not sign wanted to sign but were afraid that doing so would injure their business. Getting more specific, Judge pointed out that one man was "prohibited from signing according to his convictions by the contrary influence exerted by his wife."

Judge also encountered people with outright inflammatory and prejudicial views concerning the case. He was told by one person that Emma Kaufmann "should have been hanged at the first without ceremony," and another who insisted that the trial be held in Hutchinson County "where the dead girl had lived, to get her justice." Judge also informed the court that many people held a "bitter prejudice against the defendant on account of the supposed wealth of her husband" and that the wife of a poor man would have had an immediate trial followed by imprisonment.[25]

Judge Smith also listened to the testimony of proprietors of the two Sioux Falls daily newspapers, the *Daily Press* and the *Argus-Leader*, along with representatives from four weekly newspapers, including Ross and his *Critic*. Each man had to explain the distribution of his newspaper, including the number of subscribers. Every article that each newspaper published about the death of Agnes Polreis was introduced into evidence for the purpose of showing the nature and depth of the reporting on the case, much of it inflammatory and prejudicial. And if this wasn't enough to convince Judge Smith, he was reminded of the display of Agnes' tattered and bloody clothing that took place at the Cataract Hotel. Emma sat quietly while her counsel argued that "some of the papers tended to inflame the public mind against the defendant." For this reason, she could not get a fair and impartial trial in Minnehaha County.[26]

Ross was singled out by Aikens for special scrutiny and ridicule. With Ross on the hot seat, and feeling vulnerable, Aikens "put on his deepest tones of sarcasm," questioning the reluctant witness while reading excerpts from *Critic* articles, many of which were harshly critical of the defendant. People in the audience felt the tension between the two men and watched and listened carefully as Aikens lashed out at Ross with his "stinging tongue."

But Ross apparently maintained his composure and later wrote a detailed article about the hearing for a change of venue. Ross pointed out that, plainly visible in Aikens' argument, was his desire to get another continuance as well as a change of venue. Aikens told the judge he was not ready for trial because he had a "very material witness" and needed more time to secure his presence. Egan countered this by saying that the prosecution was ready and eager to go forward with the case, noting that nearly a year had gone by since the death of Agnes Polreis and that the defense had been granted one long continuance.

The judge was in agreement and ruled out any further continuance, but he granted a change of venue. The trial was then scheduled for June 4 in the city of Flandreau, Moody County, just to the north of Minnehaha County. Upon learning that Flandreau would host the trial, the *Flandreau Herald* signaled that the choice was a good one, "a compliment to our county and our people." The *Herald* assured everyone that Mrs. Kaufmann, "who bears the presumption of innocence," would get a fair trial in Flandreau. The judge was commended for his selection of Moody County, "the best place for the trial."[27] It was a settled fact, a court order. Flandreau would be the location of what many believed would be a hard-fought and drawn-out legal battle, one that promised to loom large in the history of American criminology.

Ross had plenty of time and opportunity to size up the principal lawyers on the case. He concluded that Egan, a "Celtic and born orator," had "so far shown ability and tact but he is meeting in Judge Aikens a foeman in ability and resources worthy the steel of any opponent."[28] Most knowledgeable observers must have agreed and were eager to see if one or the other would deliver a knock-out blow.

According to a report in the *Sioux Falls Journal*, there was a literal attempt to deliver a knock-out blow that occurred at a meeting of the prosecution lawyers. About a week before the trial started, "all kinds of charges and counter charges were said to have been made, and that even a fist fight broke out in the office of the state's attorney." There was "bad blood" among the prosecution team that had been simmering for some time and, "according to rumors on the street," it "finally culminated in a fight." The article hinted that, as a result of the fisticuffs, the Kaufmann case was firmly in the control of the "Iowa lawyers," meaning George Egan.[29]

Another story about this "bad blood" appeared in the *Sioux Falls Daily Press* a year after the trial concluded to the effect that when Egan entered the picture, a "conspiracy" was hatched by a group of Sioux Falls men who not only wanted him off the case but sought to run him out of the state. The report hints that among the conspirators was none other than Senator Kittredge and his friend Moses Kaufmann. As the story goes, E. E. Rodabaugh, the law partner of Alpha Orr, was tasked with planting a "disreputable woman" in Egan's room at the Cataract Hotel. Then the authorities would "raid" the room and catch Egan in the company of the woman. He would be arrested and, after a flurry of ugly publicity, forced to leave Sioux Falls.

When Egan learned of the nefarious plot, he obtained an affidavit, which revealed all the sordid details. He then "laid it before County Attorney Orr" in the presence of the Parkston committee. They gave Orr a choice: he could allow Egan to "make a fair prosecution of Mrs. Kaufmann" or see the "story in print." Orr chose the former and Egan was designated the lead counsel for the prosecution.[30] The report, which originated from a source favorable to Egan and the progressive, anti-Kittredge wing of the Republican Party, was never corroborated but is a reminder that desperate times breed desperate measures.

The Kaufmann case may have been in the hands of Egan, but it was Ross' *cause de célèbre*, an epic piece of history in the making that would make him or possibly break him. To say that he was obsessed with the case is an understatement. He used the case to showcase his politics, to bolster his support for the underdog, and as a cudgel to pound his opponents, those whom he believed truckled to money and therefore bowed and scraped at the altar of wealth. No one had to tell Ross that money was the root of all evil. It was a belief that burned in the core of his soul.

Although Ross' arrows of indignation were hurled far and wide, Charles Day of the *Argus-Leader* was the leading target of the surly editor's barbs of anger and retribution. But Day ignored the piling on of hateful, insulting articles. So Ross kept up the pressure, as if he were trying to get some reaction from Day, some show of fight. But the only thing he got was silence, and silence was taken as a sign of disrespect. In the eyes of the *Argus-Leader*, Ross and his *Critic* were little more than an annoyance. With his rantings against the rich, Ross was digging a hole from which he might someday be unable to extricate himself.

Deeply troubled by the Kaufmann case, Ross could not simply let it play itself out in court. He seemed haunted by the specter of Agnes Polreis, the beaten and tortured immigrant girl whose innocent life had been one of strife and denial. In his mind she had become a symbol of the struggle that ordinary people waged against the institutionalized power of wealth and privilege. He could not bring her back and he could not undo the harm and misfortune that had befallen her, but he could hammer away at those whom he believed were responsible, along with the men who supported them.

So he continued to strike at the *Argus-Leader* and to a lesser extent the *Journal*, heaping new and more vicious insults on their editors. These two newspapers, Ross insisted, had, in their "favoritism for the accused," shown prejudice to the "cause of the state, and have almost reached the stage of abuse." They were "cowardly sycophants" to the rich and powerful, ignoring the "unspeakable suffering of this innocent child of poverty and toil." In doing so, they have "done more to injure the fair name of this city than all other things combined." He saw cultural degradation in Sioux Falls everywhere he looked and blamed "the moral cowardice of newspapers" for allowing it to enter society and fester. Ross believed newspapers should lead for the sake of morality, something the leading newspapers of Sioux Falls had failed to do.[31]

Ross did have a valid point. There was a tendency for western newspapers to downplay crime, a practice that started during the frontier era. This reluctance to fully report crime, especially violent crime, came about because the town boosters believed that such reports would inhibit economic development.

Eastern newspapers did, in fact, report incidents of crime in western communities to discourage residents from migrating west. Too violent, too dangerous, don't go there was the message. Editors of newspapers in struggling western communities, therefore, felt they had to guard against the negative publicity that might result from criminal activity. They in turn emphasized progress, publishing articles about the prospect of a railroad, good crops, growing businesses, political events, new settlers, literary societies, and other positive developments. When they did report crime, they did so in a way that showed the law triumphing over evil.

The Parkston people, themselves, were determined that the law would triumph over evil and there would be justice for Agnes. To that end, they rolled up their sleeves and raised the sum of $700 "by popular subscription."[32] But that money was used up very quickly, and as the time for the trial approached, the Parkstonites cranked up their solicitation of funds. They targeted Sioux Falls businesses, "flooding Sioux Falls jobbers and wholesalers with copies of a letter prepared at the direction of the citizens committee." The letter, as reported by the Yankton paper, contained a stern but slightly veiled warning that, should contributions not be forthcoming, businesses would face a boycott. The strong-armed solicitation created a bit of a sensation in Sioux Falls, for, "when read between the lines," the circular made it clear that those who did not contribute would "suffer a loss of trade." The letter pointed the finger of blame at Sioux Falls and boldly stated that, had not the people of Hutchinson County acted, "the murderer of Agnes Polreis would have escaped."[33]

The letter reminded the wealthy businessmen that the Polreis family was poor. But "poverty gives, or should give the poor as much a right to live as a wealthy person." Sound reasoning, of course, but the plea was met with rejection by the Sioux Falls businessmen, who reminded Parkston that businesses paid their full share of taxes, and taxpayer dollars from Minnehaha County would, in the end, pay for the trial. Hutchinson County, therefore, would not be responsible for the "payment of a single penny."[34]

Coming so close to the trial date, the imprudent letter seems more like an expression of anger than a request for funds to pay the Iowa, and other, attorneys. But funds were greatly needed, as the Hutchinson County Commissioners "refused to do anything in this respect," leaving it up to the citizens of the county to find money to pay the special prosecutors.[35]

~

On June 4, 1907, in the Moody County courthouse at Flandreau, about thirty-five miles north of Sioux Falls, the trial of Emma Kaufmann for the murder of Agnes Polreis opened to a packed house. Judge E. G. Smith of Yankton was about to preside over "the most famous criminal trial in the history of the courts of South Dakota." The *Argus-Leader* signaled that it would depart from its erstwhile subdued reporting. Although they would avoid the blood-curdling articles in the *Critic*, Day and staff were about to hold nothing back. After all, the case had been so widely and sensationally reported in newspapers throughout the country that it would be foolish to soft-pedal the news at this point. The *Argus-Leader* even referred to the defendant as a "wealthy Sioux Falls woman," the wife of one of the most "prominent and best known citizens in the state."

Emma Kaufmann, without a veil this time, sat quietly with her husband and son on either side of her, directly in front of the judge's bench. Western Union had installed two extra operators in Flandreau to handle "the large amount of wire news incidental" to the case. As was to be expected, a large number of correspondents from out of state newspapers, including men from Sioux City, Minneapolis, and St. Paul, were in attendance with pad and pencil.[36] The *Argus-Leader* was represented by A. L. Buckholder, whose duty it was to send back to Sioux Falls "an uncolored and truthful report" of the proceedings. "It will be full and complete but not yellow."[37]

The *Argus-Leader* editor, Day, apparently felt the need both to defend his paper's reporting on the case and make a plea for calm. He acknowledged that there were sensational newspaper reports, and much was said that was "unfair to Sioux Falls." Day pointed the finger of blame not at Ross but at Sioux City, Iowa, a town about eighty miles to the south, which had "a direct interest in lodging prejudice against the good people of Sioux Falls" by suggesting that there had been an attempt to cover up facts in the case. While admitting that some reporting—by newspapers he chose not to name—did cause harm and prejudice, thus ensuring a change of venue, Day insisted that the *Argus-Leader* consistently published facts without regard to whether they favored one side or the other. Having rejected all notions that he favored the Kaufmanns, Day wrote rather bluntly, "It is now time to drop 'the Kaufmann case' out of politics and out of business." Taking the ethical high ground, Day stated that every decent and honest person wanted the defendant to get a fair trial, nothing more, nothing less.[38] However, Day's editorial exposed his belief that political repercussions were in the making and that one or more of his friends were at risk.

The trial about to begin was to determine the guilt or innocence of the accused, Emma Kaufmann. That should have been the only concern for people living in a free society where an accused person is presumed innocent until proven guilty beyond a reasonable doubt. Still, it was probably expecting too much of people to simply view the matter in rational terms. In a larger sense, the case was a human tragedy that could be felt on a personal level, something that touched a somber chord in everyone. The event was like some intangible, animal force on the loose that inspired both sadness and anger in the divided community, promulgated by countless newspaper articles appearing in competing publications, which fought among themselves like wild dogs over carrion.

But what could one expect in the era of "yellow journalism"? Why should Sioux Falls journalists be expected to behave in a civilized manner when the New York City newspapers operated by William Randolph Hearst and Joseph Pulitzer were locked in a struggle to out-scandalize and out-shock readers who never seemed to get enough of the swill dished out daily? Neither publisher came across a murder case he didn't like; each seized upon a scandal and whipped it into a frenzy to sell more papers. People died strange and tragic deaths in New York City at a high rate, and undertakers' wagons roamed the streets night and day, transporting the dead from place to place. All this meant that Hearst and Pulitzer would never run out of material.

There had been, of course, well-publicized murder cases in South Dakota, but none like the Kaufmann case with its cast of characters. The victim: an unsophisticated immigrant girl who died a terrible death. The accused: an eccentric, mysterious woman, the wife of a rich man who made a fortune running a brewery. Add to these forceful, ambitious, and flamboyant lawyers, quirky, biased newspapermen, and intense public fascination, and all good sense and social order was sent whirling in mid-air, ready to crash down upon everyone.

CHAPTER 8

THE FIRST KAUFMANN TRIAL: THE CASE FOR THE STATE

There is not the slightest doubt that the trial of this case will prove to be the most famous murder trial in the history of South Dakota.

The Daily Argus-Leader
June 5, 1907

If the Kaufmann trial occurred in the twenty-first century, it would be covered by the press but probably not given front-page or breaking-news coverage. Today, a murder trial could be upstaged by events of national or international importance. Not likely in 1907, when murder trials were pulsating community events of utmost importance, which held the attention and captured the imagination of the public. Criminal trials, especially death penalty cases, were great theater when other forms of entertainment were limited. They attracted a cross-section of the community, sometimes with men seated in one section and women in another, all dressed for the occasion.

Like spectators in a theater, waiting for the curtain to rise, attention was focused on the accused, the "star" of the show, although many others had important roles in the drama. The judge, the court clerks, the stenographer, the bailiffs, and of course the sheriff who, while he sat quietly, might be thinking about the prospect of putting a rope around the neck of the defendant, should there be a conviction and a death sentence.

And then there were the lawyers, often the greatest entertainers in a courtroom and always full of surprises. How would the confident and able prosecution team consisting of the Minnehaha County state's attorney, Alpha F. Orr, the Moody County state's attorney, Ira F. Blewitt, special prosecutor George W. Egan, and attorney W. J. Hooper, from Bonesteel, South Dakota, perform? Among this group, Orr didn't have a ringing endorsement from the *Sioux Falls Journal*. As the time for trial was drawing near, the *Journal* observed, "Orr had such a bad time getting anyone convicted that he quit trying cases."[1] That same newspaper also slammed Egan, calling him a "pompous Iowa lawyer," a superfluous presence who would make no impact on the outcome of the case.[2]

But Orr and Egan, both imposing six-footers, approached the Kaufmann case with an air of confidence, although they did not like nor trust one another. They had to put aside their differences and find a way to work together because a bitter legal duel was expected by all court watchers. For more than a year, the wife of a "rich brewer" had been considered guilty in the public mind, but no matter how much she was hated and vilified, she still wore the presumption of innocence, guaranteed by the Constitution.

The prosecutors wanted to expose her to the world as a cruel, fiendish killer of an innocent servant girl. Their goal: a conviction for murder in the first degree for which the punishment was death by hanging or life in prison. The electric chair—introduced as a more humane form of execution than hanging, which often went awry—had yet to make an appearance in South Dakota, although it had been used to execute many condemned prisoners in New York starting in 1890.

Executions in Sioux Falls had been few and far between, the most recent was held on December 5, 1902, when George Bear was hanged for the murder of two men. That execution probably didn't linger too long in the minds of the people, but there were many old-timers who recalled the city's first execution: the horribly bungled hanging of Thomas Egan in 1882. Egan, an Irish immigrant, had been wrongly convicted of murdering his wife. An innocent man was put to death and those responsible had to bear the twin burdens of shame and guilt.[3] Should it come down to a conviction and death sentence for Kaufmann, a woman, would the city have the stomach for it? Quietly and solemnly, observers had to weigh the various possibilities as to the punishment, should there be a conviction.

The indictment of Kaufmann was a wordy document that twisted and tortured the English language almost beyond understanding. It charged her with murder that was committed "willfully, wrongfully, unlawfully, feloniously, and with malice aforethought, and with premeditated design to effect the death of one Agnes Polreis . . . with some dangerous and deadly instrument and weapon . . . unknown." It alleged that the crime took place on May 31, 1906, and that after inflicting "three (3) mortal wounds" on "the top and back of the head" and "two (2) other mortal wounds . . . upon the shoulders and body of . . . said Agnes Polreis," she "languished" and "did on the first day of June 1906 . . . die." It was signed by Alpha Orr, State's Attorney for the County of Minnehaha.[4]

Orr and his fellow prosecutors planned to try the case with a combination of direct and circumstantial evidence. There would be testimony to the effect that Agnes Polreis was a healthy, robust girl when she was hired to be the Kaufmanns' live-in maid. This would be followed by evidence showing that a teenaged Agnes, a virtual prisoner, died after having suffered abuse and beatings at the hands of Emma Kaufmann, her employer. While the true motive for committing the heinous acts was unknown, it was believed that the prosecution would introduce evidence of the defendant's cruel treatment of other domestics through the testimony of some of her former female employees.

Peter Erickson, just twenty-five years old and still referred to as the "star witness" for the prosecution, was expected to testify as an eye-witness to the cruel treatment of Agnes by Mrs. Kaufmann. He was expected to testify that the defendant threw hot water on Agnes, bathed her feet in ashes, applied turpentine to her wounds, and struck her with a broomstick. Erickson would also tell the jury about the time he saw Agnes on her knees, as if begging her tormentor for mercy.

After Erickson made his appearance in Flandreau, he was carefully watched by both the prosecution and the defense. Described as "tall and massive, broad of shoulders, a head with a mane of hair, big browed and big featured,"[5] Erickson, like Egan, was an imposing presence, and his frank, straight-forward manner of speaking made a good impression on listeners. He had the attitude and demeanor of a confident, trustworthy man.

The Parkston delegation kept tabs on him, for some believed that "an effort might be made to spirit Erickson away from Flandreau."[6] Such an undertaking, however, would be very risky, and wiser heads did not believe that the defense would engage in witness tampering at this stage. No doubt Aikens believed the better strategy would be to grill him without mercy on cross-examination and destroy his credibility.

However dramatic the testimony of Erickson or other lay witnesses might be, the outcome of the trial would likely come down to a battle of experts. The prosecution was prepared to introduce medical testimony from Sioux Falls and Parkston doctors to explain that the forty-nine wounds on the dead girl were caused by violent, external forces. It was expected that these doctors would say, under oath, that Agnes Polreis did not suffer from diabetes and that she had no heart problems.

And if the prosecution wanted to create a sensation in the courthouse, the mother of the dead girl could be placed on the stand. Should that happen, because her mind had been drastically affected by the loss of her daughter, some believed that "a scene seldom seen in court will be enacted."[7] No one liked it, few understood it, and some resented it, but the capacity of poor women to endure suffering seemed infinite, and if Theresa Polreis spoke in court, her heart-rending words would likely burn a hole in the collective conscience of those present.

Anticipation was running wild, fueled in part by press coverage in other states. The *Bismarck Daily Tribune* called the defendant "**A FIEND**,"[8] and a Cairo, Illinois, newspaper warmed up its readers with the headline, "**NORTHWEST IS AROUSED**" over the trial of a "rich woman" for killing her maid.[9] "**TORTURED TO DEATH**" was the headline in the *Marlboro Democrat* in Bennettsville, South Carolina.[10]

John Ross of the *Soo Critic* was more than ready for some kind of grand spectacle. Opposing his hated rival, Mark Scott of the *Sioux Falls Journal*, Ross believed that the evidence against Kaufmann was "exceptionally strong," and the talk on the street was that "escape from conviction was practically impossible." Ross was betting on the riveting cross-examination skills of George Egan, one of the "best in the west." His commanding presence, his ability to grill witnesses combined with his oratorical skills meant Egan was in a position to deliver a conviction, so "the interests of the people are in safe hands."[11]

The defense team of Frank Aikens and his partner, Harry Judge, recognized as two of the most talented criminal attorneys in South Dakota, was beefed up by three Flandreau attorneys, George Rice, Fred Warren, and Edward Jordan. Rice, originally from Iowa, was an experienced attorney. He came to Flandreau in 1878 and immersed himself in civic affairs. He was the Moody County state's attorney for eight years and also served in the territorial legislature. He was involved in the organization of two Moody County banks and was a state railroad commissioner at the time of the Kaufmann trial.

These lawyers had been curiously silent as to their strategy, but the general consensus was that they would try to prove that the girl died from disease and therefore her death resulted from natural causes. Their medical expert witnesses would provide testimony to the effect that Agnes suffered from anemia and diabetes. The defense experts would testify that these maladies caused Agnes to weaken and fall, injuring herself. They would explain that the wounds, bruises, and gashes on her head, arms, and legs were the result of these frequent falls, not from blows struck by their client.

A source close to Moses Kaufmann told a reporter for the *Press and Dakotan* that "the defense will be insanity." The source seemed quite certain that this would be the strategy because "very quietly it came out" from a "friend of Mr. Kaufmann" that "a psychological condition" due to "natural causes at her age in life" was at the root of Kaufmann's strange behavior.[12]

If she had experienced an episode of insanity, Kaufmann had seemingly recovered. She was said to be "fully prepared" for the trial of her life. She was in "good spirits," and having escaped the mental maladies of the past, she was confident of acquittal.[13]

But would the defendant be called to testify on her behalf? This was the question on the minds of all court watchers. For while it would be risky, it might be necessary for Kaufmann to give her version of what went on inside the Kaufmann house in order to refute the very damaging testimony expected from Erickson.

There was some thought that the defense counsel might try to convince the jury that, rather than beat and torture Agnes, Mrs. Kaufmann actually tried to care for the girl who was seriously ill. Of course, that would be a tough sell since it could be argued that a caring, rational person would have called a doctor long before the teenager was helpless and near death. The mere presence of so many sores, cuts, and abrasions would have alerted anyone who saw them that something was terribly wrong. Why didn't they contact the girl's family? No, it didn't look promising for the defendant, and Ross informed his readers that they could expect "a write-up of the case that no one will want to miss."[14]

Several witnesses had gathered in the unpretentious courtroom by noon on June 5, 1907, and were nervously waiting their turn on the stand. The Moody County courthouse was described simply as "barren." Nothing "hangs on the walls of the room to break the line of vision. Just four bare walls [that] extend from side to side."[15] Built in 1882, it was less commodious than courthouses in other towns, though it had a pleasing exterior and good acoustics. This was a plus since the audience expected a serious battle as both teams of lawyers were eager and full of fight. Spectators could look forward to many "lively tilts." Throughout the trial it would be "steel and steel."[16]

The *Argus-Leader* had the case sized up correctly, but its rival, the weekly *Sioux Falls Journal*, thought it was a certain victory for the defense. After considering the evidence in the arsenal of the prosecution, the *Journal*'s Mark Scott declared that in no way would there be a conviction. For this reason, he favored having the trial in Flandreau. It would be better if a jury from a county other than Minnehaha acquitted Kaufmann, "for then it cannot be laid up against this [Sioux Falls] city."[17]

Tension was rising in Flandreau as the time for hearing testimony approached. Both sides were busy spying, sleuthing, and inform-

Moody County Courthouse, Flandreau, South Dakota.
Courtesy Moody County Historical Society.

ing. The large Parkston delegation was especially vigilant about important state witnesses, keeping the prosecution team "posted as to the movements of the enemy." One reporter said that "both sides are watching each other like cats watch mice."[18]

Members of the press, including reporters from outside of South Dakota, were in attendance in great numbers. Among them was a young woman from Flandreau, Annie Russell, who was seeking a career in journalism, an avocation usually restricted to men only. A graduate of the University of South Dakota, she was representing the *Flandreau Herald* at the trial.[19] While Russell was busy making history, she and others were reporting on what "is now known throughout the country as 'the Kaufmann case.'"[20]

~

But before one side or the other could pounce, they had to select a jury. Jury selection began when the clerk of court drew the first twelve names out of a cigar box labeled "Colorado Claro's."[21] There were a total of one hundred men in the jury pool, an unusually large group of potential jurors. But observers believed that it was necessary in order to find twelve men who had not been unduly influenced by the press or had not in some other way formed an opinion as to guilt or innocence. It would also be important to learn about a potential juror's views on the death penalty.

On day three of the trial, before Judge Smith, the lawyers were still questioning and challenging potential jurors while the jury pool steadily decreased. Taking it all down was stenographer Carlotta East from the first circuit in Yankton.[22] Listening to the rather tedious questioning, Emma sat calmly with her lawyers, paying close attention to the proceedings and even breaking into a slight smile when someone made a witty remark. Her cheerful attitude at her trial was taken as a sign that she was confident of acquittal. Those who had attended the preliminary hearing in Sioux Falls, when she was somber, dazed, and distracted, were struck by the wholesale changes in her demeanor.

Since her arrival in Flandreau, she along with her husband and son, Charles, had been staying in an apartment at the residence of Mary Mead, across the street from the courthouse. Flandreau, originally "Flandrau," was founded in 1857 by the Dakota Land Company from St. Paul, Minnesota, making it one of the earliest town sites in the Dakotas. The Big Sioux River passed through the town site, named after Charles E. Flandrau, a prominent Minnesotan and shareholder in the Dakota Land Company. Flandreau was vacated and then destroyed in 1858 by Dakota Sioux who regarded the settlers as trespassers, but it was given new life after treaties and pressure by the military put an end to hostilities. Thereafter, it grew and thrived on the bountiful prairie soil. According to the census of 1900, Flandreau had 1,244 people.

During the early stages of the trial, Flandreau residents paid little or no special attention to their notorious guest; they allowed Emma to come and go in peace and privacy. Dr. George Pettigrew, a Sioux Falls resident, said that after a short visit to Flandreau he came away feeling that the local inhabitants had only "passing interest" in the case. He was at the Flandreau depot when Emma, Moses, and Charles Kaufmann arrived, and he estimated that only about fifty people were present and no one made any demonstration.[23]

In fact, even the newspapers reported that people seemed disinterested. Although clearly everyone understood the serious, historic nature of the case, no one was about to be swept up and carried away by the dramatic life-or-death struggle unfolding in their town. It was springtime in Flandreau and there was a sense that the joys of the season trumped the excitement about to play out in the courthouse.

Flandreau residents surely recognized that the trial was bringing hundreds of people into town, making merchants happy. Hotels, including the popular St. Vincent Hotel, and boarding houses were full, and patrons who were lucky enough to get accommodations paid a premium price. There were no bargains to be had. One hotelier had to turn away about 150 potential guests because his building was full. Many homes with rooms to spare were opened to visitors. No one complained about Flandreau hospitality.[24]

St. Vincent Hotel, Flandreau, South Dakota.
Courtesy Moody County Historical Society.

Flandreau also played host to a high-profile visitor that June in the person of U.S. Senator Alfred B. Kittredge.[25] He huddled with the defense team, sparking the false rumor that he was about to join them. But it was known that Kittredge and Moses Kaufmann were friends and political allies and it was believed that the senator was "connected with the Sioux Falls Brewery."[26] Prior to becoming a U.S. Senator, Kittredge served in the state legislature, and during legislative sessions, when the subject of prohibition came up, both men were on the same side. They were stalwart "wets" and opposed the "drys" most strenuously.[27]

They did so with great frequency, too, because South Dakota had long been buffeted by the winds of temperance, starting back in the territorial days. Prohibition had steadily gained ground in many localities. However, alcohol had been a part of frontier life for so long, and mixed with politics, it was a practice that was hard to outlaw. Failing to ban consumption, non-drinkers had to be satisfied with strict licensing laws. For example, after eighteen years of prohibition, the town of Canton in 1904 legalized alcohol consumption—and five licensed saloons quickly opened up. This caused one wiseacre to declare that Canton was making up for "lost time."[28]

While Kittredge was never charged with excessive drinking, he most certainly sympathized with his friend, the brewer, when it came to keeping booze legal. Nevertheless, he was far too astute even to appear to take sides in the case against Kaufmann. There was an attempt to keep his Flandreau visit strictly a private matter, and "friends" advised him that it could hurt him politically, especially if the Parkston people knew he was talking to Kaufmann and Aikens. Kittredge quietly left Flandreau as the trial went forward. Still, his appearance caused curious reporters to wonder why "a United States Senator from South Dakota was sent for" by the defense.[29]

The *Argus-Leader* had an answer. The senator was merely "mingling with friends" and nothing more. Always ready to defend Kittredge, the journalist called it "a yellow report," one that caused the defense attorneys to laugh. The senator paid a visit and left the next day and "that is all there is to the report."[30]

On June 6 Mrs. Polreis was seated in the back of the courtroom, having been subpoenaed to testify when the evidentiary phase of the trial started. During a lull in the proceedings, when the prospective jurors were out of the courtroom, but with the judge on the bench, the mother of Agnes Polreis, still grieving, stood up and walked toward the front of the room. When she reached a point about fifteen feet from Emma Kaufman, whom she had never seen before, Theresa Polreis stopped and got down on her knees. Bowing her head, she paused for a moment. Then she looked up, crossed herself, and with her arms raised above her head she said in German:

> Mary, Mother of Jesus, Lord Jesus Christ. Have mercy upon me. Forgive, I pray Thee, all those concerned with the death of my beloved daughter, Agnes. Lord forgive them as I do. Forgive mine enemies. Lord, look down upon me and give me rest.

It was a spontaneous, stunning, heart-rending scene "without parallel in the minds of everyone who saw the act," which brought "tears to the eyes of both men and women." Her daughter "tried to restrain and soothe her mother" and did so up to the point when Theresa assumed the position of prayer. Then the "girl's head fell like that of Millet's peasant woman in the famous picture of the Angelus." She remained motionless until her mother finished praying and then "gently but firmly . . . assisted her mother from the courtroom to the balcony." The judge, who was also taken aback, advised the court officials to watch Mrs. Polreis and make sure that there were no further demonstrations.[31]

Two days following the dramatic courtroom prayer scene, a picture of John and Theresa Polreis appeared in the *Sioux City Journal*, along with a photograph of an impressive monument on the grave of their daughter.[32] Anyone who saw the photograph might conclude that, although she had suffered in life, she was honored in death.

As a precaution, and on the advice of the prosecuting attorneys, Mrs. Polreis was taken back to Parkston. She was not going to be a witness. Her mental condition was deteriorating, so it was determined that for her sake, and to prevent any further interventions of praying, she should stay home.[33] The interruption halted the jury selection process for a short time, and after the pool was depleted, the court adjourned without a complete jury.

Jury selection was taxing the patience of the judge, lawyers, and spectators. Anxious to get into the meat of the case, George W. Egan rather testily asked one potential juror, "Does your corn need plowing?"[34] Regardless of whether he answered yes or no, tending to recently planted fields was surely on the mind of every farmer in the jury pool, for whom the Kaufmann trial was becoming a major distraction.

It turned out that the farmers and other citizens of Moody County were heavy subscribers of newspapers. After reading newspaper accounts of the case, many had formed strong opinions and were therefore disqualified. The tedious questioning of prospective jurors was relieved a bit when one man quipped, in response to a question about knowledge of the case, "I don't think a juryman should be totally ignorant." The off-handed remark evoked broad smiles and scattered laughter. Among those smiling was the defendant, who took great interest in the questioning of jurymen, her chair turned toward the jury box "the greater part of the afternoon."[35]

It was clear that some men told the court they were convinced that the defendant was guilty so they could be excused and attend to field work. Several other men revealed, however, that the sensational demonstration in Sioux Falls against Emma Kaufmann at the preliminary hearing influenced their view of the case. And since the defense was essentially silent at the preliminary hearing, people were left with the impression that their case was weak.

All this meant that Moody County Sheriff George Hoskins was busy serving summons to round up another forty men. He was hampered by heavy rains that made some roads impassable, thus slowing down his mission. He managed to get twenty out of the forty in court but told the judge that he probably could not have the entire contingent present until Saturday morning. While the defense was willing to proceed with just half of the special venire, or jury panel, the prosecution objected. Judge Smith adjourned the court, after which Emma, showing some evidence of strain caused by the delay, retreated to her rooms at the Mead house.[36]

The *Sioux Falls Journal* mocked both the jury selection process and the case as a whole. The June 7 edition of that weekly newspaper reported, "There really has been little accomplished, although the string fiends have loaded newspapers down with a vast amount of fiction." The *Journal* was primarily a commercial publication whose purpose was to be a cheerleader for commerce and business; it had little time or respect for social or legal matters.[37] For the most part, the *Journal* sulked on the sideline while other local newspapers presented the case with great relish and in fascinating detail.

Once the special venire of forty men had been sworn in, questioning began and by the afternoon of the 8th, a jury of twelve men had been selected. It was called "A Farmers Jury" by the *Argus-Leader* because eleven out of the twelve were full- or part-time farmers. The following men had the arduous task of deciding the historic case:

Sever Benson, farmer

Ed Benwise, farmer and school teacher

William Cone, farmer

C. Buck, farmer

Eben Nace, farmer

Irving Stombaugh, farmer

Christian Lea, farmer

Elon G. Pettigrew, farmer

George Pearly, farmer (foreman)

Ray Pierce, farmer

B. F. Nichols, carpenter

A. G. Platts, carpenter and farmer[38]

One minute they were just ordinary, hard-working farmers without expectation of having their names on the front page of a newspaper. The next minute they were standing at the threshold of notoriety, charged with finding guilt or innocence in a sensational death penalty case, knowing that their decision would be minutely scrutinized by friend and foe. America was watching.

Nor would they be treated like most jurymen during the course of what promised to be a very tense and possibly long trial. "Extra precautions" were announced, meaning that an effort would be made to prevent communications between jury members and outsiders. The sheriff was ordered to keep jury members together and away from outside influences. Judge Smith issued strict instructions to the jury: they were not to discuss the case in any way among themselves nor were they allowed to express any opinions.[39] They were expected to listen to the evidence with an open mind, unencumbered by emotion or feelings of favor or prejudice.

The jury in the first Kaufmann trial.
Courtesy Moody County Historical Society.

~

Monday morning, June 10, 1907, George Egan stood up in court and gave what was described as a detailed and dramatic arraignment of the defendant. Next he presented the opening statement for the prosecution. What the jury and spectators saw was a man of star quality, his large physique and massive head covered with long, black hair, take control of the stage where the terrible drama was about to begin. With his distinct "Celtic mould," quick mind, and unsurpassed eloquence, Egan had the unique ability to attract and hold attention, to convince and draw people to his side. He was instantly likeable and popular.[40]

Egan told the jury that the prosecution would prove that a young, strong, plump, and healthy Agnes Polreis went to work for Emma Kaufmann and a relatively short time later died on a hospital bed from wounds inflicted by the defendant. He made it clear that the testimony of the nurses who treated Agnes would carry a great deal of weight in showing the type and location of wounds on the body of the girl. Egan said there would be evidence introduced that Mrs. Kaufmann forced Agnes to scrub the floor with "Gold Dust when her hands were in a terrible condition and the strong powder took the skin off her hands."[41] Testimony would also show that "Mrs. Kaufmann made statements showing her animosity toward the girl" and that the defendant displayed alarm for "her personal safety when she heard the girl was dead."

It was a scathing review of the circumstances of the death of Agnes, but Emma could only sit, uncomfortably, and endure the stern, damning lecture from attorney Egan. She wasn't smiling anymore. During the powerful opening statement, Egan frequently turned and pointed directly at the defendant, as if his finger of guilt was none other than the light of truth—the absolute, golden truth that would be used to convict her and send her to the penitentiary for life or to death on the gallows.[42]

During the course of Egan's long and melodramatic opening statement, Aikens rose and objected several times, insisting that counsel for the prosecution had exceeded the limitations of the law and was in fact arguing the case. There was a fine line between making a plain statement of what one intends to prove and giving a summation of the evidence, and Aikens insisted that Egan had crossed that line time and time again. Nevertheless, the judge allowed Egan to continue, overruling the objections.[43]

The first witness for the prosecution was Arthur Snashall, an embalmer employed by the Miller undertaking firm. His testimony was brief, telling the jury that he was called to the Kaufmann house to take Agnes to the hospital, and while in transit, she "gave utterance to several exclamations in a foreign tongue."[44] Later, after he learned of her death, he took her body to the undertaking facility to prepare it for burial.

Next, three nurses from the Sioux Falls Hospital offered testimony. The first, Jeannette E. Larson, the head nurse, testified in detail about the wounds, cuts, and gashes on Agnes' head, limbs, and other parts of her body. The substance of her testimony was that Agnes was in a critical, life-threatening condition when she was brought to the hospital. Agnes, she said, was clad in a "man's nightshirt" and around her neck was a "blue kitchen apron." She was not wearing shoes. Larson described the patient as "very emaciated and black on the limbs," with shoulder blades also black and gangrenous in appearance. Further, "the third finger of her left hand was disjointed "with the bone protruding," and the "epidermis was off the feet and ankles and the flesh underneath was raw." The patient "was perfectly hopeless up until the time she died." Her only words were in German and she mumbled that her stomach and head hurt, saying, "I ache all over."

Attorney Egan tried to pull a fast one on the defense. He asked Larson if she had an opinion as to the type of blunt instruments that were used to cause the wounds. But Aikens was ready to interject. He jumped to his feet and objected vociferously, insisting the question was without foundation because the witness was not an expert. The judge sustained the objection.

On cross-examination by Judge Aikens, Larson was asked if the wounds were gangrenous. She responded by saying they had the "appearance" of being gangrenous but she stopped short of stating they were gangrenous. Overall, her testimony was credible, professional, calmly delivered, and helpful to the prosecution.

Miss A. M. Thornburg was the nurse who had "personal charge" of Agnes during her short stay at the hospital. She offered testimony about the condition of her patient, describing the wounds on her body. She said she undressed Agnes, whose hair was "snarly" and "matted with blood." There were three wounds on the top of her head and the "epidermis was peeling off" her left foot. Thornburg thoroughly corroborated the testimony of Larson when she described the weak and horrible condition of the body of the sixteen-year-old girl who had suffered terribly.[45] Thornburg recalled that Agnes "talked some" but in a language that the witness did not understand.[46]

It was reported that on cross-examination, Thornburg was "something of a tartar to Judge Aikens." When he asked her about the size of the wounds, she replied briskly, "I didn't measure them." She also said that she saw no gangrenous wounds on her patient's back because she did not "turn her over." She added rather saucily,

"I was more surprised at the clothing she had on." Clearly, here was a witness who had less than a favorable view of Aikens' client.[47]

Miss Fayola E. Couts, an undergraduate at the nurses training school at the Sioux Falls Hospital, added further testimony about the cuts, gashes, and wounds on the body of Polreis. When she was asked if the wounds "were unusual," she answered, "remarkably so."[48] She apparently proved to be less contentious when cross-examined. At any rate, she and the other hard-working nurses were to get her wounds bandaged and then moved to a private room. But due to Agnes' horrible condition, she died alone at the Sioux Falls Hospital on June 1, 1906.

Having put critical nursing testimony into the record, L. D. Miller of the Miller undertaking firm in Sioux Falls, and also the county coroner, took the stand. With Egan still asking the questions, the witness told those present about "taking the body of Agnes Polreis to his undertaking rooms and giving it the customary examination." He described the overall condition of her emaciated body, including the wounds. He was not asked anything on cross-examination.

Following Miller, John Polreis, father of the victim took the witness stand. Speaking through an interpreter, he told the court that his family had immigrated to America, arriving in Parkston on November 1, 1905. He described his daughter as not tall but solidly built—the picture of good health when she went to work at the Kaufmann residence. Agnes had not experienced the usual childhood maladies such as chicken pox or whooping cough nor had she ever been "doctored or taken medicine." She once had a toothache and a sore throat but no health problems. John Polreis testified that his daughter was "not quite seventeen years old" at the time of her death.

William Moeller, a Parkston businessman was next to testify for the prosecution. He explained that it was he who arranged to have Agnes employed by the Kaufmanns. Another Parkston resident, Dr. H. B. Schofield, was called on to testify. He told the jury that he conducted a postmortem on the body of Agnes Polreis and described his findings. Crucial to his testimony was his belief that some type of blunt instrument caused the wounds on the head and shoulders. He also said that as a result of his examination, he determined that the heart, liver, kidneys, and other organs were found to be normal. Dr. Schofield "gave the impression that the wounds on the head...

were sufficient to cause the death of the girl." This critical piece of testimony was entered into the record after the judge overruled a "strenuous" defense objection.[49] When the doctor was asked what caused the wounds, he replied, "external violence."[50]

Dr. Thomas J. Billion testified in a manner that corroborated the testimony of his colleague, Dr. Schofield, insisting that the girl died from acts of external violence. He recalled his examination of the body done a year ago and that he had found no sign of diabetes. On cross-examination, the *Sioux Falls Daily Press* reported, Dr. Billion "bristled like a cat" and admitted that he was "prejudiced in the case." There were "certain things in the case that made him so."[51] He did not elaborate on what those "certain things" were but he did say, in response to Aikens' questioning, that it was after he had participated in the examination of the victim's brain that he made up his mind that she died as a result of "external violence."[52]

The steady rain over five days finally stopped, and on June 12, in the warm glow of sunshine, Moses and Charles Kaufmann escorted the defendant to her courtroom chair. They were about to listen to the testimony of Mrs. Cordelia Udell, who once lived in the Kaufmann cottage next to the Kaufmann mansion. The first witness of the day, Udell told the jury that she "occasionally saw Agnes at work around the Kaufmann premises." At one time, when she was in the Kaufmann home talking to the man and lady of the house, she heard "the rattling of a door knob" followed by "an indistinct cry of 'Frau Kaufmann!'" Moses Kaufmann asked his wife about the noise and she said something about "that stupid girl." She went upstairs and in a loud voice said something in German and then came back downstairs. Udell once again heard a voice from upstairs saying "Frau Kaufmann!" Udell saw Emma Kaufmann going back upstairs and then left the house.

Udell further testified that, during the week before Agnes died, she saw the girl walking downstairs with a pail of water. Agnes was so weak that she had to "support herself with one hand on the side of the house." After she reached the foot of the stairs, Agnes tipped the pail over and re-entered the house, going back up the steps "with the greatest of difficulty." It was the last time Udell saw her alive.

More startling was her testimony that one evening she saw Agnes jump off the porch of the Kaufmann house and run toward her cottage. She was followed by Emma Kaufmann, who came rushing out of the house and "went hurriedly in the same direction" until she caught up with the girl. The witness watched as Emma Kaufmann marched the girl back to the big house. Udell closed her testimony by recalling that, on the afternoon of the day Agnes died, Moses Kaufmann asked her to stay with his wife because she "did not like to stay at home alone."

The Forest City, South Dakota, paper thought Mrs. Udell was "the best witness the state has had so far," noting that her testimony caused Emma Kaufmann to show "some excitement" while her neighbor recited facts according to her recollection. During the recess the defendant nervously looked around the room at the faces of the spectators "as if to see what affect the witness had had on them."[53]

Although her testimony was damaging, Udell was only a warm-up for the next witness. Peter Erickson, the former handyman at the Kaufmann house, now a farmer from Alpena, in Jerauld County, South Dakota, came to the stand and, under oath, began telling the enraptured jurors and audience what he knew about the case. In the beginning his testimony was consistent with what he said about a year ago at the preliminary hearing. He grabbed the attention of those in the courtroom when he said Agnes was "jostled to the floor" by Mrs. Kaufmann. In a weakened condition Agnes was unable to get up and when asked if he tried to help her stand up, Erickson said Emma Kaufmann prevented him from assisting the girl. At this point hisses came from the audience, though these were quickly gaveled into silence by Judge Smith.[54]

The next morning Erickson returned to the stand. With the audience on edge, he continued to relate the facts as he knew them, responding to questions by prosecuting attorney Egan. Erickson testified that on a daily basis he and Mrs. Kaufmann would drink beer together over lunch. During these "beer fests," Agnes "scrubbed and did other domestic duties." She was never allowed to join them.[55] Erickson testified that he "never saw Agnes have any lunch."[56]

The reporter for the *Argus-Leader* noted that Erickson "kept a cool head" as he testified, building the case for the state while swaying the mood of the Flandreau crowd away from the defendant. All eyes were on the plain-spoken, big "Norse" as he began a detailed recitation about what he witnessed in the Kaufmann house concerning the steadily deteriorating condition of Agnes and the manner in which she was treated by her employer.

There was the matter of the turpentine, a liquid derived from the resin of trees, mainly pine trees. The potentially toxic substance, which causes skin irritation, was widely used in America as a remedy for abrasions and sores on the body.[57] Someone who was "intimately acquainted with Mrs. Emma Kaufmann" told a reporter that turpentine was "her favorite remedy for 'ills of the flesh.'"[58] Erickson told the jury that Mrs. Kaufmann applied it to Agnes' limbs to reduce the "inflammation."[59]

"Don't touch her as she can get up herself if she wants to—she is only working on your sympathy," exclaimed Kaufmann to Erickson when he attempted to pick Agnes up after the defendant had "jostled" her to the floor. Erickson testified that she was too weak to get up on her own. And when Agnes tried to use the screen door knob to pull herself up, the defendant roughly jerked her hand away.

Erickson referred to an incident in the kitchen when Agnes was on the floor in a pool of water. Emma Kaufmann told him that she had poured hot water on her to make her get up. He was ordered to "shake the girl" to get her on her feet, which he did reluctantly. He "reviewed many instances of punishment," including seeing Mrs. Kaufmann "often" punch Agnes with a broom handle. He recalled that on many occasions Agnes was on her knees, crying out repeatedly, "Frau Kaufmann, Frau Kaufmann!"[60]

The handyman-turned-farmer also testified that Mrs. Kaufmann once told him, "Now I don't want you to say anything to the people you board with about this." Then she added, "I don't want anyone to know that I have had trouble with this girl."[61] The prosecution viewed this as evidence of a cruel woman who had a guilty conscience.

On the day of her death, Erickson recalled that Agnes was "semiconscious," that her "cheeks were sunken and her eyes glazed." He noticed "blood in the matted hair of the girl, and asked Mrs. Kaufmann about it." She told him he should pay it no mind but rather "go on with his work." And after it was learned that Agnes had died, Mrs. Kaufmann said in the presence of Erickson, "What shall I do? What shall I do?"[62]

What they did do, according to Erickson, was clean all the blood stains from the floor and walls and tear off the wallpaper in Agnes' room, testimony that elicited loud noises from the audience. Altogether, Erickson offered shocking and dramatic testimony, which appeared to have a "telling effect" on the audience that, up to this point, had shown "no pronounced sentiment one way or the other."[63] No doubt it was influencing the jury, too.

The most stunning testimony from Erickson came on cross-examination by Aikens, who asked about accepting a bribe. Erickson denied asking Moses Kaufmann for $500 in exchange for testimony. Then Aikens asked him if he were ever offered any money to testify. He promptly replied, "Yes," and went on to say that "Yourself [Aikens] and Mr. Kaufmann" offered him money for favorable testimony. "You [Aikens] told me that if I would treat Mrs. Kaufmann right they would treat me right and give me anything I wanted." This conversation, he explained, took place in Sioux Falls at the Cataract Hotel before the preliminary hearing.[64]

News of the Cataract conversation brought down the house. The entire audience came to its feet and erupted in cheering and wild applause. The crowd was loving the show. With great difficulty, the judge quieted the assemblage and restored order. But the defense had been dealt a blow by the "boomerang" testimony from Erickson, and it was clear from the spontaneous explosion that the crowd favored the prosecution.

When Aikens recovered from his surprise, he accused Egan of undignified showmanship for "trying to bring about applause from the crowd." Egan sprang to his feet not to defend himself, he said, but to protest that counsel for the defense was trying to cast aspersions on "the good men and women of this beautiful little city of Flandreau," all of whom came as good citizens to view a public trial, as was their right.

This grandiloquent outburst from the Iowa lawyer set off the audience again. As Egan took his seat, all the spectators left theirs and let out a collective roar, with loud cheers accompanying pounding applause that "lasted several minutes and only ceased after stern rapping by the court." Judge Smith, his patience severely tested, addressed the audience, reminding them that while it was their right to attend the public trial, they had no right to cause a disturbance, and should there be another outburst, he would clear the courtroom.[65]

This shocking testimony about an attempted bribe was like an adrenalin rush to publisher Ross, who loved hearing Erickson's damaging testimony. Ross called it "one of the most dramatic scenes ever witnessed in a courtroom." For that reason he could not pass up the chance to poke some fun at Aikens. Driving his verbal knife in to the hilt, Ross wrote, "In his usual sarcastic and overbearing manner," the learned attorney asked the money question and got an unexpected answer, one that caused the audience to break out in "loud applause."

Although the defense had not yet put on its case, Ross was absolutely certain of a conviction, and he proceeded with his own closing argument. Summing up all the lurid details of the maltreatment of Agnes in the house of horrors, Ross said that Egan had performed flawlessly and with matchless skill: "The people here [Flandreau] will always believe her fully guilty. That jury will never acquit."[66]

Cartoon of George Bessler's trial testimony, the *American Republic*, January 22, 1915.

The jury had more direct testimony to hear and mentally digest. Following Erickson's exit, George Bessler, another Kaufmann employee, moved into the witness circle. He said he first met Agnes Polreis "at a masquerade ball," at which time she looked "healthy and plump." On subsequent trips to the Kaufmann house to deliver beer, Bessler noticed that Agnes had changed: "there were black spots on her face beneath her eyes" that Mrs. Kaufmann described as "an old country disease." Bessler recalled hearing Mrs. Kaufmann say that Agnes was so stupid that "I feel sometimes like killing her." As did Erickson, Bessler saw the defendant "poke the girl with the broom handle" and act "very cross with the girl." On cross-examination, Bessler admitted that he once said he knew nothing about the case but explained that he expressed himself in that way because he "did not want to get mixed up in the case." Mrs. N. T. Grosz was eager to get "mixed up" in the case. A friend of Agnes, she testified that when the girl left Parkston for Sioux Falls, she was "robust, healthy, plump and strong."[67]

The people of Flandreau and throughout Moody County were now fully engaged in the case. Folks flocked into town from the outlying communities and waited, sometimes for hours, to get a seat. Their earlier indifference had become replaced by intense, even morbid curiosity. During the evening of the 12th and the next morning, Sheriff Hoskins had to disperse a crowd of "several hundred people" who had gathered in front of the courthouse to get a glimpse of Emma as she and her entourage walked to the Mead house. Truly, the spectacle had lived up to its billing.[68]

~

Agnes' brain had been in the custody of Dr. Schofield in Parkston. Having become a prosecution exhibit, it was brought into court in a six-quart tin pail filled with embalming fluid. It had been cut into quarter sections, with wooden toothpicks connecting the pieces.[69] Two medical experts, commonly referred to as "alienists," were about to give their opinions on the condition of the brain on behalf of the prosecution. Their examination of the brain had been done "under the permission of Judge Smith."[70]

The first was Dr. Arthur Sweeney of St. Paul, "a specialist in nervous diseases." Prior to his appearance as a witness, he had conducted a "microscopic examination" of the brain of Agnes Polreis at the St. Vincent Hotel. He testified that her brain was in "healthy condition." He found no sign of disease.

Egan asked Dr. Sweeney if the many wounds on the head and body of the girl were sufficient to cause her death. The defense objected but was overruled. Sweeney replied that the "blood clots on the brain" were the result of blows to the head done by a blunt instrument. The doctor concluded: "The existence of the many wounds upon the head and body was sufficient to cause death."

Following Sweeney's powerful testimony, Egan called Dr. Frank E. Coulter of Omaha, a specialist in "mental and nervous diseases." He had assisted in the brain examination, and his conclusion "was along the same line as that of Dr. Sweeney." Dr. Coulter stated that the cause of Agnes' death was "hemorrhages" from wounds "caused by external injuries." There was no cross-examination of the experts by the defense. Having put on a forceful and convincing case, the prosecution rested,[71] confidentially offering the defense's medical experts the opportunity to examine the victim's brain. It would be in the possession of Dr. Schofield, who also had custody of her heart.[72]

~

George W. Egan had done very well in his first South Dakota murder case. He had lived up to his Iowa reputation as an outstanding attorney. It had been bantered about that "Judge Aiken would make Mr. Eagan [sic] look like thirty cents," but from the outset he had impressed all observers. The admiring editor of the *Critic* opined that Egan had made Aikens look "something like a 5-cent piece."

But for Ross and his newspaper, the case was all about money. It had been about money and power from the outset, and nothing in the developments to date changed his mind: "This is a case of money and long political influence, ramifying the whole state." He stated that this testimony will be followed "by other astounding revelations which will awaken the people as they have never been before."[73] Ross had a habit of making predictions about future earth-shaking revelations—most of which failed to transpire.

The trial, however, did deliver. For three days the jury and the spectators had listened to riveting testimony from the prosecution witnesses. The tension was palpable as evidenced by the loud cheers from the spectators whenever they were moved by sensational testimony. Judge Smith responded to the outbursts by "smartly" rapping his gavel and finally declaring that unless the exhibitions ceased, he would "clear the courtroom."[74] He most certainly knew, though, that more fireworks would erupt in the days ahead, for the defense would soon be called to establish its case.

The prosecution rested at 10:55 A.M and Judge Smith adjourned the case until 4:00 P.M. At that hour Judge Smith re-entered the courtroom followed by the jury. With the audience in a "deep hush," the judge "rapped for order." The first person to stand was not Aikens, as expected. Rather, Egan rose and addressed the court as follows: "The importance of this case is such that the counsel must use much candor toward each other and with the court. Since the state rested its case this morning, something has come up, and matters of importance have developed, and a contingency has arisen which may make it necessary to again ask for a continuance of the case." Hearing this, and there being no objection by the defense, Judge Smith granted a continuance until 9 o'clock the next morning.

Hinting that he may have rested pre-maturely, Egan set the rumor mills in motion. What was this mysterious "contingency?" Did Egan have a secret witness he wanted to put on the stand? All dramatic productions employ twists and turns to engage the audience, and spectators and reporters alike were left guessing as to the state's strategy. Among the tantalizing possibilities was that Maggie M. Ross, wife of the *Critic* editor, was going to be a surprise witness. After she arrived at the courthouse, she "was at once closeted with Attorney Egan."[75]

If Mrs. Ross was under consideration as a witness for the state, Egan nixed the idea. The mysterious contingency Egan mentioned amounted to nothing more than titillating speculation. When the court convened the next morning, the defense began its case. Except for rebuttal witnesses, the prosecution was finished.

Chapter 9

The First Kaufmann Trial: The Defense Opens

"The defense in this case is that we deny everything."

The Daily Argus-Leader
June 13, 1907

Anyone who purchased the *Sioux Falls Daily Press* of June 13, 1907, must have been surprised, even shocked, by the headline: "**MRS. KAUFMANN ON THE WITNESS STAND**." A reader could not help but think the remarkable case had taken a strange turn. Would she actually testify on her own behalf? Would Aikens take that risk? But there it was in black and white: "Mrs. Emma Kaufmann will take the stand in her own defense in the trial for her life."

Perhaps the editor or a reporter for the *Daily Press* had some inside information about the defense strategy, but this was mere speculation and could lead to embarrassment. On the other hand, "the great army of readers" clinging to every word of every newspaper article on the great trial would probably just lap up each titillating detail, waiting to gulp down more.[1]

The astute Frank R. Aikens had other ideas. He began the defense of the Kaufmann case by first reminding the jurors of their promise to wait until all the evidence was in before they made a decision. Then he made the bold statement, "The defense in this case is that we deny everything," a remark that found its way into the eastern press, including the Washington, D.C. *Evening Star*.[2]

No doubt the prosecution understood this as a refutation of their case to convict, such was the confident nature of the former judge. With a wave of the hand, Aikens figuratively cleared the table of all the debris left by his opponents. From this point forward, he coached the jury with this remonstrance: Listen, be informed, and be convinced. He was a man who hated to lose, and he was about to show his hand—but his client would not testify.

Every lawyer knows that truth is the guiding star in a trial and that steering a jury toward that star in a manner the jurors find acceptable will win their support. Every lawyer also understands that there is "truth" and there is "proof," and they may not always be the same thing. So a wise lawyer acknowledges that, however elegant the actual truth, that which he can actually prove may be the best he can do. And if he is convincing, his proof may be taken as truth and it may be enough to carry him to victory.

If ever a lawyer understood that distinction, it was Frank R. Aikens. He was a careful, calculating attorney, a shrewd litigator for whom knowledge of the finer points of law came as second nature. Over his years of practice, he had built a solid reputation as one of the best lawyers in South Dakota.

As the jury and spectators waited in respectful silence, Aikens made it clear that he was not going to offer an insanity defense. Rather, he would show through expert testimony that Agnes Polreis was not murdered, nor did she die as a result of maltreatment by Emma Kaufmann. She died of natural causes, from a terrible disease called diabetes. There were no wounds on her body; the marks and abnormalities on Agnes were caused by diabetes, a debilitating disease.

He went on to say that "we will show that the disease will account for the blood clots on the brain . . . and we will show the disease leaves the body in a condition that the least scratch or bruise will produce wounds." Agnes, he said, had been taken to a doctor too late to reverse the deadly effects of the disease. Then he added, somewhat esoterically, "It is always too late." Aikens said that the defense would also rely "on the improbabilities and inconsistencies of the case presented by the prosecution."

The first defense witness was Dr. William A. Germain. He told the jury that he had been a practicing physician in Sioux Falls for the past twenty-five years and during all of this time he had known Emma Kaufmann. Consistent with his testimony at the preliminary hearing, he said he was called to the Kaufmann house on the morning of June 1, 1906. Upon his arrival he was directed to a second-story bedroom and found Agnes Polreis lying on her bed. She was weak and emaciated. Her body temperature was normal but her tongue was coated. At first he thought she had typhoid fever but later rejected that diagnosis. Dr. Germain explained to the jury the nature and location of the wounds, "largely in pairs," on the girl's body. He also said that the "flesh" on a finger, "nearly severed," was "parted to the bone."

He testified that he left the Kaufmann house following the cursory examination of the patient. Not to have insisted that Agnes, in such a horrible condition, go immediately to the hospital must have caused observers to wonder. But the question was apparently not raised on direct examination. Dr. Germain testified that he made a second trip to the Kaufmann house that same afternoon and found Agnes "in a rather nude condition." She was "eating voraciously," which he explained was a symptom of diabetes. He insisted at this point that she be taken to the hospital. He "covered her wounds with bandages," put a night shirt and stockings on her, "and got her ready to go to the hospital."[3] But he also testified that "the body was partially dead" because of the gangrene and dead tissue.[4]

The witness said he understood the German language and recalled that Agnes told Mrs. Kaufmann, in German, that she did not want to leave the house. "I don't want to go to the hospital. You must go with me," she insisted. Dr. Germain testified that both Agnes and Mrs. Kaufmann were weeping when he took the distraught girl away, in his company, to the hospital. After arriving at the hospital, he instructed the nurses to bathe and care for Agnes. At about 6 o'clock in the evening, he returned to the hospital and was informed that Agnes had died.

Aikens asked Dr. Germain if in his opinion the wounds on the girl's body were caused by "external causes," to which the doctor replied that he believed they resulted from diabetes.[5] This testimony placed him in direct contradiction to what he had told a reporter for the *Yankton Press and Dakotan* the year before. In that interview, Dr. Germain admitted that he had mistakenly relied on what Emma Kaufmann had told him and that he truly believed Agnes Polreis had died from wounds inflicted by "some blunt instrument."[6]

Diabetes was a point of contention from the beginning of the case. The disease has been known since ancient times. A diabetic's body does not produce insulin or, in less severe cases, does not produce enough insulin because the immune system, which normally fights disease, destroys the insulin-producing cells. Common symptoms are frequent urination, increased thirst and hunger, unexplained weight loss, fatigue, blurred vision, and slow-healing sores.[7] In 1906 there was no treatment to stop or mitigate the "wasting" fatal disease since insulin was not developed until 1921.

Childhood diabetes was rarely diagnosed in the nineteenth and early twentieth centuries, but its symptoms were recognizable and the victim died rather quickly following onset of the disease. But the scarcity of cases meant that doctors had relatively little evidence to examine. By 1913 a professor of medicine from Harvard University claimed "personal knowledge of 19 cases of childhood diabetes."[8] These statistics and Dr. Germain's hasty conclusion, along with his earlier determinations, cast a shadow of doubt over his new diagnosis.

~

To no one's surprise, Dr. Germain became the object of blistering cross-examination by George W. Egan. The trial was shaping up to be a battle of experts and Egan wanted to make sure that Dr. Germain's credibility was ruined, or at least further diminished. Described by the *Argus-Leader* as employing "rapid fire" questions, Egan sought to pressure the witness, confuse and confound him, hoping the doctor would answer in a way that would impeach part or all of his testimony. Egan got Germain to admit that he was once called to the Kaufmann house to see a girl other than Agnes, but the witness could not recall that he ever went to the house to see any other girls. A portion of the testimony was published verbatim in the *Argus-Leader*:

Q: Who was at the Kaufmann home when
you were called there?

A: Mrs. Kaufmann.

Q: Anyone else?

A: No.

Q: Was not Agnes Polreis there?

This question, directed at Dr. Germain, resulted in an outburst of laughter from the people in the courtroom, thus causing an angry Judge Smith to demand that the spectators quiet down and remain silent lest he deem it necessary to clear the courtroom.

Of course, Agnes was there and everyone knew that Dr. Germain misspoke, but his lapse of composure showed that Egan was grinding away at him, making the doctor look nervous and silly. The crowd seemed to favor Egan and the prosecution. Although any trial was serious business, the spectators found the Kaufmann trial entertaining. Egan kept hammering the witness:

Q: Did Mrs. Kaufmann tell you that she had
thrown hot water on the girl?

A: No.

Q: Did she tell you that she had chased the
girl across the lot?

A: No.

Q: Did you direct the putting on of the
poultices that were put right down in the
joints?

A: No. Mrs. Kaufmann stated that she put
the poultices on the girl.

The question about the poultices on the fingers of Agnes was cleverly stated, for in order to answer it, Dr. Germain had either to deny seeing it or put the blame on someone else, in this case, the defendant, for had he not done so he would risk incriminating himself. The witness was taking a beating and probably wished he was luxuriating on his Mexican estate.

Special prosecuting attorney George W. Egan in his office.
Courtesy Ed Monson Collection.

Egan continued his forceful cross-examination. He asked Dr. Germain if Snashall, the undertaker from Miller's, had refused to bury the girl because Snashall believed that it "was a case for the coroner." Dr. Germain replied, "I told him there was no occasion for an inquest."[9]

Egan had cut to the heart of the matter. Dr. Germain, a physician of high repute in the community, had examined a girl with wounds, cuts, and bruises all over her body. It had never occurred to him that she might have been the victim of foul play and therefore he should have sought a coroner's inquest? The judge, the jury, and the spectators all probably disagreed with Germain's tepid response to an obvious emergency. To any reasonable person, Agnes' condition and subsequent death would have looked suspicious. Law enforcement and the coroner, charged with investigating all suspicious deaths, should have investigated. Through Dr. Germain's admission that he did not alert the police or ask for an inquest, Egan had planted the possibility of a cover-up in the minds of the jurors.

The *Argus-Leader* reporter had words of commendation for attorney Egan, noting his skill in the art of rigid cross-examination of a witness and also his knowledge of "technical terms." Still he had to admit that Dr. Germain "stood the grilling well," despite his frequent reference to lack of memory and his fumbling over important matters such as the "authorities and statistics of the disease [diabetes]."[10]

The *Parkston Advance* analyzed the testimony differently, insisting that Dr. Germain was thoroughly discredited by Egan, the "master of the art of cross-examination" and "the intellectual corkscrew." Applying these skills, time and time again, he elicited statements "of the most damaging kind to the defendant." The *Advance* also noted that "Mrs. Kaufmann sat as hypnotized, her eyes fixed upon Mr. Egan. She never took her eyes from his face." Germain was the target of Egan's assault, and the nervous defendant was reacting to the "human Gatling gun" that was "tearing down the main witness for the defense."[11]

Dr. Germain really had a tough time on the witness stand. This pleased Ross, who watched the spectacle with special glee: "His [Germain's] demeanor on the stand showed guilt. He denied, he hesitated, he stammered, he was cornered, impeached, he writhed, twisted, turned, he looked anywhere but at the jury."[12] Ross dismissed as hogwash the doctor's ham-handed attempts to describe what he believed to be the cause of Agnes' death, and compared it to the testimony of medical experts who actually examined the critical organs of the girl's body. In Ross' mind, Dr. Germain was guilty of malpractice, perjury, and complicity in the death of a girl who had enjoyed good health all her life until she entered the Kaufmann home.

Ross used the occasion to attack "Brother Day" of the *Argus-Leader* and stoke the fires of the newspaper war that he started. The *Critic* publisher denounced the reporting of his rival's newspaper, insisting that "the whole of the *Argus-Leader*'s moral force has been thrown to Mrs. Kaufmann from the first, and its course has been a shame to journalism."[13] The criticism, however, was born of hate and was off the mark. Reading the *Argus-Leader*, one concludes that the reporting was detailed and unbiased. Although Charles Day admired successful people, and may have been secretly pulling for an acquittal, his paper provided balanced coverage of the trial.

Also not revealed was Day's feelings about having been scooped again by the *Sioux City Journal*. The Iowa daily was the first area newspaper to print a photograph of the defendant. Then a year later, it was the first to feature a photograph of Agnes Polreis, who, by mid-trial, was becoming a household name throughout the country. Doubtless everyone familiar with the case wanted to see her face. A correspondent from the *Journal* explained that he spoke with the dead girl's mother and convinced her to allow him to take custody of the photograph, "the only one in existence," and make a negative. The sweet face of the unfortunate girl appeared in the *Journal* on June 16, 1907.[14]

~

With the Big Sioux River on the rise from heavy rains, Mrs. Kaufmann arrived in court on Friday, June 14. She was late and the judge did not convene court until she had arrived and was seated. No mention was made in the *Argus-Leader* about why she was late; the judge simply re-opened the proceedings, with Dr. Sydney Olney as the first witness to testify for the defense. He had assisted at the autopsy of Agnes Polreis and later testified for the state at the preliminary hearing. He was now in the opposite camp and was questioned about the injuries to Agnes' head, a key point for both sides of the case. Dr. Olney recalled that the "membranes on top of the head were matted together and showed inflammation," a condition he believed had existed for "weeks, or a month."

Aikens asked the physician to "state to the jury what effect this inflamed condition would have had on the girl," to which the witness replied, "I think it led to a bleeding and formed a clot." He went on to say that the "blood clot resulted from a diseased state of the membrane. The lacerations of the scalp seemed to be more fresh than any other—not more than two weeks old."

Dr. Olney was asked, if in his opinion, whether "the internal conditions found in the brain [could] be the result of diabetes?" His weasel-word answer was, "It is not improbable." Later he was asked if the blood clot on the brain was the cause of death, to which he replied, "Not necessarily. Sometimes there are repeated hemorrhages, forming clots in strata." Dr. Olney was not providing powerful and convincing testimony for the defense and appeared to be in over his head. Aikens plodded on and asked him to "state whether, in your opinion, the condition of the body, when you examined it at

Parkston, was such as to make it difficult to determine the conditions at death."

He responded, "The body had no chance to show conditions that could have been seen immediately after death. It was buried twice in a grave and immersed in water." He could have just told the jury that he was not an expert on head or brain injuries. But he did not, and his weak testimony set him up for a take-down on cross-examination.

Egan, anxious to unleash the hounds, picked up a transcript of the preliminary hearing testimony of Dr. Olney and used it in his cross-examination. First, he asked Dr. Olney if he had told the truth at the preliminary hearing, to which the witness said, "To the best of my knowledge and belief. So help me God." Then Egan read from the transcript Olney's answer to the question about the cause of the wounds on Agnes' head. Reading further, Egan reminded Olney that in his former testimony he said the wounds were made by a blunt instrument.

Aikens objected to the use of preliminary hearing testimony for the purpose of impeachment. He also objected to Egan's practice of interrupting the witness. Apparently, Egan was interrupting Aikens while he was talking to the judge. Finally Judge Smith ruled that it was proper to show inconsistencies but improper to interrupt.

Egan continued to look for inconsistencies. He asked the weary witness if he wanted to tell the jury that the head wounds were caused by diabetes. Olney replied, "No. Something hit the head or the head hit something." In other words he was saying the wounds could have been self-inflicted, something he had denied at the preliminary hearing. Sensing he had Olney on the ropes, Egan returned to the transcript. He pointed out that Olney had testified that he "was rather in the dark" because he had been testifying "late in the day" at the preliminary hearing.

> Q: Are you in the dark now?
>
> A: I am not in the dark.

Dr. Olney may not have been in the dark but he was in a state of discomfort, feeling the sting of Egan's sharp questions. Egan reminded the witness that at the prior hearing he declared that "the external injuries" were the cause of the blood clots, whereas on direct examination by Aikens, Dr. Olney said the blood clots "resulted from a diseased state of the membrane." Egan had the doctor trapped between two opposing causes: disease or external injuries.

Egan asked, "Doctor, tell me as an expert what there is in medical jurisprudence that would enable you to reach a different conclusion at that time than at the present time?" The witness replied that "the testimony given at that time was tentative."

> Q: You did not get any history of the case since last June 13, 1906?
>
> A: No.
>
> Q: What has caused you to give different testimony now?
>
> A: I had not had time to consider at that time and being badgered by the lawyers was not able to answer fully on the spur of the moment.[15]

Dr. Olney was on the witness stand for a full seven hours, during which time he was pulled one way by the prosecution and another by the defense. He was asked to explain the manner in which a limb can become gangrenous and how it might be possible that the wounds on Agnes Polreis were self-inflicted. Through it all he answered the hard questions with a mixture of responses that were at times decisive and at other times evasive. Overall, his testimony did more harm than good to the defense. In the battle of experts, Dr. Olney added very little expertise.

Dr. Frederick A. Spafford, a Flandreau physician since 1884, was the first witness in the afternoon session of June 14. Aikens expected that Dr. Spafford's testimony would support the defense's contention that Agnes died of diabetes. Getting right to the point, Aikens asked, "Would it be possible for a person to die of diabetes mellitus and a post mortem examination of the urine fail to disclose sugar?" The witness said, "Yes." He added that it was common for young diabetics to become emaciated, and upon further questioning, Dr. Spafford said that diabetes could cause blood vessels in the head to erupt.

Moving on to the skin, Aikens asked: "What effect does diabetes have upon the skin?" Dr. Spafford replied that it was "a well established fact that the resistance of the skin in diabetes is considerably lessened. Slight abrasions are followed by suppuration, destruction of tissue and gangrene," including deep sores. Citing an example, the witness recalled a patient, a "traveling man," who first lost a toe, then a foot, and finally a leg, due to what he thought was merely a "soft corn." Doing better with this witness, Aikens brought up the much discussed subject of turpentine, asking if it was commonly used as a remedy. Dr. Spafford said it was a common remedy. Then when asked if ashes and water was also a common remedy, Spafford responded in the affirmative but added that he was aware of it being used only for "a felon."

Aikens then led Dr. Spafford through an interrogation of the cause of death of a diabetic. His line of questioning was for the purpose of establishing that, following her admission to the hospital with a blood clot on the head, Agnes was able to talk, took nourishment, then lapsed into a coma, became paralyzed, and died a natural death. First of all, Aikens asked the doctor the hypothetical question as to whether a person in good health in the morning, admitted to a hospital in the afternoon, spoke, ate, then suddenly died, could have succumbed to a brain injury. The answer was, of course, she could not.

The seemingly irrelevant question misstated the facts of the case because Agnes was not in good health when she checked in to the hospital, but there was no objection, and Aikens asked Spafford the following, rather inscrutable, hypothetical question:

> Q: Do you mean, doctor, that a person who has had inflicted upon the head by some blunt instrument a blow or blows sufficiently hard to make three wounds on top of the head, and to produce a blood clot of sufficient size to cause death, what would be the conditions immediately succeeding death if the blood clot extends an inch in one direction and an inch and a half in another?

A: If death was the result within a short time there would be found coma and paralysis. If death was delayed there might be an interval and sometime before death there would be coma and paralysis.

Q: Assuming that the blood clot was the immediate cause of death, do you think death could have occurred without coma or paralysis?

A: I do not think it was possible as a result of the clot.

Q: Could the clot form without external violence?

A: It might.

Aikens seemed to have completed his direct examination of Dr. Spafford with satisfactory results, if the jury was able to understand the confusing dialogue between the two men. Egan certainly was not enlightened, nor was he satisfied, and he began a determined cross-examination of the learned witness who was undoubtedly well-known to the people of Flandreau, including members of the jury.

Egan pressed Dr. Spafford on the matter of whether a person might die of diabetes mellitus when there was no sugar in the urine. Since the doctor had answered in the affirmative, Egan asked for written medical authority on the subject. The authority was produced and Egan immediately began reading as if he were in a library all by himself. The judge then suggested that the court recess while "counsel is studying medicine." This brought forth a murmur of laughter from the audience and broke the tension. A jocular Judge Smith made no attempt to "suppress the merriment in the audience."

After reading to his satisfaction, Egan admitted that Dr. Spafford was right and proceeded with his questioning. He then went on to score a major point for the prosecution when the doctor admitted that diabetes does not cause wounds. He also said that in all his years of practice, he had never seen a diabetic with wounds and cuts all over her body. Then he informed the court and jury that cases of diabetes mellitus were increasing.

There was a "lively passage at arms between attorneys" when Aikens objected to Egan forming a hypothetical question on the prior testimony by Dr. Germain. Egan perked up and said, "I would not insult the integrity of Dr. Spafford by basing a hypothetical question to him on the testimony of Dr. Germain." It was Egan's way of issuing a back-handed insult at Dr. Germain, who had made a poor showing in court.

~

The next day, the 15th, Aikens and Judge brought in their big guns, that is to say, hired guns—real medical experts, not locals. They were Dr. Albert S. Rider, a graduate of the prestigious Rush Medical College in Chicago, and brain specialist Dr. Leonard C. Mead, the superintendent of the South Dakota State Mental Hospital in Yankton, also an alumnus from Rush Medical College.

Dr. Rider was first to testify. He was asked a complex and awkwardly worded hypothetical question by Aikens designed to elicit testimony to the effect that Agnes Polreis died from disease. When all the factors were considered, including the wounds described in detail, the doctor concluded that wounds "might have been the result of disease."

But he waffled a bit on cross-examination. Egan pressed him on the causal issue and Dr. Rider said, rather esoterically, "I did not say the disease caused them [the wounds]; it could be caused by the disease and the result." Then Egan asked him point blank, "Could the disease be caused by diabetic causes?" to which Dr. Rider replied, "In my opinion it could have been caused by diabetic causes and its result." The net effect of this imprecise exchange was probably confusion in the minds of the jurors.

Dr. Leonard C. Mead, the nationally known "alienist," was next. On direct examination, he "described the covering of the brain in detail and the causes of the various hemorrhages and stated that subdural hemorrhage is usually caused by disease." When it was Egan's turn, he took the witness "through a long siege of technical questions as to the structure and formation of the brain." Egan was trying to get Dr. Mead to admit that the damage to the girl's head was due to external violence. "In examining the brain, if we find a blood clot and no evidence of meningitis," he asked, "and directly on top of the head where the blood clot started we find evidence of external violence, would we not say that in all probability the blood clot was caused by external violence?"

Dr. Leonard C. Mead, witness for the defense. *Courtesy Yankton County Historical Society.*

Dr. Mead answered, "I would take that into consideration." Then like a man carefully walking a horse into a stable, Egan asked, "can you conceive of a case like the one named where you ascribe the cause to external violence?" Dr. Mead answered, "Yes." It was the answer he wanted; Egan had fought Aikens to a draw. There was equivocation in the defense expert testimony, something Egan could use when arguing the case to a jury.

A none-too-happy Dr. Olney was given another turn in the witness stand during the Saturday afternoon session of court. "Wood ashes and water" was the first topic on Egan's agenda. He asked Dr. Olney whether feet bathed in a solution of wood ashes and water would "result in taking off the skin?" As though he were finally getting accustomed to Egan's persistence, the doctor said, "It would depend upon the amount of ashes and water."

> Q: Will ashes and water form lye?
>
> A: Yes
>
> Q: Will lye take off the skin?
>
> A: It might if strong enough.

Egan could have asked if it would cause pain, but he did not. Still he was on to something, so he stayed with the line of questioning: "If the feet of Agnes Polreis had been bathed in wood ashes and water strong enough to remove the outside skin, would you still insist that the condition was caused by diabetes?" Dr. Olney replied, "Partially so assuming there was also disease." Dr. Olney was not willing to back away from diabetes as a cause of death.

Staying with the subject, Egan persisted: "And there was nothing to indicate to you that there was diabetes?" The beleaguered witness would not go that far, but he did say, "Yes, there was a condition that I could not explain any other way. It took me a long time to make up my mind." When asked how long, he said, "Several months." Dr. Olney confessed he was a slow man who worked deliberately.

The question-and-answer exercise did not yield the kind of clarity that observers were hoping to hear. But they could tell that Egan was both wearing Olney down and inching him closer to the desired admission. And finally, after about half an hour of "fencing medical terms," Egan asked Dr. Olney, "Would you be able to say by examining the body of a 16 year-old girl, emaciated, with deep cuts on the body and head, burns on her body and the skin off the feet, and without making any further examination, that the person had diabetes?" The answer was, "No."

Egan had reached a major accomplishment. In getting that answer out of Dr. Olney, Egan had destroyed the testimony of Dr. Germain. And noting the hour was approaching 6 o'clock, Egan suggested that the court adjourn for the day. The judge was satisfied with the request and the court was adjourned until nine the next morning. Before leaving, Egan said he might want to cross-examine Dr. Olney for another half a day longer.

While Egan could be hot-headed, even offensive, in his approach, his ability to cross-examine the doctors was very impressive to all present. The *Argus-Leader* was especially impressed with Egan, who "demonstrated his ability . . . to dissect a cranium, take out the brain" and "tell the symptoms of the disease." Egan was praised for his skill, noting that he "kept two of the best physicians of the state on the rack for hours." He never seemed to lose sight of his objective, never hesitated, but rather asked question after question in a logical order that showed he had extensive knowledge of the human body. "His work was brilliant and it is doubtful if a case involving technical medical knowledge was ever conducted with more regard to detail."[16]

According to a report in an Iowa newspaper, George Egan had taken a course in medicine and he was therefore familiar with medical terms, and he used that skill while cross-examining the defense doctors. When the day's courtroom theatrics ended, Egan proudly received praise from people favorable to the prosecution.[17]

Egan was emerging as the star performer of the great trial. He and the other attorneys, along with the witnesses, more than held the interest of the people in Flandreau and others around the state. While the medical testimony, in its technical monotony, droned on and on, men and women stood in the aisles in rapt attention. Everyone was impressed with the patience of Judge Smith, who was taking an even-handed approach, understanding the historic nature of the trial and his role in it. Outside the courthouse, the influx of witnesses and interested parties livened up Flandreau's hotels and other businesses. Everyone knew that the national spotlight shone on little Flandreau, and no matter the outcome the community understood that sooner or later all the attention would vanish.

Until then the courtroom would be filled to capacity by a cross-section of the community. The kindly Sheriff Hoskins continued his role of finding chairs for the elderly and infirm. For his efforts he was "winning votes," proving that campaigning never ends. "Peanuts, oranges, bananas, and chewing gum" were the "staple refreshments of the crowd . . . during the session," and the "girl with the candy is always surrounded" by hungry court watchers.[18] Outside the temple of justice, in the streets of Flandreau, someone was selling photographs of Agnes Polreis and George W. Egan.[19]

There were other diversions in Flandreau, more suited for relaxing. When court was not in session, groups would gather and see the sights, including the Flandreau Indian School. Some took automobile rides around town, known for its shade trees and fine residences, to relieve stress and pass time. In the evenings band concerts under the direction of Professor Van Court were a regular fare.[20]

When the Saturday court session resumed, Aikens continued with the case for the defense. He called John Krust, a salty German immigrant who was once employed as a foreman of the bottling department at the brewery. Krust's testimony, in broken English, was expected to impeach that of Peter Erickson's. Aikens asked Krust if he had heard Erickson ask Mr. Kaufmann for $500 to "keep still." Krust answered, "Yes." In response, Kaufmann had reportedly said he would not "give him [Erickson] a cent."

According to Krust the conversation with Erickson had taken place in early August 1906. The veracity of this testimony seemed questionable, for if Krust had had the conversation with Erickson in early August, it would have taken place well after the preliminary hearing. It seems odd that Erickson would have undermined his own testimony at the hearing, thereby destroying his credibility, by trying to bribe Moses Kaufmann. The timing was all wrong.

The next witness for the defense was Moses Kaufmann, the man everyone respected for standing by his wife. Aikens began by asking Kaufmann if Erickson did ask for money to buy his silence. The witness answered in the affirmative. Then Aikens went on to questions about Agnes Polreis. Kaufmann said he knew Agnes, that he talked to her in German, and that as time went on he noticed that she was "losing flesh," so he asked her if she wanted to go to a doctor. Agnes said no. He also asked her if she wanted to return to Parkston, to which, according to Kaufmann's sworn testimony, Agnes said "she never wanted to go to Parkston again." On the contrary, she said that "Mrs. Kaufmann was very kind to her and she would rather stay with her." He further testified that he never saw his wife do anything unkind to Agnes. Rather, she "always treated her as her own child."

The witness was turned over to the prosecution for cross-examination by Egan:

> Q: What is your occupation?
>
> A: I have none.
>
> Q: What was your former occupation?
>
> A: I was connected with the Sioux Falls Brewing and Malting Company.

Egan then elicited testimony to the effect that Kaufmann had met Agnes at Salem, South Dakota, that she was healthy and "fairly bright," and that she had immigrated to America from Hungary just a few months prior to his hiring her. Not long after she entered the Kaufmann household, Mr. Kaufmann testified, Mrs. Kaufmann took Agnes to a ball at Germania Hall in Sioux Falls.

Then the questioning moved to Agnes' death. Egan handed Kaufmann a diagram of his residence and asked the witness to point out the room Agnes had occupied. This he did, but Kaufmann said he was never in the room with Agnes. He went on to say that on the Saturday before she died, he saw her in the kitchen and that his wife said she was not feeling well. Kaufmann said that he had only two conversations with Agnes and that he was in Menno, South Dakota, when the girl died. He knew nothing about it until he got home. It was then that he met Erickson, who told him the girl had died. Erickson then said, "Well I guess I'll go home."

Kaufmann testified that he went to the Miller undertaking firm and ordered the "best coffin he had." Later, he was present at his home when Dr. Germain telephoned and asked Mrs. Kaufmann for the name of the dead girl.

Egan asked Kaufmann, "What were you paying the girl?" But before he could answer, Aikens objected to the question; the objection was sustained as immaterial. In so doing, the judge denied the world knowledge of how much Agnes earned as the live-in maid at the Kaufmann house. Still, no matter the amount of money earned, it was certainly not enough considering her fate as a Kaufmann employee.

When asked if Kaufmann paid Snashall, the undertaker, Aikens again objected, but this was overruled, and the witness answered in the affirmative. Egan asked Kaufmann if he saw the body of Agnes Polreis after it left the hospital, to which the witness said that Snashall offered to let him see it but he declined.

Moses Kaufmann was handling the questioning quite well, so Egan hammered away. Getting back to Erickson, he asked Kaufmann if the Norwegian ever said anything about seeing any "improper relations between Mrs. Kaufmann and the girl." His answer was, "No." He also denied saying anything to Erickson about wanting to "protect his wife."

Egan switched from Erickson to George Bessler, the other brewery employee who had testified earlier in the trial. He asked Kaufmann if he spoke to Bessler about putting the "bedding and bed clothes . . . in the alley." He answered, "Not to my knowledge." Next, Egan asked, "Did you tell Bessler to find who hauled the bedding and bed clothes away . . . and not let anyone know?" The weary witness answered that he might have but didn't remember.

Aikens wasn't finished with his witness and, exercising his right to re-direct, he asked Kaufmann if he really only spoke to Agnes two times, to which the former brewer said, "No." Aikens then questioned Kaufmann about a telephone call to Parkston, during which time Kaufmann said that Agnes had died of heart disease. Kaufmann explained this by saying that he was confused about what Dr. Germain said concerning the cause of death, thinking the doctor may have indicated that it was, indeed, heart disease.

Egan then took one more kick at the cat, as if he was determined to get in the last word. He asked, "When did you first think of this other talk [with Agnes] that you did not tell me about?" Kaufmann answered that the other speaking occasions were not conversations, but merely, "Hello" and "Good-bye." In other words, the girl was barely visible to Moses Kaufmann during the three-and-one-half months she workd at the Kaufmann residence. He only had two conversations with her, and so it went into the record that way.

The *Argus-Leader* reporter commended the witness for having withstood several hours of examination. While Moses Kaufmann resorted to lack of memory or other uncertainty, he did not weaken nor did he become angry and lose his temper. Overall, he impressed the jury favorably. If they were expecting an ogre, they were disappointed.

The court adjourned at 4:50 P.M. that afternoon. The judge announced that the trial would resume on Monday morning at 9 o'clock. The trial was progressing at a faster rate than expected, and the judge was pleased with the pace of the testimony. But he probably wasn't prepared for what happened when the court reconvened.[21]

On Monday, June 17, 1907, Emma Kaufmann breezed into the courtroom looking "fresher than the end of last week." But the room quickly heated up and Charles "fanned his mother with a blotter." This kind act was but a prelude to the performance that was about to begin. For the jury, the audience, and the reporters were treated to what was described in the *Sioux Falls Daily Press* as "Celtic Clashes" between two Irish lawyers. Strangely, the defense had called as a witness none other than Joe Kirby, the firebrand Sioux Falls attorney, "the wit, the lightning golfer and 18 karat entertainer," who had secured the indictment of the defendant. For the occasion, he was dressed like "an English butler."[22]

About a week before he mounted the witness stand, Kirby was on the phone talking to a reporter about the "rumor" floating about that he was to be called as a witness for the defense. He laughed it off, saying that since he had worked for the prosecution, it would be impossible for him to be a witness for the defense. He did, however, admit that he received subpoenas from both sides.[23]

And yet there he was, in court, and the collision of egos that resulted was called a "sensational tilt," as the headline in the *Argus-Leader* announced: "**KIRBY AND EGAN LOCKED HORNS.**" Aikens' unorthodox strategy was to use Kirby's testimony to damage Erickson's. Kirby was called to say that "he did not attempt to induce Erickson to suppress facts . . . and also that Erickson had told Kirby that what he testified to at the preliminary examination was all that he knew about the case."[24] Impeach Erickson and get an acquittal was the plan.

This was a gift from the gods to Egan, the man who so unceremoniously replaced Kirby as special prosecutor. The Iowa attorney first encountered Kirby in May while preparing for the Kaufmann case. He later wrote, "I met Joe Kirby for the first time, looked him over, made up my mind that if he was not a crook and a thief he could sue his face for libel."[25] Doubtless, Kirby looked upon Egan with an equal measure of disdain.

The tension in the courtroom was palpable as the two Irishmen made eye contact, signaling that the clash of egos was about to begin. Wasting no time, Egan reached into his bag of dirty tricks and asked Kirby, "Have you ever been convicted of a felon?" The question, of course, was intended to dredge up the case many years ago involving the stolen postage stamps. Kirby replied, "No." He went on to explain that though the public might say that he was a felon, a lawyer would say no, "as for yourself for instance." Kirby's answer was an obvious reference to Egan's own legal problems with the two Iowa women.

Egan then asked Kirby whether he had been kicked off the Kaufmann case because it was believed that he had sold out. Kirby answered sarcastically: No, the people in Parkston wanted a "more able counsel; they stated there was one man who wore a charm that entitled him to practice in any court of the United States and they wanted him; that he had been connected with so many murder cases." This was a knock against Egan's oversized self-importance and flair for the dramatic. The *Argus-Leader* reporter, with tongue firmly in cheek, wrote that there were "further displays during which the lawyers paid their respects to each other."[26]

Some years later, Egan revealed his own characterization of the titanic duel of egos. He said that his cross-examination of Kirby was so fierce and intense that the latter "writhed and twisted till he became . . . a pitiable object." Egan claimed he showed no pity and kept pounding away, question after question, until Kirby's brow broke out into "great beads of sweat . . . and tears streamed from his eyes as bitter as those that cursed the face of Josephine."[27]

Assuming Egan's selective recollection of the incident was true, Aikens—smart lawyer that he was—would never allow a witness to leave the stand in disgrace. And on re-direct examination, Kirby was able to explain his old legal troubles in greater detail and in a manner that was anything but felonious. He also testified that he had never represented the Sioux Falls Brewing Company or Moses Kaufmann and that the $5.00 he received was for a witness fee and mileage.[28]

The *Sioux Falls Journal* weighed in on the Kirby/Egan dust up clearly on the side of Kirby. Mark D. Scott of the *Journal* loathed Egan, whom he referred to as an "Iowa attorney imported" by the state because of his supposed magical powers over a jury. But in the verbal duel with Kirby, Scott declared that Egan had "met his match."[29]

And after the tense but brief Kirby episode on the witness stand, calm was restored in the courthouse and the trial resumed. J. H. Ramsey of Sioux Falls came forward and testified that he sold three pairs of shoes to Agnes while she was in his store along with Emma Kaufmann, but he wasn't sure if they came in a carriage or by other means. On cross-examination, Ramsey was unable to say with certainty that the girl he served was actually Agnes.

Next, Joseph Schwarz, an architect from Sioux Falls, took the stand and explained the building plans for the Kaufmann house, which he designed some years ago. His testimony focused on the heat radiators and the slant of the roof in the room once occupied by Agnes. Aikens intended to show that the layout of the room was such that she could have injured herself on the radiators and the roof.

The last witness of the day was none other than Frank R. Aikens, proving the strangeness of life and litigation cannot be measured. In a courtroom now accustomed to surprises, he was sworn in as a witness for the defense. On direct examination he stated that he had once met Peter Erickson at the Cataract Hotel in Sioux Falls. On that occasion Aikens informed Erickson that he was about to be arrested. But he was not to worry because Aikens would protect him. While the relevance of this was certainly questionable, Aikens also denied ever having told Erickson that "if he would treat the Kaufmann's right they would treat him right and would give him anything he wanted." Clearing this up under oath must have relieved Aikens of a great burden.

Egan could not let this chance pass: "You never had seen Peter Erickson until this [case] came up?" Aikens answered, "No." Egan then asked, "Where did you first find out there was such a person [as Erickson]?" Aikens provided a rather evasive reply: "On the street, in the newspapers and everywhere I went."[30]

The exasperated attorney, who had worked relentlessly to prove his client's innocence, clearly wished that the damned Norwegian, Peter Erickson, had never existed, or at least had never come to South Dakota. For it was this handyman, who was actually born in Illinois, the much heralded "star witness" for the prosecution, who stood between Emma Kaufmann and an acquittal.

Chapter 10

The Verdict

The verdict will stand and the common people of this great state will know that the humblest as well as the most exalted can and will have justice.

The Flandreau Herald
June 26, 1907

During the morning hours of June 17, 1907, while George W. Egan and Joe Kirby were locking horns in the Flandreau Courthouse, a lively event of another type was unfolding in Sioux Falls. U.S. Secretary of War William Howard Taft arrived by train at 8:30 A.M. in the company of South Dakota Senator Alfred B. Kittredge. A large reception was held at the depot where the mayor and others greeted the secretary with appropriate honors, followed by breakfast at the Cataract Hotel. They were joined at the hotel by Sioux Falls luminaries Bishop William H. Hare, E. A. Sherman, and Charles M. Day. Next, Taft and Kittredge were feted in the hotel rotunda by a large delegation of Sioux Falls men. After a carriage ride to the Milwaukee Depot, they boarded the train for a trip to the Black Hills.[1]

Taft's short visit in Sioux Falls was merely coincidental to the great trial that was working its way to a conclusion in Moody County, and no doubt seeing a celebrity politician was a pleasant diversion from the stress of the Kaufmann case. A criminal trial for murder always ends with sadness for one or more of the families who have a stake in the outcome. While the decision of the jury to convict a defendant means the imposition of a sentence on the guilty party, another sentence, in the form of anger, grief, and defeat, is imposed on others whose emotions were trampled by the judicial process.

No one knew it, but Taft was on his way to being elected president of the United States in 1908, at a time when many people intimately connected to the Kaufmann case had their lives suspended. Worse yet, some were destined to experience a dismal future, for the trial was a transformative event. What had started out as a murder trial had become "a great human interest story" with a competing cast of characters to determine "what caused the death of the household drudge at the Kaufmanns . . . the little Parkston girl, Agnes Polreis."[2] As the air temperature reached ninety degrees on the afternoon of the 17th, many in South Dakota and the surrounding areas still yearned for the latest report from the trial scene.

The defense was in its final phase, its string of witnesses coming down to the last knot. Defense attorney Frank Aikens called George W. Bray, a liveryman who boarded the Kaufmanns' horses, to the stand for the purpose of showing that Agnes and Mrs. Kaufmann had spent time together outside of the house. Bray said that he had sent a team to the house six or seven times but that he saw the girl and the woman only twice, both times on 9th Street riding in a carriage. Apparently, he never knew Agnes personally because he said he recognized her only afterwards, when he saw her name in a newspaper sometime later. Bray testified that he once heard someone in front of the Bee Hive department store call out to Agnes. His only conversation with the two ladies was to say, "Good morning." All in all, Bray offered no compelling testimony, but it was a little slice of immortality, enough to get his name on record in the sensational criminal trial.[3]

At the conclusion of Bray's testimony, Aikens announced that the defense would rest. This brought a murmur of disappointment from the audience as they now knew they would be denied the pleasure, and high drama, of seeing and hearing the defendant on the witness stand.[4]

The termination of the defense's case meant that it was time for rebuttal. George Egan recalled Arthur Snashall as witness. Aikens objected and it was sustained. A woman in the audience registered her disapproval by calling out, "Let him tell the truth." The voice was that of Alice Wilcox, a moralist who had been an inmate at the state mental hospital in Yankton because of her anti-saloon rampage in Flandreau in 1904, which resulted in $1,500 in damages. For this she earned the title, "Carrie Nation of Flandreau."

Apparently, her stay in the asylum did not cure her. In 1907 she was back, and in the manner of the militant Carrie Nation—that infamous, hatchet-wielding saloon-hater from Kansas—Mrs. Wilcox smashed the window of a local saloon and attacked a cigar store, tossing cigars on the floor. She was also afflicted with a "praying mania" and spent much of her time praying aloud and fervently in the streets of Flandreau.[5] The judge promptly shut her down and warned her not to make any more outbursts during the trial. It was already hot and about to get hotter.

As it turned out, the rebuttal phase was the most intensely contested part of the trial. Egan and Aikens fought like tigers, the former insisting that his rebuttal witnesses be allowed to testify and the latter strenuously resisting, arguing that the prosecution's proposed witnesses were not true rebuttal witnesses. The judge had to stay on top of his game.

In a criminal or civil trial, the party with the burden of proof is permitted to introduce rebuttal testimony from witnesses who would tend to discredit the witnesses for the opposing party. But their testimony is limited and they can't introduce any new information. If their testimony strays from rebuttal, the judge will not permit the witness to speak.

Aikens, "with all the earnestness and logic at his command," protested to the judge, insisting that Egan was trying to sneak more direct testimony into the record. Egan roared back with equal exuberance, insisting that he had every right to seat his witnesses and that they should be allowed to rebut the defendant's witnesses. In the middle of it all, Judge Smith calmly and patiently evaluated each witness based on authority from the South Dakota Supreme Court. And under this standard much of the state's rebuttal testimony was barred. Smith ruled that he would separate out all the proposed state witnesses whose testimony was likely to violate the precedent set by the highest court in the state, resulting in two witnesses being excused before they could say anything.

Among the rebuttal witnesses that Egan was allowed to question was Peter Erickson, called back to explain the conversation he had with John Krust, the former foreman of the bottling department at the brewery.[6] To rebut Krust's contention that Erickson wanted $500 from Kaufmann in exchange for favorable testimony, the "star witness" said it was Krust who suggested that the right testimony would result in a payment of $500. Erickson testified that he told Krust that he could not be bought for $500 "or any other amount of money."[7]

Erickson also rebutted the testimony of Dr. Germain, saying that on the morning when she was taken to the hospital, Agnes was not eating "ravenously" and that there was no conversation between the girl and the doctor. He also denied that Agnes "placed her arms around his neck" when he carried her outside to the ambulance. Erickson also cast doubt on Bray's testimony by stating that Agnes did not accompany Mrs. Kaufmann on pleasure rides in the family carriage.[8] Once again, Erickson came through for the state.

Another rebuttal witness was Dr. Frank E. Coulter of Omaha, the medical expert who testified earlier in the trial. The doctor was asked if a "diagnosis for diabetes can be made by inspection." Aikens launched an objection but he was overruled. Dr. Coulter said, "No." He also stated that "diabetes mellitus would not produce cuts and burns on the shoulders down to the bone." This was critically important testimony because it further undermined Dr. Germain's opinion that Agnes had diabetes and that it was a cause of her death.

On cross-examination, Dr. Coulter said that he had appeared as an expert witness on "about fifty different occasions" and of that number about twelve or fifteen were in criminal cases. Aikens did manage to get in a favorable concession on cross-examination when Dr. Coulter admitted that skin is "peculiarly sensitive to diabetes, so that trivial injuries may result in gangrene."

After a recess, Egan recalled Mrs. Udell, the neighbor of the Kaufmanns, to the stand: "Did you hear any peculiar noises while living near the Kaufmanns?" She didn't get a chance to answer, for Aikens objected, and after protracted arguments, Judge Smith ruled the interrogatory was not proper rebuttal, thus stopping another round of fireworks.[9] But Mrs. Bernard of Parkston, who had roomed with Agnes when both worked at a Parkston hotel, was allowed to state that she saw and heard Agnes often singing "little Hungarian folk songs." This showed that at one time Agnes was both healthy and happy.[10]

With heightened anticipation, the spectators looked forward to the closing arguments. The courtroom was packed and many "women and young girls stood through the long hours of the trial," listening intently to the testimony and to the fiery back-and-forth arguments of the attorneys. It was generally conceded that Aikens did better than Egan during the rebuttal session, as he succeeded in keeping out many of the state's rebuttal witnesses. It had been a good day for the defense team.

The case came to a close a 9:37 A.M. on June 18, 1907. The prosecution wanted a continuance to wait for the arrival of a doctor from Milwaukee, but the request was denied. The judge wanted no further delays. And although there would be no more witnesses to entertain the crowd, the show had yet to come to an end. The last act, the closing arguments, was about to begin.[11]

~

Minnehaha County State's Attorney Alpha Orr was the first to argue before the jury. He spoke for an hour and a half in what was termed "an eloquent and impressive" summation of the prosecution's case. Orr told the jury that Moses Kaufmann was his friend but that his duty as the state's attorney was paramount and it trumped friendship: "I am not conscious of a single official act that infringes on the rights of the defense. I recognize the deep interest of the defendant and their family, but I also remember that in 1895, there came from Hungary a man named John Polreis to make his home in the land of the free and the home of the brave."

Actually it was 1905 when the Polreis family came across the ocean to America, but the error was entered into the record harmlessly. Orr went on to state that he was not trying to pit rich against poor, but insisted that Agnes Polreis, a poor girl, had the same rights as any other person and that her poverty in no way diminished her rights under the law. He went on to say that when Agnes arrived in Sioux Falls to work at the Kaufmann mansion she was in good health, "to all outward appearance." And yet on the first of June 1906, after but three and a half months on the job, she was taken to the Sioux Falls Hospital and within a few hours "she was numbered with the dead."

Next, Orr turned to the preliminary examination and told the jury that "it was incumbent upon the state to prove that death was brought about by the acts of Emma Kaufmann," and he declared that the state had met its burden. He reviewed all the testimony, starting with Arthur Snahsall, who refused to embalm the body until he had a death certificate. Orr then described, in graphic detail, the horrible wounds that Snahsall and others had found on the body of Agnes.

The state, he said, provided testimony from two South Dakota physicians, Dr. Schofield and Dr. Billion, along with two other expert medical witnesses, all of whom examined the brain "and other vital organs" of the girl and found them to be normal. This meant that she did not die of disease but from external violence. Then to drive the point home, Orr said, "The state has shown that the defendant, Emma Kaufmann caused the death of Agnes Polreis, and a weeping mother is waiting to know whether justice is to be done [for] her daughter."[12]

Orr was especially harsh on Dr. Germain, whose weak and forced testimony was "contradicted by six or seven witnesses." Since the doctor was the personal physician of the Kaufmann family, he would naturally be inclined to favor them in his testimony. As an example, Orr brought up the controversial death certificate signed by Dr. Germain. It was a contrived document that formed the entire basis for the defendant's case.

In another jab at the battered doctor, Orr mentioned that, when Germain telephoned for an ambulance to take Agnes to the hospital, he gave the street address of the house, rather than simply saying that she was at the Kaufmann house. This was another indication that what was first and foremost in the doctor's mind that day was his desire to shield the Kaufmanns from suspicion.

Overall, Orr's presentation to the jury was calm and measured. He was courteous toward his adversaries and the judge and gracious in his appreciation of the work of the jurymen called on to hear the case. Orr concluded by insisting that the jury decide the case based solely on the evidence presented, without prejudice and on the principles of justice.[13]

Next to speak for the state was Ira F. Blewitt, the state's attorney for Moody County. He made an impassioned plea for conviction, giving a "painstaking review of the evidence." To make his point, in a moment of high drama, Blewitt turned directly toward Emma Kaufmann and angrily shook his finger in her face, for Agnes Polreis, an innocent girl, had been cruelly murdered and Emma Kaufmann was responsible. "There is no parallel in criminology," he thundered. The girl had arrived at the Kaufmann house in good health and with a "cheerful disposition" only to become a "mutilated corpse" a short time later. Blewitt asked the jury to consider the awful harm the defendant had done to send "the soul of Agnes Polreis on the long road to eternity."

He went on to remind the jurors that Agnes was forced by the defendant to scrub a floor using "strong Gold Dust" on her hands and knees with bones protruding from her fingers. Rubbing it in further he declared, "The soul of an honest man or woman revolts at the treatment this woman gave [to] this helpless girl." Then he mocked the testimony of Dr. Germain, who could not "remember the three wounds on the head, the matted hair, but remembered the tender expressions of the dying girl for this woman." Hammering away at the principal medical witness for the defense, Blewitt said, "Dr. Germain's statement that the girl died of diabetes mellitus is just about as valuable as his diagnosis." It was a very animated and emotional speech that apparently touched the heart of at least one person in the audience, for the sound of weeping was heard in the courtroom.[14]

At the conclusion of Blewitt's address to the jury, George Rice, the first attorney for the defense, began his argument for an acquittal. He expressed his pride for having learned from the jurymen that not "one of them took a daily newspaper." Rice conceded that the newspapers worked hard to report on crime, but in the Kaufmann matter they went too far. Don't be over influenced by what you see in newsprint, he asked, for his client deserved fairness "as though she was a poor servant girl." Rice added, "I do not ask for sympathy, but for justice."

Then he declared boldly that the "case against Mrs. Kaufmann was as bare of evidence of guilt as any case can be." He made reference to inconsistencies in the testimonies of the state witnesses, many of whom, he said, gave one version at the preliminary hearing and another at the trial. Rice implored the jury to decide the case without prejudice, despite all the prejudicial press coverage. He argued that they must ignore any bias against wealth; he scoffed at the notion that under the American system of justice, Moses Kaufmann, a millionaire, could buy an acquittal.

Defense attorney George Rice.
Courtesy Moody County Historical Society.

As to the relationship between Emma Kaufmann and Agnes Polreis, Rice insisted that it was one of mutual respect. He "told of the girl going out across the lawn" with the Kaufmanns just like a family. Rice was willing to confess that Mrs. Kaufmann made mistakes "in the medical treatment she gave the girl," for it only made her worse and "aggravated the disease." But he insisted that there "was not one word to show that she ever complained to anyone about the treatment she received."

"If the walls and floor were covered with blood of her victim," he angrily asked the jurors, "do you think that she [the defendant] would have called her hired hand and Dr. Germain in to see the evidence that would put a rope around her neck?" It was a well-stated, thought-provoking approach, and he stayed with it. He asked the jury to consider that Agnes had spent six hours in the hospital, in the presence of a nurse who understood the German language, and yet she never said a word about cruel treatment from Emma Kaufmann, even though doing so would put "a rope around her [the defendant's] neck."

"Gentlemen, does it stand to reason that if this woman killed that girl, [and] she and her husband left the evidence of the crime for four days, and then have the hired man come in and clean it up, so as to be sure there would be a witness to come in and testify against her?" Rice demonstrated to all present that he understood the case and knew how to weave a set of facts into a cogent, convincing argument.

But he wasn't finished. He read from George Bessler's testimony about hearing Mrs. Kaufmann say she was so mad at Agnes that she could kill her. Rice said that he had heard parents say the very same thing, or worse, to their own children, "without having any idea of hurting them." Besides, he added, if she really intended to kill the girl, was she so foolish as to tell someone that she was about to do it? He called Bessler a liar because of inconsistencies in his testimony.

Finally, he attacked the prosecution's medical experts by arguing that they had testified based on opinion rather than facts. He argued fervently that Dr. Billion, Dr. Schofield, and Nurse Larson changed their stories, saying one thing at the preliminary hearing and another at the trial. The jury must therefore reject their testimony. Despite Dr. Billion's insistence that Agnes had been struck on her head and shoulders with a blunt instrument, Rice snarled, with great passion in his voice, he insisted that "no woman who has borne the sacred name of mother would go to the room of a helpless girl and murder her."[15]

His harangue against Erickson was especially vicious. He compared the big Norse—the world's biggest liar—to Sioux Indians whose savagery he assumed everyone could understand. Worse yet, Erickson was like a leper, forever unclean and fit only to be numbered among the outcasts, shunned and hated for all time to come. Rice "plunged and roared and splashed" as he "waded and floundered into the testimony" given by prosecution witnesses.[16]

Rice's shocking demeanor caught the attention of John Ross of the *Soo Critic*. Calling Rice's jury speech "labored and forced," Ross thought that the "fearful picture of his face" would have a negative effect on the jury. He looked as though "he must be in extreme stages of dyspepsia," and his face was the "picture of hatred" as he yelled "Liar! Lair!" when he referred to a state witness. Ross was of the opinion that Rice did not help the defense, and that any valid points he made were offset by his vitriolic anger.[17]

This was all good theater for the mass of spectators crammed into the courthouse, listening carefully, taking in every word, every gesture, despite the "damp, muggy air that floated through the windows." The oppressive summer heat was almost unbearable and yet "counsel and spectators sweltered" patiently during the long closing arguments.[18]

Anyone with a need for some comic relief could find it in the company of Powers Gourard, who was sojourning in Sioux Falls while he established residency to divorce his wife. In the evening hours at the St. Vincent Hotel, Gourard could be heard entertaining the guests with "songs and originalisms." Gourard was in Flandreau for the trial, like everyone else, but he used the sober occasion to share some joy and make friends.[19] He was an entertainer who had once performed in a New York City musical. He went on to become a pioneer radio broadcaster in Philadelphia known as the "Old Night Owl."[20]

~

On the morning of June 19 the jury was led into the courtroom, the space filled with the largest crowd yet to attend a morning session of the trial. Among them was Alice Wilcox, who seemed to be doing her best to get a ticket back to the asylum. While watching the jury enter and take their seats, she blurted out loud, "Has this jury been started right?" She demanded to know if they had "been instructed to take the bible for their guide." Getting more belligerent she insisted that there was something the jury had to know, "something about beer that should be explained." Soon, however, she was physically removed from the courtroom. Judge Smith instructed the jury that the "woman was demented" and that her remarks were to be ignored.

But Alice Wilcox was not a woman to give up without a fight. She stood her ground in front of the bailiff in the courtyard, and as the judge passed by, "she seized upon" him and begged to be admitted. She promised to be as quiet as a mouse. The judge relented, and she took a seat in the front row. Throughout the session, she kept quiet.

The man Mrs. Wilcox and everyone else were waiting to hear began talking at 9:30 A.M. on June 19, 1907. That man was Frank Aikens, who stepped forward to give the final closing argument for the defense team. All eyes were on the lead counsel for Emma Kaufmann, and after a "flutter of expectation," he started, slowly, but with purpose and meaning. "The unfortunate circumstances into which I was forced to become a witness was in defense of myself and my client" were the first words he spoke. This, of course, was a reference to Erickson's brazen contention that Aikens and Moses Kaufmann had tried to bribe him. That Aikens began his closing argument with this statement indicates how deeply he had been struck by the accusation. He needed to tell the jury—and through them the world—that even though he wasn't "morally or in any other sense immaculate," he was a man of integrity and any attack on his reputation required him to fight back.

He moved on to the meat and potatoes of the case: the character of his client and the attack by State's Attorney Blewitt, whom Aikens slammed because he pointed a finger at Emma Kaufmann while "calling her practically, a murderess." This woman has suffered terribly over the past year, he insisted, even though she may "be innocent as an unborn babe." Mrs. Kaufmann, he declared, "has been pursued as no other woman in America." He figuratively pointed a finger of condemnation at the many newspapers that eagerly indulged in the foulest forms of character assassination. Such publications, he railed, would think nothing of printing a "picture of you that looked no more like you than the wilds of Africa."

He addressed the subject of imprisonment, specifically the "horrors of imprisonment" that would crush into dust the husband and son of Emma Kaufmann should she be found guilty and sent to prison. Aikens painted a bleak and horrible picture of a dungeon-like realm of eternal suffering. Not only would Emma Kaufmann languish behind bars, but her son and his offspring would be burdened by the stain of her guilt. He wanted people to understand that the action of the jury had the potential to destroy lives for future generations. He left the jury wondering, can any decent man live with that on his conscience?

Aikens moved on and spoke kindly about Agnes, the poor Hungarian girl resting "peacefully in her grave in Parkston." Aikens expressed, with convincing sincerity, his regret over her fate and could only hope that she was "in heavenly chorus, singing the Hungarian songs she used to sing when on earth." Then he added that, although some may sneer, there were no two people on earth who regretted the death of Agnes Polreis more than Mr. and Mrs. Kaufmann.

Undoubtedly, there were those present who thought that Aikens was asking too much of the jury by making such an appeal.

From his diction and tone they could tell that he was being sincere, even passionate, about his belief in his client's innocence. But he also challenged the jury to think logically and sensibly. "I believe," he declared, "that every fact and circumstance in this case points away from guilt." "No one," he said, "commits a crime and then calls others to see the evidence of the crime. No human being commits a crime without a motive." Aikens admitted that the reactions of the people of Parkston to the condition of Agnes' body was not unjustified; in fact, he didn't find fault with it. But then he paraphrased Shakespeare: "Judgment has flown to brutish beasts and men have lost their reason."

No doubt the Parkston people in the courtroom thought that using that particular quote from *Julius Caesar* was an overstatement, if not an insult. Nonetheless, its effect on the jury might have been just what Aikens wanted.

But what Aikens wanted even more desperately was to discredit Erickson, the one witness whose testimony had the terrible potential to brand Emma Kaufmann a felon. "If Peter Erickson's story is true he is an accomplice in the crime and his evidence is not sufficient to convict this woman." What kind of a woman do you, the jury, think she is? Is she the kind of woman who would commit an atrocious crime and then invite someone like Erickson to view the evidence? "Would she put her life and liberty into the hands of Peter Erickson?"

Aikens had become obsessed with Erickson, whose shadow haunted the defense's arguments day and night. "I admit that I am prejudiced against Peter Erickson. It makes me shudder to be in the same room with him." He felt that his learned opponents had the same opinion of this scourge of humanity, whom "any community would be ashamed to own."[21] Aikens spoke like a man in torment, pointing out that this damned perjurer had blatantly asked for "hush money." Aikens was constrained to confess, "I concede we are not trying him but without his testimony there would be no case against my client."[22]

And what about Dr. Germain? If he were the accomplice as stated in many newspapers and batted about among the public, why would he have taken the girl to a hospital where her wounds could be seen and examined by potential witnesses in a case against him? "It would have been wise," Aikens said, "to take the body down to the Cataract corner and put it on exhibition!" Had Emma Kaufmann struck the blows that caused the death of Agnes Polreis then, in the middle of night, she would have been on her hands and knees scrubbing away the evidence of the foul crime while Moses Kaufmann stood by with a gun to keep people away from the crime scene.

But no, none of that happened. Instead, she asked Erickson, the man who would be a witness against her, to clean up the girl's room. His emotions at a fever pitch, Aikens declared, "Show me anyone in the asylum at Yankton who would have put into the hands of a man like Erickson, their lives in the happiness of their posterity." She wasn't trying to hide anything; she wasn't making up anything. The actions of his client, Aikens contended, were examples of consciousness of innocence. Anyone who had committed such a fiendish crime, as was charged in this case, would have exhibited far more cunning.

There was, however, none of that at the friendly Kaufmann household. While it is true that Emma Kaufmann may have spoken harshly to Agnes, it was nothing more than the kind of talk commonly heard around town. "Do you think Mr. Kaufmann would have allowed anyone to be hurt" in his home, he asked, a place where the "dirtiest tramp that ever came across the prairies could find enough to eat?" Aikens was doing his best to humanize the Kaufmanns by portraying them as generous citizens and good neighbors.[23]

He did his best to dehumanize the medical experts who testified for the prosecution. Drs. Sweeney and Coulter were "a class of fakers who sell their services and opinions" to the highest bidder. He mocked their so-called examination of the brain "that had been soaked in formaldehyde for a year," using only their "naked eyes." They were "professional paid witnesses," ready to swear to an opinion and send someone to the gallows for the right price.[24]

Aikens returned to the question of motive. Why, he asked, would Emma Kaufmann want to torture and kill Agnes? She was not jealous of her. Rather, she had everything: wealth, a beautiful home, and a loving husband and son. Was there anything in her personal makeup that would cause her to throw all this away? No, of course not, according to Aikens. Furthermore, Mrs. Kaufmann was a mother who loved her boy to "idolatry," as much as she loved her little girl who tragically died and "is sleeping in the grave." She most certainly would not want to commit a crime that would brand her loved ones, for all time to come, with such an awful stigma.[25]

As Aikens neared the end of his long oration, nearly six hours in duration, he was clearly drained of energy. His voice had lost its sound and fury from the stress and strain. Yet he begged the jury to blame any mistakes on him, not on the defendant, saying, "Don't let her suffer for my mistakes." If his harsh comments on Erickson had caused the jurymen to sympathize with him, "charge it to me and me alone." He also reminded the jury to avoid prejudice by not bearing hostility toward Kaufmann because she is a Jew married to a wealthy brewer or because Agnes was a poor servant girl. Instead, judge the case based on "cold, naked facts." Then he added:

> Gentlemen, I belong to no church but I believe in a Supreme Being and that where two or three are gathered together he hears their petitions and having been associated with the Kaufmann family as I have for the past year, knowing them and loving them as I do, if it were permissible in this place, I would feel like getting down on my knees and asking God to help you see the truth as I know it to be.

As Aikens concluded, many in the audience were weeping, as were members of the jury and the Kaufmanns. It was a pure and natural courtroom scene that few are ever privileged to experience; nothing was contrived. "I want to thank you all," he said, with tears rolling down his checks and his voice faltering, "for this is the last effort of my life in a case of this kind. I could not stand the strain of another." He had been preparing for this trial for more than a year, and like the true lawyer and fighter that he was, he had given his all for his client and cause.[26]

The *Yankton Press and Dakotan* called his speech "true and natural," like a "last appeal for mercy" that "touched the mind and the whole emotional system." Aikens had delivered what many believed was his greatest effort in a court of law. "If he had been pleading for his own life he could not have been more natural, earnest and dramatic."[27]

The practice of law is not an art; it is the tedious, incremental connecting of dots, stringing them together in a convincing manner to lead to the desired outcome of a legal problem. Although he may or may not have loved Shakespeare, Frank Aikens was good at connecting the dots, and he did so in a way that resembled art. That is to say he used words, phrases, and posturing to create figuratively a thing of beauty, a form, a picture both melodious and dramatic. He succeeded so well that he became the most tragic figure in his own creation.

Later that day, while Judge Aikens was relaxing in a comfortable chair on the veranda of the St. Vincent Hotel, Moses Kaufmann approached and offered his hand. The two men shook, a long and strong handshake that spoke volumes about their relationship and the ordeal they had gone through together. They were, however, speechless, and both men "broke down and wept."[28] There simply was nothing more to say.

That Aikens had poured his heart, soul, and his powerful intellect into his closing argument no one could dispute. All were impressed, even John Ross, who had for so long in his columns dragged Aikens through the mud. As much as he hated Aikens, Ross wrote that the lawyer's address to the jury was splendid. "It is doubtful if it could be much improved."[29] Still Ross was betting on a conviction. For as much as Aikens wanted an acquittal, Ross hungered for a guilty verdict to quench his thirst for justice for Agnes. He believed it would be a blow struck for common humanity. That one rich family was suffering, and would be made to suffer even more, gave Ross some pleasure.

~

Ross was counting on George Egan to bring it all about. The much-heralded oratorical skills of the Iowa lawyer, Ross believed, were superior to Aikens and the other defense lawyers. On June 20, 1907, a crowded courtroom was waiting for Egan to dazzle them with his silver tongue, quick wit, and flare for the dramatic. Truly, his fame and reputation had preceded him, for he was a celebrity almost from the very day of his arrival in South Dakota. Everyone believed that Egan would deliver a masterful performance, with a knock-out punch at the end.

At 6 A.M. people began filing into the courtroom, willing to sit and wait for the star attraction, for nothing in their mundane lives had aroused such high expectation. Soon every seat in the courtroom was taken and another 150 people stood in the aisles.[30] Others sat on the floor or on the platform at the feet of the judge. Some folks even "climbed into the courthouse on ladders from the outside."[31] People had come to town from out in the country, as far away as fifteen miles. Alice Wilcox was on hand, but having been so disruptive during past sessions she was kept out. Everything was ready. It was a public trial like no other in the West.[32]

Outside of the courthouse, activity in the town of Flandreau came to a halt. Businesses closed down, shopkeepers pulled their shades and locked their doors; banks closed. The streets were bereft of people except for the occasional pedestrian. "Everything was at a standstill in Flandreau because this orator [Egan] of country wide fame was to make his closing argument in this celebrated case."[33]

Judge Smith was feeling the tension, too. As though expecting some kind of disruption, he reminded everyone that "it was absolutely important for them to refrain from any sort of demonstration," for an untoward outburst could result in a new trial. Should any demonstration occur that might influence the jury, he would order the courtroom cleared of all spectators.

Exuding power and confidence, Egan rose and addressed the jury at 9:15 A.M. He re-introduced himself, saying proudly that he was from Iowa, and though a stranger, he shared with everyone present the same attachment to the Creator. He reminded the jury of their sacred oath, and that in doing their solemn duty they should rise above the ordinary and "do complete justice to the defendant and to this commonwealth." This seemingly ordinary day, he said, would be the "greatest day of your life."

Egan said that he harbored no ill-will against the defendant, but it would be wrong for him not stand up and address the many falsehoods made by the defense. Aikens, he said, accused him of using certain testimony from Erickson to play a trick in court, and that somehow the people of Flandreau were participants. He argued that Aikens "came in here and shed crocodile tears." The people of Flandreau, Egan said, were not the sort who would "pour hot water on a helpless girl."

He commended the work of his colleagues, Orr and Blewitt, and then got to the heart of the case, Erickson's testimony: "I do not want to see Peter Erickson abused for his honest testimony." Such tactics were unworthy of honorable men and, Egan declared emphatically, no one should stoop so low as to "abuse a witness." No, he would quit rather than resort to such tactics. Erickson a liar, he asked? Who believes it but Aikens? If Erickson gave false testimony, if he lied, why on earth would it be necessary to bring in Krust in an attempt to impeach him? Erickson, he thundered, had been labeled a liar because he "turned on his heel there in the Cataract and left Judge Aikens," who had offered to protect him.

Egan went further, saying he really didn't need Erickson's testimony to convict Emma Kaufmann. The jury could disregard Erickson's testimony altogether and still convict her based on other evidence. And in that vein, Egan turned to Dr. Germain, a key defense witness. He reminded the jury that under rigorous cross-examination the doctor's body language was akin to that of a worm acting out its final agonies while impaled on a fishhook. Egan then linked Germain to the death of Agnes by arguing that his neglect of her condition was a factor in her death. He implied that a conscientious doctor would have taken a more active role in treating her instead of dumping her off at the hospital. "Where was Dr. Germain," he asked, "from the time he left the girl until she died?"

He brought up the death certificate signed by Dr. Germain, which listed the cause of death as anemia. Diabetes, Egan said, came into the picture when the doctor realized that more was needed to make a "strong defense." More than that, Egan said, Germain wrote an incorrect name on the death certificate, even though he knew her name. Egan wanted the jury to think that Dr. Germain was a bumbling incompetent or, worse yet, an accessory to the crime. The doctor suspected that something had gone wrong at the Kaufmann house, but rather than confront Moses or Emma Kaufmann, he sought a way around the problem so as not to incriminate his friends.[34]

Egan insisted, and stated with damnable certainty, that Dr. Germain's plan was to "bury the girl under a false name" on a death certificate that stated a false cause of death. He asked, "Doesn't this show signs of guilt?" The girl, Egan continued, was the victim of murder, and Dr. Germain knew the truth of it.[35]

And what about that gangrene that Dr. Germain mentioned? Egan boldly stated that "the only gangrene I have seen in this case was when Judge Aikens asked Erickson if the Parkston people had offered him any money and he said 'the only money offered was by you and Kaufmann.'" Egan said that hearing Erickson make that statement caused Aikens' face to get "so black that I thought I should diagnose it for gangrene."[36]

Egan praised his own experts, Dr. Sweeney and Dr. Coulter. He was willing to let the jury weigh their testimony, confident in his belief that the state had the superior medical experts. He went on to mock Aikens, who had asked for mercy, saying the state would not sink that low. He challenged Aikens' opinion of Erickson and his relationship with the Kaufmann family. The reason, Egan insisted, that Emma Kaufmann called on Erickson to help her with Agnes was because she deemed him trustworthy. Therefore, she had no problem with Erickson seeing Agnes on the floor in wet clothes. "Who would she tell but the man both she and her husband trusted?"

Furthermore, Erickson had given truthful testimony when he said that he called at the house and saw Agnes in wet clothes, for Mrs. Udell, the neighbor, had testified that the day before Agnes died, Mrs. Kaufmann was seen spreading wet clothes on the lawn. This, Egan declared, means Erickson told the truth, and there was enough truth in the state's case to put "the noose around the neck of this defendant." As to the foot bath of water and ashes, said to be an old German remedy, Egan off-handedly remarked that he had always believed that Germans had as much "sense as anyone else."

He argued that the only reason Agnes was sent to the hospital was because they didn't want her to die in the house. If that had happened, Egan suggested, all the money Moses Kaufmann had could not save his wife from conviction. Then he asked the jurors what their wives would do had their servant girl been in the same shape as Agnes. Of course, Egan had an answer: their wives would have provided her with the best care available to them. Any woman of compassion would have done so.

"I challenge all the pages of literature to show me so sad a case and so awful a case." Emma Kaufmann, Egan roared, was a woman who never experienced "the flower of sympathy." Compassion was not a characteristic of her personality. If she truly believed that Agnes was suffering from a deadly disease, why didn't she say, in the presence of Erickson, "Great God! Erickson, this awful disease is killing this girl!" But that was something Erickson never heard.

Egan was getting inside the heads of the jurors in a mesmerizing closing argument while the enthralled audience was standing by, waiting for the knock-out punch. At several points during the special prosecutor's blazing speech, Aikens launched strenuous objections, contending that Egan was inflaming the jury or that his closing argument had gone beyond the bounds of what the law allowed. But time after time, Aikens was overruled by the judge.

Given free rein, Egan continued apace, as though within his powerful prose was some divine force carrying his message on its wings. Expecting that the jurors would want to understand motive, Egan, in a seeming fit of passion, declared that he could think of no reason why a woman would want to scald a girl like Agnes. How do you assign motive to such a horrible crime? He advised the jurors to look to the human heart, for there and there alone is the "one standard to measure people." As for Emma Kaufmann, the keeper of the "death bastille," Egan had painted a portrait of a heartless, depraved human being with sadistic tendencies. In all the history of criminology, Egan said, there is no comparable case: "Where is the motive of Jack the Ripper? England had her Mrs. [Brownrigg], Italy her Lucretia Borgia and South Dakota her Emma Kaufmann!"

Aikens, Egan reminded everyone, had started the case like a "Roman, with his chest out but he ended down on his knees almost, begging for mercy." Egan responded to his plea to "Show mercy and I will show you mercy." And while there had been no mercy bestowed upon the suffering Agnes Polreis, Egan, in his concluding remarks, reminded the jurors that their ruling must be strictly in accordance with the law and based on the facts in evidence. It had been an explosive trial, one of high drama and emotion, and yet the jury had to decide guilt or innocence, rejecting undue passion and bias by applying the law to that which had been brought into the record as evidence.

Egan turned to Aikens and, looking directly into his eyes, said, "Great lawyer that you are sir, I acknowledge it gladly and am proud to sit at your feet, but I know that you have only one idea in this case—to confuse two or three of the men and have them hang the jury." While this clever remark was, on the surface, a personal message of praise for his opponent, it was meant for the jury to hear and take into account during their deliberations. It was a warning not to be indecisive. Deliver a verdict of guilty, he pleaded, for a hung jury would be a dishonor to justice.

In his final pitch, Egan stated, "Mrs. Kaufmann has committed a murder. Gentlemen of the jury, I leave this case with you. When you think of sympathy, think of Agnes Polreis, suffering more in those few weeks than the Kaufmanns could suffer in a lifetime."[37] It was a lot to think about, and most people expected the jury to think about it for a long time.

~

Egan concluded at 2:30 P.M. and Judge Smith gave the jury a complex and lengthy set of instructions that would govern their deliberations. He explained the charge of murder, which could carry either the death penalty or life in prison, along with the lesser charges of manslaughter in the first or second degree. There were two separate parts needed for a conviction: "First, death by criminal means, and second that death was caused by the accused." He gave the jury the meaning of premeditation.

Concerning the death of Agnes, should the jury believe that she had a disease and that an "act by the defendant hastened her death, she would be just as guilty as if the deceased was in perfect health when the crime was committed."

Importantly, he informed the members of the jury that they could not be swayed by any matter outside the scope of the evidence presented. They must reject all matters of sex, race, and wealth, as well as public anger, prejudice, demonstrations, and opinion. The burden of proof is always on the prosecution and the defendant need not prove how death occurred.

The jury was reminded that this was a circumstantial evidence case, as there were no eye-witnesses who testified to seeing the blow or blows that killed Agnes Polreis. In order to "warrant conviction it must be shown that the evidence is well substantiated and must exclude all other hypothesis." The state must prove, beyond a reasonable doubt, that death did not result from disease or other circumstances.

Judge Aikens made a request for a special instruction: that the jury not draw any negative inferences from the fact that Emma Kaufmann did not testify at the trial and that her not-guilty plea meant that she denied all the essential elements in the charges against her. The health of Agnes and her ability to escape must also be considered, if in fact, the jury believed she was in good health and had opportunity to escape. Finally, as Aikens had requested, the judge instructed, "It is not sufficient to establish a probability, but guilt must be established to a moral certainty."[38]

The jury retired at 3:37 P.M. on the afternoon of June 20 to begin deliberations. It didn't take them long to reach a decision—just five hours and two ballots. No one was expecting the jury to work that fast. But according to the *Sioux Falls Journal*, the jury had decided on guilt even before the closing arguments.[39]

The surprising speed with which the decision was reached meant that it took some effort to round up all those who were required to hear the verdict. Judge Smith was notified by telephone at 8 o'clock and soon "a strange procession, consisting of the principal actors," was seen walking toward the courthouse. Once seated, the gathering waited quietly in eerie silence for eight minutes, during which time the Flandreau band could be heard playing "a strangely incongruous two-step" outside the courthouse.[40] Finally, at 8:45 P.M., in a hushed, dimly lit courtroom, the clerk, William Kellogg, revealed the jury's decision: guilty of manslaughter in the first degree.

Upon hearing the verdict, Emma Kaufmann, clad all in black, showed no emotion but for "a slight compression of the lips and a slight increase in the pallor of the face." Overall she exhibited the same poise and composure that characterized her conduct throughout the long and painful ordeal. The *Argus-Leader* reporter could not help but admire her "magnificent nerve." She shed no tears but both her husband and son "broke down and sobbed audibly."[41] Was their outburst triggered by their dogged belief in her innocence or because, in their heart of hearts, they knew she was guilty?

On the first informal ballot, without previous discussion, the vote was eleven to one, all for conviction. But juror William Cone voted for murder while the rest voted in favor of manslaughter. Since they had a conviction, the jury then proceeded to a unanimous decision. By 6:30 P.M., the jury was ready to reveal the decision, but Judge Smith was out attending the Flandreau horse races and could not be found. They finally got word to the judge with a message simply asking for more information. The jury used this feint to avoid having a large crowd on hand with the potential for a noisy demonstration.

Although there were no celebrations, the people of Flandreau favored the jury's decision. There was a great deal of handshaking and expressions of "Well done" in the courtroom. The *Sioux Falls Daily Press* published a photograph of the proud twelve. The men who had given up seventeen days of their time in doing their duty could now walk the streets of Flandreau with their heads held high. Each man was paid $68 plus a mileage fee for his service.[42]

After hearing the dreaded guilty verdict, Aikens quietly and immediately notified the judge that he would move for a new trial. October 10 was the date set by Judge Smith for the hearing on the motion. He did not pronounce sentence. The Kaufmanns quietly left the courthouse for their boarding place. The rich woman walked away a convicted felon, released on the original bond, and the Kaufmanns were left to labor under the unpleasant knowledge that the sentence for manslaughter in the first degree was a range of years in prison from four to life.[43]

The mood in Flandreau—and Sioux Falls as well—was that the verdict was just and that it should stand against any attempt to get a new trial. The *Flandreau Herald* firmly believed that Emma Kaufmann received a fair trial. "Twelve of the best men in Moody County, men of mature judgement and good intentions, sat on her case." She had outstanding legal representation and the judge was imminently fair, and he was careful to see that nothing "detrimental or prejudicial" was entered into the record. "What more could she have had?"[44]

Of course, everyone knew that the defense team would do its utmost to keep her out of prison. Still, the Kaufmanns and their attorneys departed the Flandreau courtroom under a cloud of gloom. Meanwhile, the jurors gathered around the triumphant George W. Egan "and congratulated him upon his wonderful and illuminating speech." At long last released from those responsibilities mandated by the American legal system, the jurors dispersed to their homes.[45]

Chapter 11

The Fallout

Counselor George W. Egan, who prosecuted the charge for the state has been showered with congratulations every minute since he finished his great address to the jury.

The Sioux Falls Daily Press
June 22, 1907

In the course of participating in any great event, the lives and fortunes of people can change dramatically. For George W. Egan, the future looked positively golden. His work as special prosecutor in the Kaufmann trial catapulted him into the stratosphere of public opinion and adoration. Even though during the trial a newspaper called him "George B. Logan,"[1] his correct name was on the lips of the multitudes. He was a hero, a wonderful orator, a conqueror of evil, and a coming man. Opportunity opened up before him like a treasure vault, and he had only to choose from among the vast array of gems spread before him.

Congratulatory telegrams were sent to him from all over the West. Admiring Flandreau women sent bouquets of flowers to the St. Vincent Hotel, where he shared a room with his wife. Words of praise gushed forth from a host of new admirers, including the foreman of the jury. He described Egan's closing argument as "not only the greatest speech ever made in this state, but in my judgment at any time and at any place in a murder trial." The jury liked his style, his powerful but affable manner, and they believed him.

A "delegation of brother Irishmen" presented Egan with a "fine blackthorn cane" imported from Ireland. Ira Blewitt, the Moody County state's attorney, hosted a dinner party in Flandreau to honor the victorious attorney. The "most prominent residents of Flandreau and Moody County" attended the gala event. The guest of honor received a "handsome and costly cut glass vase" along with other gifts. And if all this wasn't enough to satiate Egan's ego, he and his wife were extended "invitation after invitation" by other Flandreau folks in the days following the conclusion of the famous trial.[2]

Egan's trial mate, State's Attorney Alpha F. Orr, the less flashy, introspective prosecutor, had also made a good impression. He had done his job calmly, despite the incessant chatter of mean-spirited critics accusing him of being incompetent, uninterested, and weak. In his own quiet way, he had proved them wrong.

The public and the jury believed and trusted the prosecution witnesses, especially the nurses and medical experts. And they really took a liking to Peter Erickson, whom people were calling "Big Pete," or the "Big Norse." The jurors found him to be forthright, honest, and credible, a sympathetic witness whom many believed the defense had been unfairly maligned. He emerged unscathed, vindicated, and happy with the outcome of the case. He harbored no ill-will toward Emma Kaufmann, but rather "was pleased because the jurors believed him." Erickson, from the beginning the "star witness," found himself, at the end, surrounded by admirers at the hotel. With a crowd of well-wishers gathered around his carriage, he departed Flandreau for his parents' farm in Alpena.[3]

The residents of Flandreau wanted to return to normalcy. With the hot air gone, the town became deflated, as all the visitors, the lawyers, and witnesses hurriedly boarded carriages, trains, and automobiles. The sudden, mass exodus left the town's residents wondering whether there had been any real benefit to having hosted the famous trial. The influx of people created an anxious flurry of activity, and money was spent. But the trial was actually disruptive to normal business activity. Potential customers were so mesmerized by the trial that routine matters were forgotten and consumer spending lagged.[4]

Not all of the non-residents, however, left Flandreau. It was learned that the Kaufmanns had not checked out of the Mead residence. In no hurry to abandon small town life, Emma Kaufmann needed time to recover from three weeks of a grueling trial. A South Carolina newspaper, the *Manning Times*, inaccurately informed its readers that Emma Kaufmann, "a very rich woman," was carted off to prison to serve time for having "cruelly tortured to death" an "old maid servant, whose mother, in open court," begged God to forgive the doer of the evil deed.[5]

The guilty verdict, while certainly a crushing blow, had no such effect on Emma Kaufmann. Because of the appeal, she did not go directly to prison, though there were undoubtedly some folks who thought she should be locked up and made to suffer. The beleaguered Kaufmann family stayed in Flandreau, away from the hornets' nest in Sioux Falls. It came as a mild surprise that instead of retreating to some quiet eastern resort, the Kaufmanns chose to spend the rest of the summer where they felt at ease and welcome.

They arranged for an extended stay in an apartment in the "handsome residence of Miss Mary Mead," directly opposite the courthouse where all the drama had so recently occurred. Everyone needed respite, and the town of Flandreau was "enjoying the first quiet it has known since the beginning of the famous Kaufmann trial." While all the hubbub was over, there was "still interest in the movements of the Kaufmanns."

Emma Kaufmann was said to be moving around, enjoying herself, making new friends from among the "prominent ladies of the city." She went "driving every day" and joined a group of people who took a "touring jaunt" out into the countryside. She also had a relaxing time on the Big Sioux River, cruising for a few miles and then fishing with some ladies.

Young Charles Kaufmann stayed in Flandreau with his mother and father and was making friends from among the townspeople who regarded him as a "fine young fellow." He received and accepted invitations from the "best people here," and "despite the cloud" that hovered over him, he was in good spirits. Charles and his father had their driving teams brought up from Sioux Falls so they could while away the time exploring along scenic country roads.

Moses Kaufmann "has a wide acquaintance among the residents of Flandreau," and the people openly expressed their sympathy to him. "The pronounced prejudice which was created against Mrs. Kaufmann during the trial is dying away." All this had led to an improvement in her health and outlook on life. Truly, as there was balm in Gilead there was healing, peace, and quiet in Flandreau, according to an article in the *Argus-Leader*.[6]

While the Kaufmanns were rusticating under the beguiling spell of the undulating prairie, the public was informed of the cost of the trial. An itemized bill was published in the *Argus-Leader* with a total of $6,880.08. The figure raised eyebrows, but the high cost of the trial was not an issue that would have any lasting effect on the people of either county, though the participants would not easily be forgotten.

George Egan was so impressed with the effect of his closing argument that he wanted to share it with the public. He had it copyrighted and printed in a bound pamphlet that included pictures of key figures in the trial. By the end of August, it was out and selling for fifty cents a copy. The *Soo Critic* was offering it for sale and advised interested parties to read it and learn how and why a conviction was secured.[7] As the publisher, John Ross looked up to Egan, whom he held in high esteem, a man ready to hit the lecture circuit.

Such braggadocio was a bit too much for the Sioux Falls folks who put out the weekly *South Dakota State Forum*. They wanted peace and promised to remain calm throughout the ordeal, hoping that the agony would not extend far into the future. Under the guidance of H. C. Sessions and his son, the *Forum* reminded its readers—in the midst of the newspaper madness—that "we have always tried to picture the pleasant side of life as we saw it." Sessions sought to elevate his newspaper's coverage, stating that it would ignore "the horrible riff-raff gossip of the saloons and . . . the washerwoman's clubs" and instead "give the people a paper that is fit to be read in the home."[8]

Many agreed with this approach because there was an abundance of good things to talk about. Sioux Falls bore the appearance of prosperity in the summer of 1907. It was an attractive place in the mind of Egan and other ambitious men. One Sioux Falls newspaper boasted that the city was "the best built town" in America "for its size." With five railroads huffing and puffing, fifty-two trains went in and out of the city's busy depots every day, including twenty-two passenger trains.[9]

Although Sioux Falls had missed out on the excitement of hosting the Kaufmann trial, there were other diversions. On June 24 the "Pawnee Bill Historic Wild West Show" came blazing into town. Among its highlights were bucking broncos, "the great train robbery," and "aborigines fresh from prairie wigwams."[10] It was a show tailor-made for folks who didn't get enough of the frontier experience while it was happening all around them. And if Pawnee Bill left the city wanting, the Barnum Bailey Circus did a one day show on July 15, featuring an unforgettable, circular bicycle ride called the "Dip of Death."[11]

~

The Kaufmann family returned to Sioux Falls before the summer ended. A Flandreau letter to the *Critic* from "A Resident" said, "The Kaufman[n]s have gone and the air is no longer polluted by the breath of a murderess." The writer, who claimed to be supported by many others, went on to criticize the *Argus-Leader* for its story about the "entertainment of Mrs. Kaufman[n] by the best families" because there was very little truth to it. She had been called on by just a few maudlin women, but "the people in general do not wish to be classed with the worshippers of the doers of such fiendish deeds." According to the "Resident," the trial and conviction settled the matter once and for all in the minds of "justice loving people."[12]

But the fallout was far from over. The date for the hearing on the motion for a new trial, October 10, was approaching. Until then most newspaper coverage of the trial would diminish or cease, with one exception: the *Soo Critic*. Ross was unwilling to be silent on the matter and was driven by an insatiable desire to keep the story in print.

After the verdict of guilt was announced, Ross paused and in a moment's reflection, while feeling some sympathy toward the defendant's husband and son, expressed hope that the sentence would not be long in years. But when Ross learned that Frank Aikens had made a motion for a new trial, the fiery editor did an about face and called for a severe sentence. Kaufmann had refused to accept her role in Agnes' death. She refused to take her medicine and Ross wanted it poured down her throat.

Receiving apparently numerous inquiries from his readers, Ross penned another angry article about the Kaufmann case. Will she get a new trial, he asked? He was worried that State's Attorney Orr would simply capitulate. He started his analysis by stating that it was doubtful that Judge Smith would grant the motion, for he had presided over a fair trial and had been careful in his rulings. Ross expressed some concern over demonstrations that occurred during the trial, such as Mrs. Polreis' prayer in the courtroom, the applause during Erickson's testimony, and the disruptive ranting of the demented Alice Wilcox. Still, these matters should not have unduly influenced the jury, for "if a juror is convinced as a man, he must also be convinced as a juror," and there was "nothing in reason and common sense in any of these [demonstrations] to cause a new trial to be granted." A new trial was uncalled for, according to Ross, and an unnecessary expenditure to the taxpayers.

The country as a whole, Ross argued, "is suffering from too much leniency shown toward criminals." The verdict had been widely applauded and so should withstand all challenges. Emma Kaufmann could have pleaded insanity but she did not and it was too late to do so. Everyone, including Kaufmann, should step back and reflect on what had just transpired in Flandreau. Ross declared that a jury of honest men could never acquit based on the evidence presented. But if there were to be a new trial, the evidence to be presented would need be far greater than that which the jury heard at the first trial.

Ross had a penchant for tossing out sly warnings about the revelation of some shocking developments that were just waiting in the weeds. He was convinced that there was much more to the case—more than that which had been revealed at the trial. But, he added, it will never be known unless there is an "effort made to get what can be had." This was an obvious allusion to the perceived lack of interest on the part of law enforcement to do their duty. Ross claimed that he had "knowledge of what evidence was not secured for the trial, but which can be secured." Without naming names or giving specifics, something even he was reluctant to do, Ross postulated that if a new trial were held, there would be multiple defendants and a "conviction of murder." His readers could bet on it.[13]

Lives are shaped by the random coming together of unrelated incidents over which individuals have little or no control. Decisions are made; action is taken. Something happens to one person, and in ways that no one can predict, another person is affected thereby. The wheel of fortune, or misfortune, spins perilously or gloriously close to each person until at some point there is contact. In the wake of that sudden, unexpected impact, the mind breaks out in thought or cringes in a spasm of emotion. But in the light of the moment, one is compelled to respond affirmatively—or run.

On Sunday evening, September 29, 1907, John O'Grady, a farmer in Mapleton Township, about four miles north of Sioux Falls, was in his house, reading and relaxing in a chair by the stove. His wife, Julia Ann O'Grady, was also in the house. Suddenly, the quiet evening was shattered by a shotgun blast. A gut-shot John O'Grady stood up, walked a couple steps, and fell dead. His bowels had been torn asunder by a "full charge of No. 4 shot."[14]

Julia Ann rushed to a neighbor's house crying hysterically, saying that someone had shot and killed her husband. The neighbors wanted to help. The first person they contacted was the coroner, L. D. Miller, at about 10 o'clock that Sunday night. Miller contacted Deputy Sheriff Eugene Reilley, and the two men drove to the O'Grady residence, where they found a man dead with a wound to his left abdomen.

The incident set into motion significant press coverage. John O'Grady, an Irish immigrant, about sixty years old, was a quiet, inoffensive man with no known enemies. He had arrived in America in 1864, and in 1866, as a veteran, became one of the very earliest residents of Minnehaha County. A member of the 22nd U.S. Infantry, he served at Fort Dakota until he was discharged in April 1869, at which time he acquired 120 acres of farmland north of Sioux Falls in Mapleton Township on one side of the Big Sioux River. He later added another 120 acres on the other side. O'Grady, described as "an industrious man, and a good citizen," was one of a small number of hardy pioneers who took land outside of the Fort Dakota military reservation.[15]

According to the *Argus-Leader*, the O'Gradys were well-known and respected, and their home, alongside the Big Sioux River, was "a most hospitable place" where people were warmly welcomed. It was also known that the couple liked "a friendly glass of beer or a glass of toddy." Mrs. O'Grady was described as being of "swarthy complexion" and was called "Black Mary."[16]

The *Sioux Falls Journal* assumed a more contemptuous posture. It reported that John O'Grady and Julia Ann O'Grady, whom the paper called his "half-breed wife," had been living "in squalor on their farm," surrounded by good land and "fat stock." They had the means to live much better, "if not in luxury," but they chose to cloister themselves in "a single room where they sleep eat and make their toilet." Their home, the paper reported, was a gathering place for disreputable people, including Indians, and it was "the scene of many rows" in which the O'Gradys were the participants. Visitors noted that liquor played a major role at the sordid events on the Mapleton Township farm.[17]

Actually, Julia Ann was the daughter of Mr. and Mrs. William Melvin, respectable pioneers who came to Minnehaha County in the late 1860s.[18] In 1868, when Minnehaha County was organized by the territorial legislature, Mr. Melvin was appointed to the county commission.[19] He was also involved in establishing the first school in Sverdrup Township in 1871.[20] His daughter, Julia Ann Melvin, married John O'Grady in the early 1870s and they apparently had a good life together until that fatal September night in 1907.

Julia Ann claimed that a man named Frank Miller, who had dined with the O'Gradys that night and then left in anger because he was not allowed to stay overnight, returned and shot her husband. Before long, two men who answered to the name Frank Miller, were found; both had solid alibis.[21] Thus the focus of the investigation by Sheriff Nelson and Coroner Miller was squarely on the new widow. The idea that a man denied lodging at a stranger's home would shoot that man wore very thin in the minds of the investigators. And if a stranger shot the husband, in a relatively isolated location, why would he leave the wife alive?

A double-barrel shotgun was found in the attic with a live No. 4 shot shell in one barrel, the other being empty. No empty shell was found. There was nothing to support her contention that the shot was fired outside the house. The authorities did not believe her story and she was arrested. A coroner's jury, led by L. D. Miller, held a hearing and concluded that John O'Grady died as a result of a homicide and that his wife had killed him.[22] Since both the deceased and the suspected perpetrator were heavy drinkers, it was believed that alcohol played a role in the tragedy.

The *Soo Critic* dove into the shocking story with an article that included insulting remarks about Julia Ann O'Grady's ethnicity. After relating some of the details of the investigation that he learned from talking to Sheriff Nelson, Ross used the shooting and arrest to remind the public that all defendants are not treated the same in Minnehaha County. Comparing the O'Grady case to the Kaufmann case, Ross noted that the sheriff did not hesitate to jail Julia Ann O'Grady and, because of it, "people are inquiring why she is treated differently from Mrs. Kaufman[n]." The people, he wrote, should bear in mind that the "purpose of the law is the equal treatment of all," but in the execution of the law "there is partiality." Pointing a stern finger at the deputy state's attorney, E. E. Rodabaugh, Ross raised the specter of a double standard.[23] Kaufmann, Kaufmann, always Kaufmann; it seemed as if Ross would shout "Kaufmann!" until the end of time.

~

Upon being accused of murder, Julia Ann O'Grady "broke down completely" and was heard to say, "You know I did not kill John."[24] In her jail cell, she was showing signs of mental instability. She retained the services of C. H. Winsor, a reputable attorney who first hung out his shingle in 1873, when Sioux Falls was a rough frontier town with many challenges and few lawyers. Winsor was able to get Mrs. O'Grady bonded out of jail and began preparing a defense. However, it was soon learned that Winsor was off the case and none other than George W. Egan was to represent her going forward. The change was so sudden that people were left wondering whether she did so of her own accord or had been swayed to do so.

The death of John O'Grady and the arrest and trial of his wife for murdering him promised to become an exciting side show. Soon, people were treated to the "O'Grady Gold Rush." It was rumored that just before his death, O'Grady inherited $20,000 from a relative in "the old country." According to a story circulated in the 1930s of questionable veracity, O'Grady converted the $20,000 into gold and hid it on his farm. Somehow word about the hidden treasure leaked to the public and "excitement developed into a fever." Predictably, a large number of people, characterized as "young and old, drunk and sober," all trespassers, were on the O'Grady farm searching frantically for the gold.

The search became so intense that "plaster was torn from the walls of the house." The house was in danger of becoming a complete wreck when the attorney for the O'Grady estate hired a security guard. It was a good idea with a bad outcome because the guard proved to be fond of strong drink, and the gold hunters made certain that he had a plentiful supply. Plied with liquor, he spent his time sitting in a stuffed chair in the living room while searchers continued their work uninterrupted. Ultimately, $2,000 in "negotiable bonds" were discovered in the stuffed chair, but no one found the gold, which according to local legend, remains somewhere on the property.[25]

Not long before taking the O'Grady case, Egan had been retained by the Parkston people to oppose the motion for a new trial in the Kaufmann case. He was also advertising his upcoming program entitled "A Great Lecture" on "The Educated Man," to be presented at the Flandreau Opera House on October 3, 1907.[26] With two sensational cases on his plate, and a lecture series about to begin, Egan was on his way to further dazzle the public with his wondrous legal and oratorical skills.

Success and widespread adulation had gone to his head, and while Egan was steamrolling into prominence, opposition was gathering. But as a narcissist with a tendency to equate instinct with wisdom, he was unable to see the danger. Egan was bright and articulate, but would he prove to be a match for those who might be scheming against him?

As the time for the hearing on Aikens' motion for a new trial grew closer, newspapers began weighing in on the matter. The *Soo Critic* was solidly against it. Arguing that no honest jury could acquit Emma Kaufmann, Ross continued his mean-spirited attacks on her while mocking the judicial process. He insisted that the motion was nothing more than an attempt to defeat justice in "the most heinous crime ever heard before a jury." He also attacked Minnehaha County officials for their lack of interest in opposing a new trial, saying their ho-hum attitude "is a shame and disgrace." But as evidence of decency in the state, he praised the valiant people of Parkston who had the good sense to keep Egan on the job.[27]

Egan would soon be in court arguing against a new trial for Kaufmann, but in the meantime, he was grappling with the ugly details of the O'Grady case. Although it promised to be another juicy murder trial, it was his fee arrangement that got immediate and critical attention in the papers. To ensure that he was amply rewarded for his legal services, he convinced Mrs. O'Grady to execute a "warranty deed and a bill of sale" to him. For the sum of "$1 and legal services," Egan was to receive all of his client's interest in the farm, including the livestock and chickens, plus a $1,000 bond and $50 in cash. The *Sioux Falls Journal* looked askance upon the questionable arrangement and blurted out that the woman would become a "pauper and Egan the richer by probably $5,000.00." In other words, if she won an acquittal, a destitute Julia Ann O'Grady was certain to become a "public beneficiary."[28] Acquitted or convicted, people would say she gave away the farm.

The unique fee arrangement became public knowledge after the deed was filed with the register of deeds. Egan was inviting trouble because this looked like he was, in fact, cleaning her out. Wagging tongues would inevitably accuse him of taking advantage of a client whose state of mind was irrational and therefore easy to manipulate and deceive. While many people thought Julia Ann had killed her husband in cold blood, there were those who also believed that she was barely able to deal with her financial affairs, especially since she was showing signs of severe mental illness. The situation was fraught with disastrous consequences.

The Minnehaha County Bar Association took notice and filed a petition with Judge Dana R. Bailey, asking that a guardian be appointed for Julia Ann O'Grady. Their petition stated that she was "for some time past" mentally incompetent and unable to care for herself and her finances. On the face of it, some may have thought their motives were pure, but in all likelihood, they were acting out of a growing dislike for Egan, whose bombastic style and egotistical ambition alienated other lawyers. Judge Bailey set a hearing in county court for October 21, knowing that Egan would fight against it with all his abundant energy. [29]

Out of town when the petition was filed, Egan arrived back in Sioux Falls and was quickly surrounded by reporters eager for a good story, knowing that the flamboyant lawyer was likely to erupt in a fountain of words. Expressing great surprise at the turn of events in the O'Grady case, Egan commented, "I am amused. It is the last effort of the defense in the Kaufmann case," trying desperately to get a new trial. But he said, "There will be no new trial." Egan wasn't finished: "How hard a little bunch of henchmen have worked to injure me only to defend the Kaufmann case." He told reporters that a plot against him had originated in the office of the state's attorney, and then hinted at a cover-up: "I hope I shall never be compelled to give the public the full details of the fight for conviction in that case."

He claimed that success "brings out rattlesnakes," meaning the lawyers ganging up on him were doing so out of jealousy, and contrary to their allegations, all his dealings with Mrs. O'Grady were open and fair. To his way of thinking, she wasn't incompetent. In response to those who thought he had taken her for a ride, Egan said, "I never robbed a widow or an orphan."[30] But he was clearly stung, for his character had been called into question.

The Iowan got some support from his admirer at the *Soo Critic*. Ross cautiously but firmly stated that "we do not believe that Geo. W. Egan would take the last dollar of any widow and leave her penniless." Egan, he insisted, "is strictly honest." All doubters need only look at the work he put into the Kaufmann case for proof of his ability and integrity. As an example of dedication to cause and client, or as a moral compass, the Kaufmann case and George Egan were inextricably blended together in a crucible of ethical purity, asserted Ross, just days before the Kaufmann hearing.[31]

But Ross could not make the O'Grady matter go away, and Egan most definitely didn't need any distractions. On October 15 the hearing on the defense motion for a new trial opened in the circuit court in Sioux Falls. And knowing that Frank Aikens would be razor sharp and aggressive, Egan had to be at his best. He would soon be fighting on two fronts.

The Minnehaha County Courthouse was not crowded when Moses and Charles Kaufmann arrived with attorney Aikens. Mrs. Kaufmann was not with them, causing Egan to demand that she be present. Judge Smith ruled that her attendance was not required and Egan accepted the ruling, having made his point for the record. State's Attorney Alpha F. Orr was also at the prosecution table, but Egan did all the talking, fending off attacks from Aikens.

The hearing, described by one paper as "dry, stale, flat and monotonous," began with a minor tilt between Aikens and Egan over

Minnehaha County Courthouse, Sioux Falls, South Dakota.
Author's Collection.

the defense's bill of exceptions. Then George Rice began a tedious reading of a large number of defense affidavits in support of the contention that the first trial had been unfair. Rice droned on and on while the mother of the late Agnes Polreis sat quietly in the front row, dressed all in black with a shawl on her head. When Rice got to the affidavit about her prayer in the Flandreau courtroom during the first trial and read the words, "Mary, Mother of Jesus, Lord Jesus Christ," Mrs. Polreis stood up and with clasped hands and bowed head, assumed the position of silent prayer. The quiet but emotional display drew an objection from Aikens, and he called Judge Smith's attention to the conduct of the grieving woman. Aikens was probably thinking, "Here we go again," but the judge said nothing, and after standing for several minutes, the haunted woman sat down beside her husband.[32]

Rice's reading went on during this brief demonstration. The affidavits of certain jurors were read to bolster the defense argument that misconduct had occurred. It was alleged that the bailiffs conversed with members of the jury about the case in violation of the law. It was also alleged that while the jurors were kept together in the Davis house, one juror was allowed to sleep on the first floor while the others slept on the second floor. Egan interrupted and insisted that the jurors could not impeach their own verdict. But Rice responded that the juror affidavits were not an attempt by them to impeach their verdict but rather to show misconduct on the part of the bailiffs.[33]

Elon G. Pettigrew,
juryman for first Kaufmann trial.
Courtesy Moody County Historical Society.

Aikens' own affidavit, read by Rice, stated that the state's medical experts, Dr. Sweeney and Dr. Coulter, took seats in the courtroom next to the jury. While Dr. Germain was testifying, the other two doctors were said to be exchanging assorted winks and nods, frowns and grimaces, with members of the jury. It was also claimed that one of the nurses, Miss Thornburg, who testified on behalf of the state, was seen talking to jury member Elon G. Pettigrew.[34]

Five members of the jury submitted affidavits alleging that a bailiff talked to them about seeing Dr. William A. Germain lurking around the house where the jurors were staying, allegedly for the purpose of bribing the jury. But it was "proven that Germain had to go to the pump in the rear of the house to get drinking water" because the place he was lodging at had no water.[35] Judge Smith admitted the juror affidavits into the record. Rice continued reading affidavits until 2 P.M., at which time he began the arguments for the defense. He did so to an audience that had diminished in size, leaving just a few of the "regulars" in their seats.[36]

On the second day of the hearing, attendance in the courtroom was again light, indicating that interest in the case had waned considerably. John and Theresa Polreis were among the scattering of spectators; they sat quietly in the front row during the morning session but were absent in the afternoon. Egan took the floor during the morning session and submitted a number of affidavits to counter the charge of bailiff misconduct. He sat down after speaking for about ten minutes. Aikens then rose and commenced a speech that would last for three hours, taking up the rest of the morning session of court. He continued his long-winded oration into the afternoon and was still talking at 3:30 P.M. with "no indication as to when he would close."

During his oratorical marathon, he freely criticized bailiffs, jurors, witnesses, and experts, but his principal target was Egan. Among the many points he made, Aikens argued that Egan's closing argument at the trial "went outside the testimony" that had been entered into the record. As an example of the misconduct by Egan, Aikens said that his reference to the Kaufmann home as a "Bastille" was improper for the house looked like anything but a jail. Aikens went on to claim that Egan had "juggled" the testimony of witnesses and instead of sticking to the record, the zealous special prosecutor "played on the prejudices of the jury and got them in such a state of mind that they could not a fair verdict render." As the close of day drew near, it was clear that Aikens was still not approaching the conclusion of his argument. The court went into an evening session, amid speculation that the decision by the judge would not be known for several days.[37] Of course, no one knew how much longer Aikens would speak.

The essence of the defendant's case, as revealed by the lead counsel, came down to four points: (1) insufficient evidence to sustain the verdict, (2) misconduct by the jurors, (3) errors of the court on evidentiary rulings, and (4) misconduct by the prosecution, meaning George Egan. In fact, Egan's trial conduct was at the very heart of the defendant's motion. During his argument, Aikens constantly needled, attacked, and abused Egan. Among the names he used to flay his opponent was "pettifogger," meaning that Egan had engaged in vile, professional misconduct. It was, and still is, one of the most insulting names anyone could call a lawyer.

Aikens attacked some of the newspaper coverage and was especially sarcastic toward the *Sioux Falls Daily Press*. He boldly declared that some of the demonstrations that took place during the trial were "worked up and brought about by the *Press* dispatches." He charged that a *Press* correspondent was in league with the prosecution and a "henchman of Egan" and that "together they sought to create in Flandreau an atmosphere detrimental to the interests of his client," so as to make it impossible for her to get a fair trial. He claimed that the people in Flandreau were "hypnotized by counsel with the assistance of his lick-spittal [*Press* reporter] Harger."

Fully caught up in the heat of the moment, Aikens poured on the vitriol. He admitted that Egan was a good orator but that he "appealed to prejudice." He asserted that Egan had "lost sight of everything but himself." He was an advocate who "prodded and goaded witnesses and then looked around for applause." Finally, something interesting was happening in the courtroom—time for the court watchers to perk up.

Aikens pointed out that when Egan called the Kaufmann residence a "palatial home," he made the remark to incite "class prejudice" because of the wealth of the Kaufmanns. Aikens also played the "J" card, claiming that because his client was a Jew, she faced automatic, institutional prejudice. It is a known fact, he lectured, that the citizens of the United States "do have a strong race prejudice against the Jews." While this was most certainly true, there was no overt or covert attempt by the prosecution to inflame the jury with anti-Semitism during the trial.

The ex-judge attacked the prosecution witnesses with vigor and indignation, especially the medical experts. "He charged Dr. Sweeney with opening a post-graduate school at Flandreau to educate Dr. Schofield and Dr. Billion." This was a reference to the collaboration and examination at the St. Vincent Hotel when "the brain of the girl was carved to bits and then put together with toothpicks."

They were charlatans, one and all. But as expected, he saved his most pernicious poison for Peter Erickson, who had what he called a "depraved" mind. Erickson had no credibility and was simply an "accomplice of the state," an outrageous charge that implied that the prosecution was involved in criminal activity. In Aikens' mind, the authorities had arrested the wrong person. The evidence of a crime, if any at all existed against the person of Agnes Polreis, pointed more toward Peter Erickson than Emma Kaufmann.

Wielding his verbal sword in a cut and slash manner, he splattered blood all over his guilty adversaries, including those in the press. But in delivering such a damning argument at the motion for a new trial, he was in effect arguing the case all over again, albeit this time to a judge, not a jury. While it was unlikely that Judge Smith would become incensed, Aikens was making the same kind of vainglorious mistakes he had just laid at the feet of Egan.

Sometime during the night session, Aikens' long oral dissertation came to an end, at which time Egan requested, and was granted, time to respond. He had a great deal of work to do in order to repair the damage leveled by Aikens' attacks. For his part, Egan appeared more subdued than Aikens. And yet in a mere twenty-five minutes, Egan got in some good jabs at his opponent. He said he was forced to confess that he here noticed a great change in the attitude and behavior of Aikens, having turned very aggressive after "weeping" in the manner of a "supplicant" at the trial. Now the great lawyer was castigating the government, the witnesses, the press, and "everyone who had the backbone to be of an opinion different to that of the defendant's counsel, and not afraid to express it." As for the accusation of being a pettifogger, Egan told all those present that Aikens never mentioned it at the trial, so why now?[38]

He defended the state's witnesses, especially Dr. Arthur Sweeney from St. Paul, noting that only during this hearing did Aikens dare attack "one of the brightest minds in the west." Far from being unethical, Dr. Sweeney was "one whose shoe laces this counsel for the defense was unworthy to loosen."[39] And yet, during the trial at Flandreau, "he [Aikens] did not have the courage to cross-examine the doctor." Egan accused his opponent of cowardly conduct for having chosen the new trial hearing as a forum to condemn and insult a man who was absent and therefore unable to defend himself.

Egan defended Sweeney and his own conduct at the trial, conduct that Aikens had just so severely censured. He claimed that "he had sought always in the trial to present the case of the government with fairness." He insisted that he did nothing to inflame the jury nor could anything be construed from his closing that would have done so. Egan implored the judge to take his side of the case, for at no time did he suggest to the jury that a decision in the case should be made for anything but actual evidence. There was no need for a new trial, he asserted, because the record reflected no substantial error that would warrant a reversal.[40]

In contrast to the relatively even-handed reporting by the *Yankton Press and Dakotan*, *Argus-Leader*, and the *Daily Press*, one of the weeklies, the *Sioux Falls Journal*, offered an extremely biased account of the hearing. Mark Scott of the *Journal* hated Egan and that hate was poured out in gallons on the page that featured the short article. He called Egan's address an empty diatribe from "a man from Iowa," who is convinced that he is "the greatest man that lived." In contrast, Scott praised the efforts of Aikens, who roasted his opponent, "getting through the hide of Egan," who could do nothing but "cringe and sneer." Scott believed that Aikens and Rice had shown sufficient grounds for a new trial, but he refused to predict the outcome, for it was impossible to read Judge Smith, "a sphinx on the bench."[41]

On October 20, 1907, the *Sioux Falls Daily Press* announced that Judge Smith's decision would be known on the 21st. The judge himself had confirmed, by telephone from Yankton, this important news to a *Press* representative. The public was on edge. A reporter for the *Press* said that telephone calls from all over the state were coming in with questions about the much-anticipated court decision. Once again, interest in the "famous" Kaufmann case was peaking.

Sioux Falls was still enthralled with the great mystery. Still, a weight pressed down on the brow of the people, the curse had yet to be exorcised. Adding to the gothic atmosphere that pervaded the city, a woman dressed in black was seen approaching the Kaufmann house one evening not long after the new trial hearing closed. The woman knelt down in prayer in front of the house and spoke in German. It was Theresa the mother of Agnes Polreis. She and her husband were still in the city, staying with a German family on the east side, waiting like everyone else for the judge's decision.

Like an animal suffering from a wound that would not heal, Mrs. Polreis had wandered off one night and made her way to the Kaufmann house. She made no attempt to enter the house nor did she knock on the door. A nearby resident called the police, and Chief of Police Wade asked the fire chief, who spoke German, to accompany him to the Kaufmann house and "dissuade" Mrs. Polreis "from making a scene." When they arrived at 7th and Summit, the woman was gone. Her strange behavior in Sioux Falls mirrored the bizarre activities in Parkston, where it was said she was so grief-stricken over the loss of her daughter that she would steal away to the cemetery at night "and sit and pray for hours on the grave of her daughter."[42]

On October 21, as promised, the decision of Judge Smith was announced in Sioux Falls, South Dakota, and then in waves, radiated out across America. "**NEW TRIAL DENIED**" was the headline from the Yankton paper. In the next instant came the notice of appeal to the South Dakota Supreme Court, which because of the appellate process, denied the pronouncement of a sentence. The attorneys for Emma Kaufmann had been expecting a denial and had their appeal papers at the ready. While the case would be moving to the state capital in Pierre, meaning another lengthy delay, interest in the case approached fever pitch, as evidenced by the numerous telephone calls coming in to the office of the *Yankton Press and Dakotan*. Questions without end, it seemed, flowed into the besieged office of the Yankton newspaper, but the overriding moral question remained unanswered: Would the law ever "mete out justice for the death of poor Agnes Polreis?"[43]

Chapter 12

A Trail of Calamities

Man's inhumanity to man has been exemplified many times since the Kaufmann case has been before the public.

The Sioux Falls Journal
October 25, 1907

The cogent message reminding people to be kind to one another came from an unlikely source: an editorial in the *Sioux Falls Journal,* a publication that ordinarily assumed a hard-handed position when it came to matters of compassion. And no, it was not a plea for justice for Agnes Polreis; rather, it was a hand-wringing lament over the sad fortune of Moses Kaufmann. His friends were deserting him, one by one.

"Men who posed as warm friends of poor old Mose[s] Kaufmann in the hey-day of his business success" had forgotten the good times and their affable friend, the former brewer. He had done nothing to dishonor or discredit himself; he had merely tried desperately to support his wife and keep his family together. And yet this hapless, good citizen, fully "entitled to the plaudits of every loving household," had become the "object of scorn and ridicule from many who used to pose as his friend." With his erstwhile friends abandoning him in his time of need, the *Journal* wondered where was the support? What happened to ordinary loyalty? The *Journal* reminded its readers that when it came right down to it, each person had very few friends he or she could depend on in a crisis.[1]

As expected, the *Soo Critic* was prepared to counter the charitable piece on Moses Kaufmann with suitable invective. The *Critic* responded with a generous measure of contempt and scorn for Moses, a rich man whom John Ross deemed unworthy of even a particle of sympathy. Fired up over the motion for a new trial, Ross raised some new accusations against the wealthy former brewer. He accused Kaufmann, and his son, Charles, as well, of allowing "torture" to occur "in that house," meaning they did nothing while Emma mistreated Agnes Polreis. Ross believed they could have stepped in and stopped it, but they did not and for this blatant failure, they needed to be held accountable.

Ross brought up other shocking incidents that allegedly occurred "in that house" on the corner of 7th Street and Summit Avenue, in a neighborhood where the upper crust resided. "When Moses Kaufmann," Ross thundered, "paid $500.00 to preserve silence on the part of the girl with the broken jaw, he should have guarded his wife." Going on with his list of accusations, Ross roared, "When the little niece, there on a visit, was put in the kitchen to work and struck vicious blows with a large wooden mixing [spoon], he should have guarded his wife." And for good measure, he had one more example of evil left unchecked. "When a sick girl was driven out of bed at the point of a revolver, he should have guarded his wife."

Although he avoided naming names, the point Ross was trying to make was that a steady stream of questionable behavior occurred under his roof, and yet Moses Kaufmann did nothing. As a result, matters got worse until Agnes became the saddest victim of all. Out of love for his wife, he turned a blind eye to Emma's habitual wickedness and acts of cruelty. No, there was no need to pity Kaufmann, for it was his lack of willpower and good judgment that led directly to the death of the servant girl. Ross declared that Moses Kaufmann and others in the household were guilty of criminal negligence.[2]

For Moses Kaufmann, the good life seemed to be over. In addition to friends turning their backs on him, friends were dying. One man in particular, Kaufmann's former business partner at the brewery, Moriz Levinger, just fifty-five years old, died November 16, 1907, on an operating table in a Chicago hospital, having gone there for treatment of stomach cancer.[3] Levinger's passing cast a pall over the city he loved, silencing a voice that might have spoken about what had occurred in the Kaufmann house.

It was the autumn of the year 1907, and it would be some months before the South Dakota Supreme Court would hear arguments by counsel and rule on the motion for a new trial for Emma Kaufmann. In the interim, Ross, his newspaper allies and enemies, and George Egan found themselves mired in another tussle, this one over Julia Ann O'Grady. It was believed that Mrs. O'Grady did not simply choose Egan to represent her, but rather "several persons had been very strennous [sic] in their endeavors to get Mr. Egan into the case."[4]

It was shaping up to be a fine mess that defense attorney Frank Aikens managed to avoid. But many of his colleagues were in it full tilt, with Egan as their target. In the minds of his supporters, Egan was on the hit list because members of the Minnehaha County Bar Association were jealous of his success in the Kaufmann case and wanted the egotistical, long-haired Iowa lawyer to leave town and never come back. Egan, however, was in the process of purchasing a residence in Sioux Falls and had no intention of leaving.

On October 21, 1907, County Judge Dana R. Bailey opened the competency hearing on Egan's client, Julia Ann O'Grady, the woman charged with the murder of her husband. His task was to determine whether she was competent to handle her affairs or whether a court-appointed guardian was needed. Egan's task was to convince the judge that she was competent, and further, that her selection of Egan as her attorney was a rational decision.

Medical experts on both sides testified that she was either mad or sane. But when O'Grady was put on the witness stand, she gave a rambling account of the events leading up to her arrest and the competency hearing. She said she was about to be hanged and the gallows were just then under construction. While she admitted that she had turned over much of her property to Egan, as compensation for his representation, she still had enough to live on. But when pressed, she said, "she did not have a cent."[5]

Judge Bailey decided that she needed a guardian, and at the next hearing he announced the appointment of W. L. Baker to that position. He ruled that "Mrs. O'Grady was absolutely incompetent." In his written order, Bailey was critical of Egan, condemning the fee arrangement with the widow of John O'Grady. Bailey concluded that "the actions of Egan are so far removed from the ordinary course pursued between attorney and client." He ruled that Mrs. O'Grady's state of mind was worse than insane, for insanity could be cured. The judge believed that she was in a class of "incurable incompetents" and should be deemed a ward of the state.[6]

It was not a good day for George Egan. He had recently applied for admission to practice law in South Dakota and a hearing in the supreme court, on that application, came on the heels of the O'Grady guardianship proceeding. In Pierre, Egan was attacked on three fronts: for "butting in" on the O'Grady case; for "moral turpitude, immorality, contempt of court and unprofessional action in court"; and for "unprofessional conduct in the Kaufmann case," as cited by George Rice and Fred Warren, Flandreau lawyers. The charges were filed to prevent Egan from practicing law in South Dakota.[7]

The complaint from his adversaries in the Kaufmann trial, Rice and Warren, consisted of a charge that Egan had published and sold copies of his closing argument in that case. This brazen act was an example of "unprofessional conduct" and was "put out in a manner of advertising it and himself."[8]

The supreme court, after considering the affidavits and arguments of counsel, granted a conditional right to practice subject to disbarment, should the circuit court find that Egan had defrauded Julia Ann O'Grady during the course of arranging for his representation of her for the murder of her husband. And it was learned that the committee from the bar association, in the name of W. L. Baker, as guardian of Julia Ann O'Grady, was preparing to file an action in the Minnehaha County circuit court against Egan.[9]

The brief reprieve allowed Egan, assisted by D. J. Conway, to represent his friend, John Ross, in the trial of the criminal libel lawsuit brought against him by Joe Kirby on December 18, 1906. The case resulted from Ross' accusatory article about Kirby's performance in the Kaufmann case. Although it was considered a minor case, the courtroom was crowded with the curious because of the towering personalities, the promise of a good fight, and of course, because of its ties to the Kaufmann case. The crowd was not disappointed. Although State's Attorney Alpha Orr was present in court, Kirby was fully in charge of his case, acting as the prosecutor and questioning witnesses. Both Egan and Kirby made strong appeals during their closing arguments. After an all-night session, the verdict came down in favor of Ross—the jury decided that he had not libeled Kirby and so was acquitted.[10] Ross was free to continue as the underdog's advocate and keep his vitriolic pen aimed at the rich.

As for Egan, the troubles continued to pile up. The circuit court, with Judge Joseph W. Jones presiding, heard arguments on the O'Grady guardianship. When it was over, the prior decision of Judge Bailey in county court was upheld, and "George W. Egan, of Iowa, had something handed to him."[11] The holiday season was anything but happy for Egan.

"Judge Jones saw Judge Bailey and went him one better," reported the *Argus-Leader*. And to make Egan's holiday even worse, Jones hinted that "the matter will be made the basis of a further action before the Supreme Court against Mr. Egan." It was a complete rebuke of Egan, one that might have shattered and humbled other men. But the proud lawyer from Iowa was too full of himself to slink away like a whipped cur.[12]

The *Soo Critic* tried to put a positive spin on the calamity. As usual, Ross tied the action against Egan, and the judge's decision, to the Kaufmann case. He insisted that the attorneys who fought against Egan did so out of jealously because of his success in getting the conviction of Emma Kaufmann. Ross went on to write, "Mose Kaufman [sic] has been trying to get some of Mrs. O'Grady's bondsmen to go off the bond." The fiery editor, always quick with a snide remark, noted that "there are a few people who believe this whole city, county and state should be run in Mose Kaufman's [sic] interest to clear his wife, but about 99 3/4 per cent don't."[13]

~

Julia O'Grady was free of Egan, but the murder charge still hung over her head. The O'Grady murder case, unlike the Kaufmann case, however, was destined to have a short life. In open court on January 14, 1908, State's Attorney Orr made a motion that all charges against her be dismissed based on lack of evidence. Judge Jones granted the motion.

After the case was dismissed, a Sisseton, South Dakota, newspaper revealed information that had not "heretofore been printed in any newspaper." On the night John O'Grady was killed, Julia Ann returned to the house with a man and a woman, nearby neighbors. "A lighted lamp standing on a table revealed the body of the old man on the floor." The neighbors did not enter the house, but Julia Ann rushed inside, raised the head of her dead husband, placed her cheek next to his, and begged him to speak to her. The author of the newspaper article believed this kind of behavior was evidence of innocence, for a woman guilty of the "wanton murder of her husband . . . would have shrank from the body" in horror.[14]

Headstone for John and Julia O'Grady at St. Michael's Cemetery, Sioux Falls, South Dakota. *Author's photograph.*

Julia Ann O'Grady may have killed her husband, but the prosecution was not prepared to put on a case. She was free and the matter of guilt or innocence would never be established. She was also free of the burdensome attorney-client agreement with Egan, as he agreed to deed her property back to her.[15] Of course, he had no choice in the matter, as there would now be no need for his services. Furthermore, all her financial and personal affairs were subject to the guardianship of W. L. Baker.

Egan hated to let go of anything. He complained that the O'Grady competency hearing had been "a farce from the beginning." He blamed a bitter and vindictive Moses Kaufmann for using his influence to get the hearing process started. Kaufmann, he said, had tried to get O'Grady's bondsmen to withdraw so she would be put back in jail. And if that had happened, she would lose her confidence in Egan. This astonishing revelation came from an interview published in the *Critic*.[16] Egan, however, was forced to quit his rant, for he and his wife were summoned to Modale, Iowa, due to the unexpected death of his father.[17]

Meanwhile, the Parkston committee—with the assistance of John and Maggie Ross—was seeking funds to fight against the appeal for a new Kaufmann trial. The general consensus was that the authorities of Minnehaha County were too sensitive to the Kaufmanns' political influence and therefore could not be counted on to act independently. Money, Ross said, "silences many good men" and "makes cowards" of others. And since it was thought that the Minnehaha County state's attorney, Alpha Orr, was no match for Frank Aikens, more firepower was needed. This required money, and Ross made a passionate appeal to the public on behalf of the poor immigrant girl who had suffered, died, and whose wounded ghost cried out to "every fireside for justice."[18]

The restless soul of Agnes Polreis needed her champion, but it would not be in the person of George Egan. With the hounds of misfortune nipping at his boot heels, disappointment continued to follow Egan. The anti-Egan *Journal* gleefully reported that while the Parkston people once considered him a "little tin god [they] have concluded that he is shortwinded [sic]" and have "dropped him entirely."[19] It wasn't quite that bad, but after a disagreement over fees and Egan's lax attitude toward the upcoming hearing, the Parkston people decided they no longer needed his legal services. They hired two new lawyers to work the Kaufmann case: Thomas H. Null from Huron and J. E. Whiting, from Woonsocket, South Dakota. They would "make arguments before the state supreme court in opposition to granting a new trial."[20]

It was Maggie Ross who spoke to the Parkston men and persuaded them that a more "close thinking lawyer" was needed. She presented the names of Null and Whiting to the Parkston committee, after which she delivered the bad news to Egan, the "world-renowned lecturer and statesman." A "little bird" informed the *Argus-Leader* that "a warm time resulted in which Mrs. Ross was quite able to keep up her end."[21] The once friendly relationship between John and Maggie Ross and Egan was fraying at the edges.

But Egan had other irons in the fire. He was a candidate for the Minnehaha County state's attorney, running as an insurgent Republican in the June primary election. He vowed that, as a candidate, he would "stand for a fearless and candid enforcement of the law" and for "rich and poor alike."[22] To the growing number of people who disliked the Iowa lawyer, this latest somersault by Egan was head-shaking, irrefutable evidence of ego and gall. How could anyone, conditionally allowed to practice law, and facing possible disbarment over the handling of the O'Grady case, be considered a serious candidate for any political office?

H. C. Sessions, the editor of the *South Dakota State Forum*, certainly didn't think so. Sessions was staunchly Republican and of the stalwart variety. He called Egan a "windbag" who had no chance at winning in the primary election, predicting that "Mr. Egan will be about the smallest potato in the insurgent row on June 9."[23]

As time for the hearing in the supreme court drew near, Ross decided to give his readers a civics lesson and, at the same time, remind them of all the sordid details of the Kaufmann case. He liked to cite examples of swift and certain justice in other states and compare them to the timid, weak-kneed pace of the Minnehaha County criminal procedure. Chester Gillette, he wrote, was recently electrocuted in New York "for the murder of his sweetheart." He killed her quickly so there was no suffering, and though evidence against him was circumstantial, Gillette was kept locked up until he was convicted and executed. Bang, bang, bang.

"Out here in South Dakota," he bemoaned, "a poor girl, unable to speak our language or perfectly understand her mistress, was tortured by her for many weeks in the most inhuman manner." The husband of the mistress knew what was going on in the house and did nothing. The family doctor tried to cover up the killing, and they had yet to spend a day behind bars. Getting himself worked up as only Ross could do, he reminded everyone that there had been twelve or more murders committed in Minnehaha County over the past fifteen years, and yet only one penniless old man sits in the penitentiary, serving a life sentence.

Ross warned his loyal readers to beware of "strong social and political influences" that had been used to prevent a conviction of Emma Kaufmann. He hinted that Moses Kaufmann had the political clout to influence the outcome of the case, for in his hey-day no man had greater access to powerful people than the popular brewer. As an example of this power, Ross said that when the governor was about to make appointments, he always counted on the counsel of Moses Kaufmann, a "practical autocrat."

The wily editor called upon all fair-minded citizens to fight against the knot of powerful men who would subvert justice, for neither wealth nor political cronyism "should have any place of influence" in the prosecution of criminals, high or low. Repeating what he stated in past editorials, he warned that further delay "means the possible death or removal of . . . important witnesses." The ordinary citizens of Minnehaha County were saddled with the responsibility to make sure that "inhuman torture, that fiendish cruelty, that diabolical crime," shall not go unpunished. Ross asked with passion, "Will the people slumber?"[24]

Should there be a new trial, Ross wanted another conviction in the worst way, and as the day of reckoning approached, he came out with another inflammatory article. Using another recent murder conviction—this one in Minnehaha County—as an example, he once again complained that the rich could count on a better outcome because of the power of money.

The murder case in point was that of John J. Steltz, a poor laborer, who confessed to killing Theodore Sothman, "who lived in a little cabin near the slaughter houses east of the city." Ross reminded his readers that when Sothman's headless body was found—the result of a shotgun blast—Chairman Thomas McKinnon of the Minnehaha County Commission promptly hired detectives to track down Steltz and get a confession. Steltz received a ninety-nine-year sentence and was sent "up on the hill" to spend the rest of his life in the state penitentiary, located in Sioux Falls. Bang, bang, bang.

After applauding McKinnon for doing his whole duty in the Steltz case, Ross asked, rhetorically, why did he not show the same enthusiasm in the Kaufmann case? Ross had the answer. The perpetrator in the Steltz case was a poor man and as such, he was an easy target for law enforcement, while Emma Kaufmann was married to a "rich brewer," whose political power and social standing were credentials that shielded him and his wife from vigorous prosecution. "No fair minded man" could look at the two cases and "have any other opinion than that the money and social and political influence of Mr. Mose Kaufman [sic] are factors in this case."[25]

~

The *Soo Critic* was opposed to all Republicans, even those who were not rich. The *Yankton Press and Dakotan*, on the other hand, was opposed to stalwart Republicans, for it supported the insurgents. Changing times caused the party to divide into two factions, insurgent and stalwart, progressive and conservative, at each other's throats, one side trying to throttle the life out of the other. Since Moses Kaufmann stood with the stalwarts, he was fair game for the *Press and Dakotan*. He was criticized for his friendship with Senator Alfred B. Kittredge, known as the "silent senator" because of his taciturn personality. The quiet, cerebral senator, it was claimed, shielded his friend from an investigation into the activities of a group of "land grabbers" of which Kaufmann was alleged to be the leader.[26]

Politics touched every aspect of life, including murder trials. If the insurgents could use the friendship between Kittredge and Kaufmann to cast both in a bad light, they eagerly did so. Kaufmann's reputation had suffered as a result of his wife's long and painful odyssey through the court system, and the Yankton newspaper was anxious to take advantage of that sad fact in order to weaken Kittredge, who was facing stiff competition in his bid for re-election to the U.S. Senate.

In the minds of the stalwarts, Kittredge was the only choice for South Dakota.[27] In the minds of the insurgents, Kittredge's loyalty to Kaufmann meant that both men were passengers on a sinking ship of fools. But Kittredge believed in the sanctity of friendship and would never desert Kaufmann. Instead, "when a friend became involved in trouble, Mr. Kittredge stuck to him the closer." Come what may, Moses Kaufmann could always count on his good friend, the senator, for support.[28]

The early vote count of the primary election of June 1908 did not bode well for Kittredge. The headline in the *Sioux Falls Journal* sounded off in a blast of defeat: "**KITTREDGE A GONER**." Although returns were incomplete, indications were that the divided Republican Party split the primary vote. The upstart insurgent tide hit the stalwarts hard, meaning both sides had elected nominees for the local, county, and state offices. In the U.S. Senate contest, it was reported that the insurgent candidate, Governor Coe I. Crawford, had a statewide majority "ranging anywhere from 800 to 3000."[29]

The only thing that really mattered was the vote total, and when the counting was done, Crawford had 35,151 votes and Kittredge had 33,086.[30] Crawford the insurgent would run against whomever the Democrats, and possibly other parties, put up to challenge him. In a stunning turn of events, the unbeatable Kittredge was beaten. The silent senator's political career was over and his calamitous defeat had "the Kaufmann case" written all over it.

Kittredge's sympathetic biographer, O. W. Coursey, did not aver that Moses Kaufmann or the Kaufmann case contributed to the senator's defeat. But the *Argus-Leader* made it clear that Kittredge was a casualty of the Kaufmann case. He lost votes in Hutchinson County on the claim that his wife had signed the bond for Emma Kaufmann, and a significant number of voters in Minnehaha County went against him because they believed he had actually acted as an attorney for Kaufmann. Both claims were false: Kittredge had no wife and did not act as Kaufmann's attorney. Nevertheless, a senator, known and respected throughout America, would not be returning to the U.S. Senate.

To heap additional pain and suffering on the conservative Republicans, Egan emerged as the nominee for Minnehaha state's attorney, having handily defeated his stalwart opponent. This double-barreled blow left the *Argus-Leader* editor, Charles Day, in a funk, and he sadly declared that "Sioux Falls has suffered severely in reputation" because of the Kaufmann case and the ill will it engendered, and that "it will take years to recover from the damage which has been done."[31]

Sessions, editor of the *South Dakota State Forum,* took the Kittredge defeat very hard but seemed to dismiss the Egan win with a shrug. When he published a list of all the Republican candidates for office at the November election, Egan was listed as the candidate for state's attorney. Apparently, a "windbag" Republican was better than a Democrat.[32]

The hearing in Pierre on the motion for a new trial did not come up in spring, as expected, but rather opened in mid-summer of 1908. It was a long, drawn-out affair, with Frank Aikens on the offensive, taking up much of the time, as though he wanted to suck as much air out of the courtroom as to leave little or no breathing room for the prosecution. The Sioux Falls newspapers offered little coverage of the proceedings in Pierre, almost as if they were suffering from Kaufmann fatigue. Ross, however, would never tire of the case, and he published a somewhat disjointed article under a banner headline: "**KAUFMANN HEARING HELD AT PIERRE**." He pounced on Aikens, who "pours our bitterness against Egan" in four days of "argument and vituperation." Aikens roasted Egan for "posing during the trial," acting as a "manager" rather than a lawyer. But Ross dismissed Aikens' angry efforts as an attempt to "make mountains out of mole hills."

Ross made it clear that Aikens would lose his motion because the facts, as illuminated by the witnesses' testimony, strongly supported a conviction. No reasonable jury could have decided otherwise. Aikens, whose "ability as an attorney no man of judgment ought to question," had simply become unhinged following the defeat in Flandreau, and was now only venting his frustration in an undignified way.

"Private advice from Pierre" stated that Orr, Null, and Whiting had made "able and dignified" arguments before the supreme court, refuting the case citations put forth by the defense team. And yet a tentative-sounding Ross closed his article with a soft coda instead of his usual bold pronouncement. "Our informant believes the verdict of the lower court may be sustained."[33]

While the supreme court was deliberating over the appeal, Egan was cut down a few more notches by the circuit court in the O'Grady case. Judge Frank B. Smith of Mitchell, acting on behalf of Judge Jones, upheld the action filed by the guardian, W. L. Baker, and ruled that Egan had taken steps to strip the old lady of her property, thus violating his duty to protect her. The property transfer deed was canceled and Egan was ordered to repay her the $1,050 she had given to him as a fee. He had shamelessly taken advantage of "a person of unsound mind," unfit to "transact business."[34]

Because of this, Egan was disbarred by the South Dakota Supreme Court. A petition to disbar was filed by Sioux Falls attorney Park Davis, Dell Rapids attorney Henry Robertson, and soon-to-be ex-senator A. B. Kittredge on behalf of the Minnehaha County Bar Association.[35] Egan claimed the petitioners were motivated by professional and political jealousy, and he promised a hard fight. But after a hearing in Pierre, Egan was officially disbarred and disgraced, although his eligibility to serve as state's attorney, should he be elected, was an unsettled matter. He stayed on the ticket backed by his band of die-hard loyalists.[36]

While such a sharp rebuke might have humbled some men, for Egan it was like a shot of adrenalin. Far from slinking off to lick his wounds, Egan booked the New Theater in Sioux Falls and gave notice that on October 16 he would deliver a lecture entitled "My Fight For Liberty, or The Kaufmann Case and What It Did For Me." Ticket prices ranged from twenty-five to fifty cents. He took the stage at 8:15 P.M., and like a pied piper from days of old, he spoke to an overflow crowd that cheered and gasped as he castigated his enemies, including the "blackmailing sheets." He lashed out at a group of lawyers, including Senator Kittredge, who had huddled on Phillips Avenue and conspired to get him disbarred, and lastly, Supreme Court Chief Justice Dick Haney, who was offered "large sums of money" to render a decision against Egan.

Egan vowed that, try as his enemies may, he would not cower, he would not quit, and he would never leave town. No, he would stay and fight for himself and the good people who supported him. Then in a breathless crescendo, he declared, "I stand here tonight to defy every cowardly enemy and assure him that I can make my living and keep my home right here in Sioux Falls and I will do it, so help me God!" Hearing this, the crowd burst into wild, thunderous applause.

It was pure demagoguery and the audience of die-hard supporters ate it up, for if the newspaper-savvy Egan was good at anything, it was delivering red meat to a hungry crowd, many of whom stood in the aisles. More than a thousand had been turned away, disappointed after the tickets were all sold and therefore unable to hear Egan's prediction. "I want to tell you," he said, "that as surely as God reigns in Israel, Mrs. Kaufmann will be given a new trial by the supreme court."[37] It was a performance that only George W. Egan could pull off. It proved that he still could count on support from people who were hearing the voice of a demagogue but not recognizing it as such.

One person who thoroughly believed that Egan was a demagogue was the tough-minded Maggie Ross, co-publisher with her husband of the *Soo Critic*, who decided to do some lecturing of her own. She was prepared to attack Egan and call "a spade a spade." She would expose Egan as the ultimate "white sepulcher," a dangerous, holier-than-thou hypocrite, deserving of unconditional condemnation.[38]

Speaking to a small but attentive crowd at the New Theater, Ross took Egan apart, telling the audience about his legal troubles in Iowa with two young women and that he fled the state to avoid disbarment. She touched on the O'Grady case, quoting a third party who said that Julia Ann O'Grady would "have taken her clothes off" for Egan had he but asked.[39] But the greater part of her address was Egan's ties to the Kaufmann case. It was avarice on the part of Egan, she insisted, that caused the Parkston committee to sever its relationship with the flamboyant lawyer. Ross told the crowd that she had been asked by him to travel around and get as much money as possible and then place the amount on a table, after which Egan would decide if the money was enough to keep him on the case.

Ross told her listeners that Egan had spurned the $400 offered by the Parkston committee to handle the appeal. He also told the lady journalist that he would eventually retry the case under any circumstances. The supreme court, he insisted, was "fixed" and would certainly rule in favor of a new trial, and since he was certain that he would be elected state's attorney for Minnehaha County, he would prosecute Emma Kaufmann and get another conviction. Ross gave a calm, masterful presentation of the evidence against Egan, who never saw himself as dishonest but, rather, as a victim.[40]

Back and forth they went, blow for blow, town to town. The dueling orators made sure the public was not without some exciting entertainment. The tiny town of Scotland had its "Jack the Peeper,"[41] and the “big city” of Sioux Falls was struggling with the proliferation of saloons, including a number of unlicensed “blind pigs.”[42] But it seemed as if all eyes were on Maggie Ross and George Egan. They took up the lion’s share of time and space until the fall election—and its surprising results.

If Egan’s bullheaded, unrelenting blame-game wasn’t sufficiently insulting to his enemies, his election to the office of Minnehaha County state’s attorney delivered a gut punch to the haters. Egan not only won the office, he polled more votes than any other winning candidate for county office. He buried his Democratic opponent by a majority of about 2,500 votes. To all appearances, he had turned calamity into victory. The win raised his spirits and sparked his determination. Shortly following the election, he announced that he would begin publishing a weekly newspaper in the near future.[43]

But life for the ex-Iowan was one of extremes, and he quickly sank to a new low when, on November 19, 1908, the South Dakota Supreme Court published its decision on the motion for a new trial for Emma Kaufmann. In doing so, it slammed Egan with another powerful dose of condemnation. Although Egan had been widely and wildly criticized by his enemies in the bar association and the press, the past rebukes paled in comparison to the scathing criticism leveled at him by the high court.

The appeal was based on attorney misconduct, and the court ruled that Egan’s conduct throughout the trial “abounded in misstatements as to the law and evidence, and was replete with appeals to passion and prejudice.” It showed that Egan, as chief prosecutor on the case, had displayed ignorance or an intentional violation of the law as set forth by statute and in supreme court decisions. In short, Egan had engaged in so many acts of misconduct that he had no business acting as a prosecutor.

Chief Justice Dick Haney wrote the opinion and when he was finished, all the fat was flayed from Egan’s ego. Haney started with Egan’s opening statement to the jury, which he called “an appeal to passion” instead of a dispassionate explanation of the prosecution’s case. Egan was “summing up, making an argument,” something that every competent trial lawyer knows is not permitted when delivering an opening statement.

Next, the court examined Egan's interrogation of witnesses and noted that many questions were artfully worded so as to excite or prejudice the jury. In this vein, the court noted that Egan had alluded to the fact that Kaufmann did not testify on her behalf and that he had asked many questions and made statements "for the evident purpose of influencing the jury." In another particular instance, Egan had described the Kaufmann house as "palatial," when in fact, it was not. And even if it was palatial, it mattered not, for Haney stated that people who live in palaces have rights, too.

Haney took a shot at Egan over the "dramatic situations and scenes" during the trial that were "calculated to appeal to prejudice." As examples, Haney mentioned the prayer by Agnes' mother and Egan's remarks about "beer." Haney stated that the dramatic acts during the trial should have been prevented or denounced by Egan and suggested that he may have inspired them. All this amounted to "pettifoggery," conduct "unworthy of an officer of the law . . . charged with the duty of aiding in the administration of justice."

The chief justice reviewed Egan's closing argument which, on the whole, he exposed as a performance "abounding in misstatements of law and evidence." From "start to finish," Egan carried on like "an egotistical, ambitious actor" who "sought applause and personal renown regardless of the consequences to anyone accept himself." Egan's audacity was unlimited. He had argued to the jury that God had guided him to evidence that Emma Kaufmann had gone to Agnes' room at night and delivered the death blows to her head. There was no testimony to support that assertion, nor was there support for several others, making it easy for the court to arrive at its decision. Haney even took a poke at Judge Smith for being asleep during the trial and allowing Egan to carry on without limit. "It is the duty of the trial judge to see that no such improper statements are permitted to be made to the jury."

The defense had preserved fifty-nine separate exceptions from the record, which in and of itself was a testament to Egan's runaway misconduct. But the court found there was no need to review each and every one of them, for to do so would take up unnecessary time and resources. It was like saying there were not enough trees in the Black Hills National Forest of South Dakota to make the paper that would be required to thoroughly address each and every example of Egan's misguided and wrongheaded courtroom tactics.

In the end the supreme court granted a new trial. Haney wrote, "To sustain this conviction upon the record before us would mean the approval of methods of procedure inevitably subversive to the most sacred constitutional rights."[44]

For Frank Aikens, it was sweet vindication and a resounding victory over his insufferable, showboating opponent. He had lost at the trial because of Egan's misconduct, but in the end, Aikens had proven his superiority as a lawyer. Each time the judge overruled his objection, the shrewd Aikens was adding a nail to Egan's coffin while he painfully endured the insulting theatrics. Having emerged the winner, Aikens could read the decision, smile, and savor victory. His long experience as a trial lawyer, dating back to frontier days, had served him well, and in all likelihood, he was reminded of the old saying, "If you give a man enough rope, he will hang himself." Although not dangling at the end of a rope, the thoroughly discredited Egan was certainly in the process of tying the knot of his own noose.

CHAPTER 13

WITH NO END IN SIGHT

Just how long the famous Kaufmann case will continue to be used as an argument for everything, this newspaper does not know.

The Daily Argus-Leader
November 20, 1908

Charles M. Day expressed feelings of extreme frustration in his *Daily Argus-Leader* editorial about the granting of a new trial for Emma Kaufmann. He believed that his beloved city and county were lost in a "crazy belt." Many people were acting like lunatics because of their tireless fascination with the Kaufmann case. Its cast of characters had taken a legion of thrill-seekers on a wild ride, and the new trial meant there would probably be more thrills and chills—and more taxpayer money spent, about $12,000, according to Day—all because of the outrageous antics of George W. Egan. It was he who had "honeycombed" the case with reversible errors that any capable lawyer would have easily avoided, and in the process, could have secured a conviction that would have "stuck." But for Egan, the madness would have subsided.

Instead of closure, life in the "crazy belt" would continue, and that made Day sad. In addition to the pain of another trial, there was the irrepressible Egan, who had, at his back, "an admitted majority of the citizens of this county who . . . take cheap talk as a substitute for ability." And soon the people would be treated to a new newspaper, run by Egan, for the purpose of convincing the supreme court to change course and permit him to once again practice law. Day was advising everyone to prepare for more "swaggering ways."[1]

The swaggering Egan was consumed by narcissism, driven by the desire to make other people adore him. Public support was the pathway to political power, and Egan was committed to following that trail, for he yearned to be recognized and honored.

If Day was simply frustrated, John Ross was deeply hurt—not by Egan's antics, but by the decision of the state supreme court. The esteemed justices ignored his wishes and ordered a new trial, and the intense pain he felt was reflected in the *Critic* article of November 19, 1908. He acknowledged that Egan had made "many errors in the conduct of the case," and regretted that Sanford H. Cochran, a more experienced attorney, had not stepped in to try the case, "as we expected him to do." Still, he was dead certain that Emma Kaufmann was guilty—"fearfully" guilty of a brutal murder—and every clear-thinking man knew it. But here was the highest court in the state reversing the jury's honest verdict on "technicalities." It was simply another victory for wealth; it was something that Ross could neither understand nor accept.[2]

Ross and Egan had parted company but editor Ross was still devoted to assisting the Parkston committee in its determined effort to find justice for one of its own, for Agnes. But Ross and his Parkston friends were faced with a strange dilemma. They had refused to rehire Egan as special prosecutor; however, since he had just been elected Minnehaha County state's attorney, it would be his duty to prosecute Emma Kaufmann at the second trial. Alpha Orr's tenure would end on January 1, 1909. How strangely ironic. A disgraced and disbarred lawyer, "not learned in the law," was about to assume the mantle of county prosecutor, a position of public trust that required a high level of professional competence.

But further changes were in the works. Sioux Falls Attorney George J. Danforth filed suit seeking the removal of George Egan from the office of state's attorney. Danforth was Egan's rival in the primary election and had been soundly defeated. But he seized an opportunity to turn the tables on Egan, charging him with incompetence, lacking in the knowledge of the law required by the Constitution of the State of South Dakota. Disbarred, with his name stricken from the roll of attorneys, Egan was both unfit and ineligible. Danforth asked for an injunction to restrain Egan from taking the office to which he was elected and that the court "declare the office of state's attorney vacant" upon the expiration of Orr's term in office.[3] Danforth, of course, wanted the job.

With the backing of other attorneys, Danforth dealt Egan's ego another hard blow. Egan's hold on the job of state's attorney was being threatened, and he could not count on the support of John and Maggie Ross and their newspaper because of his high-handed tactics in dealing with the Parkston people, as well as his personal attacks against Mrs. Ross.

The once solid relationship between the parties had unraveled. As a result, a hapless John Ross left town and Maggie filed for a divorce. Maggie first explained that her husband left Sioux Falls because he lost interest in running a newspaper but later said he had suffered a nervous breakdown because of Egan's oppressive tactics. Finally, it was learned that John had traveled to Omaha to be with a woman named Laura Turner, with whom he had been corresponding. It was because of this correspondence that Turner was charged with sending obscene letters in the mail. But Miss Turner reportedly had proper motives. She wanted to support Mr. Ross until he became "learned in the law," at which time, he would support her.[4]

It all made for juicy gossip, but for Maggie, it meant that she had to pick up the pieces of her life and move on. Maggie Ross was as strong a woman as any who dwelled in Sioux Falls, and she vowed to continue the publication of the *Soo Critic* with the assistance of her son. Could she handle the stress and strain, along with the vicious personal attacks that came with running a newspaper? The public was anxious to know the answer.

The public was also eager to know whether Egan would succumb to the pressure of another lawsuit that reflected negatively on his character. The Danforth v. Egan case came up in circuit court in Sioux Falls with Judge Joseph W. Jones listening to arguments from both sides. Egan insisted that he was, indeed, "learned in the law" and therefore he met the state's constitutional requirements.

Danforth argued that since Egan had been disbarred, it mattered not that he was, or was not, "learned in the law," for he was disqualified from holding office due to the disbarment. A state's attorney was required to make court appearances on behalf of the county he represented, and Egan could not do so because he was disbarred from the practice of law.[5]

After several days of thinking it over, Judge Jones ruled on December 26, 1908, that Egan was unqualified to hold office *before* his election and that he remained disqualified "and ineligible to hold the office of states [sic] attorney." The expectation was that the county commissioners would appoint Danforth to the office. Egan vowed to appeal the decision to the state supreme court. Even though the Kaufmann case would move on without him, he was not about to give up.[6]

Instead, he announced that he would continue the fight against the opposition, including the *Argus-Leader*, through the columns of his own newspaper. Egan was to be both the publisher and editor-in-chief of this journalistic venture. The plan, according to Egan and his backers, was to put out an evening newspaper.[7] On the first day of the new year, his newspaper would be speaking for him in a series of attacks on his enemies, such as the Kaufmanns.

True to his word, Egan launched his newspaper, the *American Republic*, on January 1, 1909, announcing that the purpose of "this paper shall be, to publish the news and print the truth fearlessly, frankly and without restraint." But readers would not have to read more than one edition of this paper to know that Egan had found a lofty perch from which he could sling poison-pen arrows of ridicule and hate at his enemies. His inaugural offering was a front-page cartoon that featured Charles Day, Maggie Ross, Emma and Moses Kaufmann, Frank Aikens, and A. B. Kittredge smiling and holding hands in a circle while they danced to "Turkey in the Straw," played on a violin by "Fiddler Joe" Kirby. They were celebrating the disbarment of George Egan, something they had all worked hard to achieve.

It was the beginning of a long series of attacks and insults from the new "progressive Republican" newspaper "for all the people." The masthead proudly proclaimed that it was "owned and edited by George W. Egan." Although he was undoubtedly the primary writer, the editorial "we" and "us" appeared in his articles and edi-

Post-trial cartoon in the *American Republic*, January 1, 1909.

torials. The paper featured newsy notes from the rural areas and small towns of the county, where Egan was popular. It is clear from volume one, number one, that the secondary purpose of the paper was to create a constituency for Egan's political ambitions.[8]

In his debut editorial, Egan expressed strong feelings of gratitude to all those good, common people who had stood by him in his time of crisis. Then he played the victim: "No man who ever sought residence in South Dakota . . . was ever besought and attacked by such a pack of unscrupulous and yet . . . powerful enemies." The leader of that pack was none other than Moses Kaufmann, a man whose "money and influence have wrought such havoc" against those whose responsibility it was to prosecute his wife for the murder of her "poor, ignorant, unlearned and helpless servant girl, Agnes Polreis." Egan unabashedly claimed that he was the man who obtained the conviction of Emma Kaufmann. And for that reason, he became the principal target of a devious plot to destroy him, one that he compared to the conspiracy to murder the Roman Emperor Julius Caesar.[9] The brazen lawyer had taken a bold, melodramatic step forward on a worn battlefield, signaling that a new and terrible war among the presses and personalities was about to begin.

Egan, not one to shrink from a fight, was determined to use the Kaufmann case as a means of opening both old and new wounds.

Unlike most lawyers, who are trained to attempt to understand both sides of a case, Egan saw only his side. He was unable to proceed with a fair amount of prudence and deliberation. Because of his single-minded approach, he was sure to stoke the fires of anger. Revenge was a dish that Egan would never eat cold.

As the start of the second Kaufmann murder trial drew closer, it was learned that Judge E. G. Smith, from Yankton, who presided over the first trial, was being considered to fill a vacancy on the South Dakota Supreme Court. Knowing this, the Kaufmann attorneys heartily recommended that Smith be awarded that high honor, meaning they didn't want him retrying their client. Aikens and company wanted a new judge for the new trial.

The people in Parkston wanted money to pay the special prosecutors. The *Parkston Advance* took up the cause and made a fervent plea to the public, asking everyday people to chip in, hoping that sympathetic men and women would assist "in a small way towards helping to secure justice for the dead girl." Parkston residents felt they had given all they could and that the rest of the state should contribute to the "just cause." The *Advance* urged people throughout the state to "get up clubs in your vicinity" and send in the money raised "at once." Anonymous contributions were welcome and secrecy was guaranteed.[10]

Defense counsel would face a new state's attorney, for the Minnehaha County commissioners appointed George Danforth to fill that position. It was settled once and for all: George Egan would not be present when the second Kaufmann murder trial began on June 1, 1909, again in Flandreau.[11] What the trial would lack in showmanship it would more than make up in professionalism. Or as the *Argus-Leader* stated, the new trial would not be a "vaudeville entertainment."[12]

Egan seemed to accept that he would not be in charge of the case for the prosecution. Furthermore, he fully expected that the trial would be delayed until the fall, or that it might never be tried. He was certain that "everything is 'fixed'" and "we are as sure as anything that the defendant will never do a day" in prison. In a passionate editorial, he predicted that the celebrated Kaufmann case would "leave a dark and lasting blotch upon the fair name of Sioux Falls and South Dakota" because the woman all knowledgeable people believed was guilty will "go unpunished."[13]

Had Egan been in a different position, he might have concluded otherwise. But Danforth had the job of state's attorney, and there was no way he would associate with Egan. Instead, he chose Huron attorney Thomas H. Null to be his trial assistant in the second attempt to find justice for Agnes. In an interview for the *Sioux Falls Daily Press*, Danforth seemed enthusiastic about the trial, hinting that it would take longer to select a jury than it would to conduct the case in chief. The confident prosecutor told the reporter that the state would present the testimony of twenty-five or thirty witnesses. He and Null would be facing the law firms of Aikens and Judge from Sioux Falls and Rice and Benson from Flandreau.[14] The article in the *Press*, while rather straightforward, suggested that another long and bitter contest was in the offing. Eager court watchers were surely left licking their chops in anticipation.

The stage that had gone dark during the interlude since the first trial was now relit. Crime and punishment were always at the forefront of public attention, simply because there was so much of it. Audiences could never seem to get too much of the misfortune and suffering of others.

While people were eager for more Kaufmann excitement, Mary Farmer, a New York State woman convicted of murder, walked "unfalteringly to the death chair, clasping a crucifix in her hands." She died "after the first shock,"[15] and in that instant, a nation of addicted crime-watchers received another jolt of vicarious fulfillment. America's bizarre love/hate relationship with crime, which thrived in the previous century, continued to thrive in the twentieth.

In early May 1909 the South Dakota State Penitentiary was deemed "unfit" for women prisoners after it was investigated by a member of a woman's organization.[16] Nevertheless, Emma Kaufmann faced the distinct possibility of joining the four women incarcerated in the Sioux Falls facility, should she be convicted by another jury. She and her husband were counting heavily on Frank Aikens to make sure that she would not have to endure punishment in that dismal place, located just a short distance away from the comfort of the Kaufmann mansion. With pressure mounting as the trial date approached, the Kaufmanns were not in the mood for news about an "unfit" prison.

Nor were they open to some of the hateful criticism that surfaced in some South Dakota newspapers. Inspired by Egan's *Ameri-*

can Republic, the *Miller Gazette* called Emma Kaufmann "the villainous, astrocious [sic], cowardly, inhuman, dastardly murderess of Agnes Polreis." And then, taking a deep breath, the *Gazette* editor suggested that she should be taken "forcibly from her luxurious home" and hanged "from the nearest telephone pole."[17]

The *Gazette's* position was so extreme that no thoughtful man, not even Egan, would dignify or approve lynch-mob "justice." Egan did, however, weigh in on the persistent rumors that Aikens and his team would launch an insanity defense. In a surprisingly sober editorial, Egan laid out the hazards of an insanity defense. To begin with, an insanity defense "admits the offense," and should Emma Kaufmann make an insanity plea, and succeed, she would be placed in the state mental hospital for an indefinite period of time, an outcome that, for her, would be the same as being in prison. The door would also, then, be left open to charge at least two other people. Both Moses Kaufmann and Dr. Germain would be dragged into the case as accessories and for lying under oath in the first trial.

Egan was correct when he stated that "a plea of insanity is always dangerous . . . and is resorted to only as a last means of saving a defendant."[18] Although an insanity defense would revive interest in the case equal to that of the first trial, Aikens and his team were not desperate and would not profit by igniting a spectacle. An insanity plea would also set in motion a dramatic change of strategy by the prosecution, causing Danforth and his allies to find experts to testify that Kaufmann was not insane and that she knew the difference between right and wrong.

Finally, June 1 arrived and the second Kaufmann murder trial was underway in the old, boxy courthouse in Flandreau—on the third anniversary of the death of Agnes Polreis. The first order of business was a motion by the defense counsel to limit the charge against Kaufmann to manslaughter only, thereby eliminating the possibility of a murder conviction. They reasoned that since she had been earlier convicted of manslaughter only, the murder charge was made irrelevant by the jury. Judge William G. Rice, from the eighth circuit in Deadwood, took it under advisement. Then the jury selection from a large pool of potential jurors began. It was expected to take all week because both sides were focused on getting a favorable jury.

The Kaufmanns sat surrounded by a cluster of lawyers giving the appearance of strength and safety in numbers. The defendant and her husband had been in Flandreau for a week, boarding in the Mary Mead residence once again. Sitting quietly in the courtroom next to his wife, Moses Kaufmann's appearance bore stark evidence of the terrible strain he had been living under for the past three years. He was a victim of the case that "has left a line of calamities in its wake."[19]

Moreover, he was a victim of the love he felt for his wife; his support of her was absolute and unwavering. Whatever he may have felt in his heart of hearts about her guilt or innocence, it did not convince him to turn away from her. Observers could read into his demeanor all sorts of questions. Was he haunted by doubt or feelings of guilt by complicity or negligence? Was his wife really insane? Was she a murderer? Did he ever subject her to questioning? Did he even want to know the answers to these questions? Did he want to learn the truth?

Aikens had added the Flandreau firm of Jordan and Warren to his retinue, bringing the defense team to a total of six attorneys. On the state side, Alpha Orr and Moody County State's Attorney Ira F. Blewitt took their places at the counsel table, hoping to use their experience in the first trial to boost the prosecution. Danforth and Aikens would be the lead attorneys for their respective sides. Other than the persistent rumor that the defense counsel would enter "a plea of insanity," it looked as though the trial might actually be a quiet affair.[20]

On day two, juror questioning continued while at the same time witnesses, including Peter Erickson, trickled into town. Erickson, whose old "star" was about to assume its former luster, had been farming fourteen miles northwest of Wessington Springs. In December 1908 he had sent a letter to his "old friend" George Egan, inquiring about the new trial, hoping it wouldn't interfere with spring planting. He stated rather pointedly, "I see that the Kaufmann clique of friends are giving you a lot of trouble, but I honestly believe that you will get the best of the whole outfit." Erickson closed his letter by offering words of praise and encouragement for Egan's newspaper venture.[21]

Although Erickson would remain a key witness for the state, Maggie Ross advised her *Critic* readers that "the state has one very important witness, who could not be found two years ago." Like her soon-to-be ex-husband, Maggie was very coy about naming names, but she was apparently referring to the "man who took the blood spattered paper off the wall" of the room once occupied by Agnes Polreis, "the poor, defenseless little girl." Mrs. Ross said that she gave the name of the man to the prosecuting attorney, but the mystery witness disappeared before he could be interviewed.[22]

On day three, the relatively small and orderly crowd of court-watchers was joined by citizens from Parkston, a group that included the father of the late Agnes Polreis, her brother Paul Polreis, and other men who had so steadfastly supported the family of the unfortunate girl.[23] They arrived in time to endure the tedious grind of jury selection.

All interest and eyes were, of course, on the enigmatic Emma Kaufmann. The take away was that she showed "even more indifference than at the previous trial," although it was noted that she devoted strong attention to "the faces of the jurors as they answer questions."[24] A member of the jury pool provided a bit of excitement. Tom Whitters, an auctioneer and well-known citizen of Flandreau, made some remarks about being biased against the defendant. That riled Aikens, who wanted to get a restraining order against Whitters to keep him silent.[25]

But the matter passed and by the end of the first week twelve men were seated in the jury box. Whitters was not among them. The court adjourned until Monday at 1:30 P.M. after the judge overruled the defense motion that Kaufmann should be tried for manslaughter only. Siding with the prosecution, and raising the specter of the gallows, Judge Rice ruled that she would be tried for murder.[26]

The *Daily Argus-Leader* promised to print accurate reports of the proceedings, "devoid of any sensational stuff."[27] This was Charles Day's signal that he was clearly tired of the mess and just wanted it to end as quickly and cleanly as possible. Once again, he would report on the case with reluctance. The *Sioux Falls Daily Press*, on the other hand, gave every indication that it was eager to provide readers with a thorough, accurate, blow-by-blow coverage of the trial. If something sensational happened, then so much the better—the *Daily Press* was ready to pounce.

Among the weekly newspapers, Maggie Ross and the *Soo Critic* were ready to dive into the fray, although with much less passion and anger than her ex-husband had unleashed in covering the first trial. Maggie didn't want her paper to be identified with the "smut mill," nor did she wish to be consumed and destroyed by the Iowa monster who drove John Ross away.

Egan's the *American Republic* promised to produce a lively account of the proceedings, all the while taunting men like Day of the *Argus-Leader*. Further, he claimed to have it all figured out: there would be a hung jury or an acquittal, and Emma Kaufmann would never see the inside of the state penitentiary. The "fix" was in.

The outside press was ready to unleash as well. Among them the *Spokane Press* was taking a graphic, almost blood-curdling approach. Just as the first testimony was about to be heard, the Washington State newspaper came out with an article that screamed, "**STRANGE CASE OF WOMAN'S INHUMANITY TO WOMAN**, a horrible story of the torture of a servant by her mistress . . . [the] wife of a wealthy brewer." Agnes Polreis was "practically a slave in the Kaufmann household" where "Mrs. Kaufmann used to beat the girl with clubs." The net effect of such maltreatment of the poor girl, who had become "a skeleton," was that she was "killed by inches."[28]

Not all newspapers were interested in accuracy and fair play. But owing to the type of publicity generated by sensational murder trials, no one was surprised by articles that presumed the defendant's guilt. It was business as usual. It was pablum for the craving masses. Reporters anxious for recognition could rant and rave without restraint, but in the end, a Moody County jury would decide guilt or innocence. Nine farmers, a laborer, and the mayor of Flandreau were entrusted with the fate of Emma Kaufmann.[29]

Chapter 14

The Second Kaufmann Murder Trial

The defendant will never do a day for this most cruel and atrocious murder.

The American Republic
March 12, 1909

At exactly 1:30 in the afternoon of June 7, 1909, in dramatic fashion, Emma Kaufmann entered the Moody County courtroom with her husband and took a seat in the rocking chair reserved for her. No word was spoken as the stately woman made her appearance, her long black hair "dressed down her neck in a striking and becoming coiffure." As becoming a woman of wealth and status, she wore a "green silk waist and a green broad cloth skirt, both splendidly tailored." Her "jet black eyes gleamed brightly as she glanced quietly around the room." The woman looked and acted as if she were about to receive an award or give the performance of a lifetime.

The defendant made her entrance and fashion statement to what was described "as an almost empty court room," with about fifty people in attendance. A puzzled reporter for the *Sioux Falls Daily Press* wrote: "Nothing could have been less spectacular than the silence of an almost empty court room when Judge [William G.] Rice announced simply proceed with the trial gentlemen."

At that point George J. Danforth began his deliberate, step-by-step opening statement, laying out the state's case. Agnes Polreis was born in 1890 in Austria. She came to America in 1905 with her family, a healthy and strong girl sixteen years of age. She was hired to be the servant of Mrs. Kaufmann, in whose employ she died a terrible death. Danforth said that the state would produce witnesses who would testify to the mistreatment and maltreatment of Agnes by the defendant, the cumulative effect of which led to the cruel death of the unoffending immigrant girl. He explained to the jury that the prosecution believed, and would prove, that Emma Kaufmann murdered Agnes Polreis with "some dangerous and deadly weapons unknown to the state."[1]

The first witness was Arthur A. Snashall, the undertaker from the L. D. Miller firm, the man who delivered Agnes to the Sioux Falls Hospital as a patient on June 1, 1906, and then took charge of her body later that same day. He described the condition of the body he embalmed, noting in detail similar to his testimony at the first trial, that the corpse was a mass of cuts, wounds, bruises, and abrasions.

Sioux Falls in 1909. Note L. D. Miller Livery on the right.
Courtesy Center for Western Studies, Augustana University, Sioux Falls, South Dakota.

Snashall was a test case for Aikens. The wily attorney put this seemingly matter-of-fact witness through severe cross-examination, forcing the undertaker to plumb the depths of his memory, hoping to catch him giving an answer that contradicted his testimony of two years ago. Since memories fade over time, Snashall could not keep from frequently saying, "I don't know" or "I don't remember."

Aikens' cross-examination strayed into subject matter that could best be described as morbid:

> Q: How did you get rid of the body?
>
> A: I put a robe on it, prepared it for burial and shipped it to Parkston, via Mitchell, at 6:35 on Sunday morning over the Omaha line.
>
> Q: Did you find water in the bottom of the casket when you opened it at Parkston after it had been exhumed?
>
> A: I did.
>
> Q: How much?
>
> A: About six or eight inches.
>
> Q: This casket had holes in it so that the water could run out?
>
> A: Yes.
>
> Q: Was the casket lined with white satin?
>
> A: I don't remember.
>
> Q: Was there any water marks on the lining?
>
> A: I do not remember.[2]

While the relevance of these questions seems dubious, there were no objections by the state and Aikens was allowed to continue testing Snashall's capacity for remembering the ghastly details of his handling of the body. Experienced criminal lawyers know that if members of the jury become overwhelmed or confused by testimony, they might simply vote for an acquittal because they lack a clear understanding of the prosecution's case.

The next witness was the superintendent of nurses at the hospital, Jeannette Eitel, formerly Miss Larson. She described the horrible condition of the patient when the servant girl arrived at the hospital, including "three wounds on the right side of the head that were deep enough to expose the bone."[3] But when asked, she could not tell Danforth where Agnes came from. In other words, she was testifying that on June 1, 1906, she did not know that Agnes had been taken from the Kaufmann house to the hospital. She did, however, give one startling piece of testimony in answer to the question that was not asked at the first trial. Danforth asked who it was that told her that Agnes was the name of the patient. Her reply: "Dr. Germain."[4]

That reply was buried in small print in the *Argus-Leader*, but it was worth a headline in the *Daily Press*: "**WHO GAVE THE NAME AGNES?**" In the first trial it was brought out that when Dr. Germain executed a death certificate, he listed the name of the deceased as "Theresa Polreis." Why would he have done that if he knew that it was Agnes Polreis who died? If he knew it was Agnes that he sent to the hospital, he certainly knew it after she was dead. The seemingly innocuous question and surprising answer further eroded Germain's already badly damaged credibility. People could not help but wonder what he was thinking about when he wrote out the death certificate.

The next day Elizabeth Polreis, sister to the late Agnes Polreis, was one of the principal witnesses called by the state. After testifying that Agnes was strong and healthy when she left Parkston, she was cross-examined by Aikens. He handed her two letters written in German, purportedly by Agnes, explaining that, in Mrs. Kaufmann, the girl had found "a second mother." He asked, "Were these two exhibits written by your sister, Agnes Polreis?" With the courtroom deathly silent, Elizabeth read them page by page while Aikens stood in front of her "twirling his spectacles." Several minutes passed and then Elizabeth looked up at Aikens and spoke in a heavy accent. She recognized the first letter as one that Agnes had written to a friend in Austria; the handwriting was that of her sister. But as to the other she said, "No, I think not. They are words my sister never did." This was deemed to be "easily the feature of the second day of the trial," for the letters had not been produced at the first trial.

Dr. H. B. Schofield was next to give testimony under oath. He talked about being present at both exhumations and explained in detail the location, size, and type of wounds on the body of Agnes Polreis. In other words, he repeated much of what he said at the first trial. He also said the second postmortem revealed that her vital organs were normal. His explanation of the opening of the skull was explicit, almost gruesome. As to the cause of death, he stated that it was the blood clot on the brain caused by external violence. The head wounds, he said, were caused by "a semi-blunt or oval instruments, used violently," as were the shoulder wounds.[5]

At the outset of cross-examination by Aikens, Dr. Schofield persisted in his belief that the "cause of the blood clot upon the brain was, in my opinion, external violence." But when pressured, he said that by external violence he didn't necessarily mean a blow to the head "which caused her death." Under further questioning, Dr. Schofield admitted that he had never before seen such a blood clot and that he had consulted medical authorities to help him understand the nature of it.

Cross-examination led to the time that the medical experts for the state examined the brain of Agnes Polreis at the St. Vincent Hotel in Flandreau, two years previous. Dr. Schofield said that he had been subpoenaed by the defense to bring the brain to Flandreau and that after the dissection some parts of the brain were "taken from a cuspidore [sic] into which they had been dumped." Aikens asked, "Did the lawyers who were present at the examination . . . put their hands into the solution in which the brain was kept?" The answer was, "I do not know." Once again the testimony strayed into the macabre.

By asking questions about hemorrhages and blood clots and a patient's reaction to them, Aikens tried to move Schofield away from his testimony as to the cause of death. But the doctor answered, "I said that this blood clot was, indirectly, in my opinion the cause of the death of Agnes Polreis." Still the defense got something out of it, for when asked, the doctor said, "I have never known any patients who died from an injury to the brain who were conscious [as was Agnes] up to time of death." Based on his experience, he admitted that at no time had he ever known of a person who died of a blood clot to the brain "who did not show profound coma before death."

Sensing that he was on to something, Aikens asked, "If a patient died absolutely conscious, you would say that she did not die from the effects of the blood clot, would you not?" Dr. Schofield answered, "I do not remember of ever having heard of such a case." The Parkston doctor, the living example of a country doctor, was clearly in over his head. He was not an expert in brain injuries.

Aikens may have had the jury thinking that there was no blood clot after all, despite the insistence of the prosecution medical experts, including Dr. Schofield. For it was clear from the way the doctor stumbled through his explanation about how Agnes would have physically reacted to a blood clot on the brain that what he was saying in 1909 differed from his testimony in 1907. When Aikens pointed out the inconsistencies, the witness said he changed his mind after doing some reading on the subject.

Although Schofield did the best he could based on his limited experience, he took a beating. Still he got in a few good licks. Aikens pressed: "I believe you have testified that this body weighed only 85 or 95 pounds at the time you first saw it. If the girl weighed 135 pounds in February, 1906, might not have some wasting condition caused the depreciation in weight?" Schofield snapped back: "Starvation would do it."[6]

Aikens may have been satisfied with his cross-examination of Dr. Schofield, but A. M. Thornburg, a nurse, proved to be a surprisingly tough witness. On direct, she came out swinging, describing the wounds and bruises. But unlike Dr. Schofield, who was examining a corpse, Thornburg was talking about attending to a living—but dying—Agnes Polreis. "The girl," she said, "had no control over her muscles. She was perfectly helpless."

On cross-examination, her testimony inadvertently strayed into new grounds, revealing that there were "open sores on the girl's abdomen." When Aikens asked if she were certain, Miss Thornburg answered rather haughtily, "Well I did not know how to bandage her she was so sore all over." Hearing this, "a flutter ran over the court room," for it was clear that Aikens had heard something that he did not like and the spectators knew it. Aikens asked the judge to strike the response from the record and the judge agreed. But on re-direct she was allowed to describe the abdomen wounds and their location by pointing to her own abdomen.[7] It was a win for the prosecution.

But it was clear from the testimony of Dr. Thomas J. Billion that the state's medical experts were not holding up as strongly as they did in the first trial. Billion described the wounds and the overall condition of the body at the time of the second autopsy. He stated that the wounds on the head were the result of "external violence with some blunt instrument." But when he was asked if the wounds and blood clot caused the death of Polreis, he faltered somewhat, saying only that "they probably were."[8]

On cross-examination Aikens pressed for more details. Billion testified that the wounds might have been caused "by violence on the part of some other person." He went on to say, "I think it must have been a sharp instrument or something with a sharp edge which caused those [head] wounds." Based on his examination in June 1906, he concluded that "the three wounds on the side of the head and the blood clot on the brain, would probably cause death." Aikens wanted to hear Billion say that the wounds and blood clot "possibly" caused the death of Agnes, but the doctor would not utter the desired word. Yet his testimony showed some equivocation.[9]

Having shaken Billion somewhat, Aikens, a lawyer with a bulldog's tenacity, wasn't willing to quit. He kept probing and finally asked a rather odd hypothetical question: "Supposing you had held a post mortem upon a person, who, in life, had been stumbling about, and you knew nothing about that person and you found, after death, a blood clot upon the brain, would you conclude that the blood clot had caused the stumbling?" Billion's terse reply was, "Yes."

It was an answer that Aikens liked so much that he went on with the examination of the hostile witness. "Now doctor, when did you determine that that blood clot was caused by external violence?" Dr. Billion seemed to regain his confidence and said, "I was never fully satisfied until I made the examination of the brain at the St. Vincent Hotel" along with the other doctors. The reply was undoubtedly not what Aikens wanted to hear, but he kept on. After asking Billion about his fees for testifying, he inquired, "Now doctor, is it usual that sub-dural clots are caused by external violence and not by disease?" The witness replied, "I think it would be quite usual for the sub-dural clots to be caused by violence and not by disease."

That ended the cross-examination of Dr. Billion, who, after stumbling around, made a strong finish.[10]

The neighbor lady, Cordelia Udell, provided a colorful recitation of what she had witnessed at the Kaufmann house in the spring of 1906. Her testimony was consistent with the 1907 trial, but she admitted on cross-examination that she reviewed a transcript of her first stint on the witness chair. She said that Mrs. Kaufmann had called Agnes a "stupid girl," and that on one occasion she heard Agnes pleading, "Frau Kaufmann, Frau Kaufmann." She described seeing the unfortunate girl more dead than alive, struggling to carry a "slop-pail." Then there was the time that Agnes attempted to escape but was overtaken by her mistress, who walked her back to the big house "close behind her" but "without stepping on the girl's heels."

According to Udell, Agnes' condition was deteriorating right before her eyes. And while this was going on, Kaufmann frequently came to Udell's back door because of Agnes. Udell stated that on one such occasion Mrs. Kaufmann came to her because Agnes was very sick. Udell asked why a doctor was not called and the defendant said, "She wasn't sick enough for that." Finally, after the girl died, the defendant told Udell that death resulted from "malignant blood poison." It was an effective testimony that once again pointed out both mistreatment and maltreatment.[11]

More important, Cordelia Udell had new information to offer. She made a rather startling revelation about something that she had never discussed with George W. Egan. On the Sunday following the death of Agnes, Emma Kaufmann paid a visit to Udell. For two hours she talked about her fear of being arrested by the authorities, saying she was being "accused of killing the girl." She seemed very upset and confessed that if she had to relive the experience with Agnes she would not "have done what she did." It was not a confession of guilt, but it was an admission of a guilty conscience.

Udell testified that Mrs. Kaufmann even admitted that she had been with Agnes the entire night before the day that the girl died in the hospital. This admission allowed the state to point out that the defendant had the opportunity to harm Agnes. Indeed, for what other reason would she have spent the entire night with her, except to inflict more punishment and pain?

The next witness, Peter Erickson, added more titillating details. He testified that on the day before Agnes died at the hospital, he assisted Mrs. Kaufmann in bandaging the girl's wounds—but there were no wounds on the head. The following day, at the hospital, the nurses found "hair matted with blood and six cuts or wounds underneath." The inference the jury could draw from these facts was that Emma Kaufmann inflicted the head wounds with some blunt instrument during the night she spent alone with Agnes.[12]

Erickson also testified that on the morning of her death, he went to Agnes' room and observed that there were blood drops on the floor and on the walls—blood drops that were not there the day before.[13] Once again this implied that some violence had occurred the night before. He also testified on direct that Mrs. Kaufmann wanted Agnes' room cleaned out thoroughly because "she did not want to have anything around that would remind her of Agnes."[14]

Other damaging testimony from the "Big Norse" was his suggestion to Mrs. Kaufmann that Agnes be taken to the hospital. Instead of agreeing, she balked and complained that she would get stuck with the $12 fee. After Erickson suggested that the county might pay for it, Mrs. Kaufmann said, since she was rich, and people knew it, she would have to pay. Later, after it was learned that Agnes was dead, she was no longer so haughty, and Erickson watched as she paced back and forth in her house, wringing her hands and repeating, "What shall I do?" and "What shall become of me?"[15]

The general consensus was that Erickson, at twenty-seven years old, was still the "star witness," although he had to admit that his memory of key events had faded somewhat. Aikens even treated him with more respect on cross-examination. Throughout it all, Erickson provided testimony in a straightforward, unemotional manner and in no way attempted to embellish or cause any excitement. He spoke in a low, calm voice, "almost a monotone," and was very effective in revealing a firsthand account of the defendant's cruel treatment of her servant girl. His testimony did not "differ in any material detail from that given in the former trial." Nor did he weaken on cross-examination.[16]

Nevertheless, Aikens tried his best to discredit Erickson's testimony and was able to elicit numerous responses of "I don't remember." Where Erickson's answers were inconsistent with the preliminary hearing or the first trial, Aikens was sure to remind him of the inconsistency. But Erickson was frank in his admission that his memory had faded, saying, "How is a man going to remember things for three years?" What he did remember was that Emma Kaufmann used turpentine to "reduce a swelling on Agnes' body" and that he saw Agnes lying on the floor of her room when he was ordered to remove her bedding. And although he was no chemist, the spots in her bedroom looked like blood and varied in size from "a dime to a dollar." While the prosecution was never able to establish a timeline to show how Agnes' condition worsened, Erickson did state that he first noticed that she "had begun to fall away" on or about on March 1, 1906.[17]

George Bessler, another former brewery employee, now a Sioux Falls grocer, offered testimony that was consistent with what he said in the first trial. One of the lighter moments of the trial came when a lady from Parkston, Mrs. Bernhardt, took the stand to affirm that Agnes was plump and healthy when she left town to work for the Kaufmanns. On cross-examination, Aikens asked Mrs. Bernhardt how much *she* weighed when Agnes left Parkston. The witness, who was "fleshy," resisted, saying that she was embarrassed at the question but admitted that she weighed 199 pounds.[18]

The state used the services of Dr. Arthur Sweeney, specialist in "mental and nervous diseases," as an expert witness. He was a distinguished St. Paul doctor and was on the faculty of the University of Minnesota. He had appeared in court as an expert 100 to 200 times. His testimony was essentially the same as what he gave at the first trial. His examination of the heart and brain of Agnes Polreis revealed that they were normal and that the blood clot was the result of "external violence." He also stated that "the girl's death was caused by the shock and exhaustion from such injury."[19]

Following Dr. Sweeney, the prosecution brought forward a new witness, one that had not testified at the first trial. Dr. W. E. Crafts explained that he began medical practice in 1890 and was a "specialist in nervous and mental diseases." To further bolster his credentials as a medical expert, he told the court and jury that he held "the chair of nervous and mental diseases" at the Hamlin Medical School in Minneapolis. He was asked a hypothetical question similar to that asked of Dr. Sweeney. Judge Rice overruled an objection by Aikens. Then Dr. Crafts testified that, considering the type of wounds to the head, it was his opinion that "external violence" caused the hemorrhage and the clot on the brain, thus causing the death of Agnes Polreis.[20]

Late in the afternoon of June 10 the prosecution rested its case. Upon hearing this, the defense team broke into smiles and handshakes, for the feeling among them was that the prosecution had presented a weaker case than at the first trial. Although Erickson had spoken with clarity and credibility, the jury heard him say many times, "I don't remember." Worse yet for the state was the testimony by Dr. Schofield, who diverted from some of his prior statements. Aikens would most certainly hammer that point home to the jury. The Kaufmanns were seen to "smile broadly," chat with their counsel, and then cheerfully walk out of the courtroom.[21]

The defendant and her party had good reason to be cheerful, according to George Egan. His newspaper rather blandly reported that the prosecution had done nothing by way of pre-trial investigation to strengthen its case. The parade of the same witnesses, mouthing their prior testimony, applied a thin, dull layer over the proceedings. Egan complained that "there is nothing at all in connection with the case that is deserving of special attention" and that the most important feature of the trial "is the lack of interest expressed by everyone."[22]

On June 11 Frank Aikens began the case for the defense by making a short statement, complimenting the attentive jury, the audience, and the participants in the "orderly" trial. He seemed pleased to point out that the second trial was a model of the judicial process done right when compared to the circus atmosphere of the first trial. "The defense," he said, "will be very simple . . . and will be an attempt to show this woman is . . . innocent of the charge which has been hanging over her for three years."

Aikens read at great length the first trial testimony of certain state witnesses, including Dr. Schofield, to point out how it varied from their sworn statements in the second trial. He also read from the deposition of Johanna Thorson of Minneapolis, a woman who had worked at the Kaufmann house when Agnes was there. She saw nothing unusual nor did she see any "ill treatment" of the girl by Emma Kaufmann. Peter Erickson's testimony, given at the preliminary examination, the depositions of a liveryman, and a clerk in a Sioux Falls department store were read into the record, too. All this was rather stale stuff compared to the eye-opening testimony of an unexpected witness.

Attorney W. J. Hooper, formerly from Parkston, who had served on the prosecution team in the first trial, took the stand as a defense witness. He testified that he once had custody of the letters, purportedly written by Agnes, and that he had received them from her mother, Theresa Polreis, while the first trial was in progress. Then on May 19, 1909—without saying anything to his former co-counsel—he gave them to Aikens, who simply asked for them. Hooper and the other prosecutors had intended to introduce them at the first trial for the purpose of proving that Mrs. Kaufmann wrote them, but they decided against it. It was Judge Smith, Hooper said, who told Aikens about the letters.[23]

The next day, the 12th, Aikens produced three letters purportedly written by Agnes Polreis, two of which had been previously shown to her sister, Elizabeth. Aikens then called as a witness Professor A. C. C. Azemar of Sioux Falls to translate and read the letters in English. The first missive was a letter written to a friend in Austria. In it Agnes cheerfully told her friend how much she liked America, and with a sense of pride stated that in two months "in service" she had earned $16. The letter made it clear that for her Germany was in the past, even though one must learn, for instance, that in America, "there is no black bread, only white."[24]

The second letter was sent by Agnes also to a friend shortly after her employment at the Kaufmann house began. It describes her experience in coming to Sioux Falls and working for Mrs. Kaufmann in grand and glorious terms. She was happy and her life was one of pure joy. Her employer was good and kind to her and bought her nice things. All in all, she was like a second mother. Then Azemar said that the letter appeared to be dated November 22, which seemed odd because Agnes did not start to work at the Kaufmann house until February 17, 1906, and she died on June 1, 1906. The November date was not within Agnes' employment timeframe.

The third letter, undated, was from Agnes to her parents. In it she said, "I let you know I never felt to[o] well in my life. The mistress and master look so for my health as if I were their own child. The mistress is so kind . . . there is no lady in South Dakota who has everything so nice and so clean. She is so good as my mother would be." Agnes continued in euphoric terms: "I drove down into town with my mistress with the finest carriage in all South Dakota. I will remain with my mistress my whole life for she is so good to me as my mother."

After a brief cross-examination of Azemar, the judge asked, "Is there any dispute as to the authorship of these letters?" to which Null replied rather oddly, "There is no denial that Agnes wrote these letters, but there is a question as to their composition."[25] The letters were admitted into evidence.

By waiving any objection as to the authenticity of the letters, the prosecution saved the defense the cost of hiring a handwriting expert. But Danforth and his team were not simply caving in. They believed that the jury should see all relevant evidence. Further, they thought that the letters actually supported their case because they were proof that Agnes was happy and healthy when she went to work for Mr. and Mrs. Kaufmann.

Aikens showed the jury that he was not finished with surprises when, on the 14th, his first witness of the day was the defendant. With only about a dozen spectators present, but all listening attentively, she was asked five questions in a rapid-fire manner: Did you see any wounds on the girl's head? Did you ever strike her with any instrument? Did you pour hot water on her? Did you poke her in the side? Her demeanor reflecting composure and her eyes looking directly at the jury, she answered "No" to each question. Aikens said, "Cross-examine?" and after a brief conference among the state's lawyers, their response was, "No questions."

Danforth and his fellow prosecutors declined to cross-examine because they would be very limited in the scope of their questioning and, besides, her "No" answers were essentially another "Not guilty" plea and nothing more. Furthermore, if they did cross-examine and their line of questioning strayed from the limited scope allowed, they would give Aikens grounds for an appeal. Aikens had cleverly set a trap but Danforth didn't take the bait.

The next witness was Dr. William Germain, the Kaufmann family physician who sent Agnes to the hospital on the day that she died. On direct examination, the much maligned doctor spoke out aggressively and with confidence, answering questions forcefully as if he had been thoroughly prepared and rehearsed. Recalling his first visit to the Kaufmann house early in the morning of June 1, 1906, Germain described the condition of Agnes Polreis in graphic, explicit terms. She was "thin, emaciated, her eyes were shifty," with dark spots surrounding them. There were sores on her shoulders, both elbows, and her hands. Her right knee was badly swollen "and looked like it was ready to break down and rot." The skin on her feet was "rotten." A finger on her right hand was "in the process of disintegration." However, her heart and lungs were normal. After he had finished his cursory examination of Agnes, Germain testified that he prescribed "wine and a tonic" to "brace her up."

When asked by Aikens if the "sores" he described were caused by external violence, Germain replied, "It would not be possible for external violence to cause them." When asked if he noticed any wounds or cuts on the head, he said, "I saw none," and it was only after he read about the head wounds in a newspaper that he was made aware of the claim. As to what he thought was wrong with her at the time of the first examination early that morning, he considered "several diseases" or "possibly some kind of blood poisoning."

After he returned to the Kaufmann residence for the second time that day and saw Agnes eating "heartily of crackers and milk," he decided Agnes had diabetes mellitus or anemia because it was "characteristic" for diabetics to eat and drink "all the time." As to the cause of her death that evening, Germain said it was diabetes mellitus. Unlike his testimony at the first trial, in answer to Aikens' question about the cause of death, Germain said that he only came to that conclusion after consulting medical authorities.

On cross-examination by Thomas Null, Germain stated that on his first visit to the Kaufmann house he insisted that Agnes be sent to the hospital. But it wasn't until the second visit, hours later, that an ambulance was summoned. Null probed Germain about his diagnosis, asking, "When did you make up your mind the disease was diabetes?" He answered that when he went to the hospital after the girl had died, he "thought it was diabetes or anemia" or possibly Bright's disease. "It was a difficult matter to say just what was the diagnosis." Germain said that he had "no idea she would die so soon."

Germain did offer a definition of diabetes and its causes. He called it "a disease of the kidneys and a passage of sugar through the spleen. The seat of the disease is in the blood. The presence of the disease may be manifested through the condition of the organs or it may not. The liver manufactures the sugar which is the cause of diabetes."[26]

Null kept the pressure on, asking if Germain had tested the girl's urine during the second visit to the hospital. The doctor admitted that he had not. Null then moved on to the infamous death certificate. This set off an alarm, and Aikens launched an emphatic objection when Null asked the witness about the cause of death that he certified on the death certificate. A heated exchange followed, with Null insisting that prior inconsistent statements as to the cause of death were relevant and admissible evidence. Aikens countered by stating that "what a physician might write into a death certificate is not in any way binding on this defendant."

While it might not be binding on the defendant, it was definitely binding on the credibility of the witness. Nevertheless, Judge Rice sustained the objection, thus blocking the prosecution from drawing out testimony about Germain's inconsistent pre-trial statements about the cause of death. It was an odd exchange of legal points of view, but stranger still was the judge's ruling. Prior, out-of-court statements, inconsistent with testimony in court, are normally admissible to test a witness's veracity. But Null did obtain an important admission from Germain. He asked the doctor if, as the Kaufmann family physician, he had taken a close interest in the case on behalf of the defendant. Germain responded, "Yes, sir."[27]

Although Germain held up better under cross-examination during the second trial, his testimony abounded with examples of shoddy practice and professional incompetence. The jury was treated to a performance by a doctor who displayed an open and blatant indifference or, worse yet, an uncaring attitude toward Agnes. Here was a doctor, a heartless man, testifying in court to protect his friends after he fumbled and bumbled his way through a cursory and inept examination of a girl in a critical condition—according to the nurses who attended her at the hospital. And yet Dr. Germain made a very poor attempt to save her life. Maybe he didn't think she was worth the effort.

The defense presented two other medical experts, Dr. A. Rider and Dr. F. A. Spafford, both well-respected Flandreau physicians. Their testimony closely mirrored that which they gave during the first trial. To wit: the girl died of disease. Taking into consideration the "symmetrical distribution of the lesions of the skin," they both ruled out external violence. They were both unshakeable under cross-examination.[28]

Dr. Spafford testified as if he had hit the textbooks to prepare for his testimony. He declared that he had been practicing medicine since 1874, and during that time, he had treated forty or fifty diabetics and had five under observation. Spafford was seemingly holding court on the witness stand, offering a variety of information about diabetes. It was a "wasting disease" that could be contracted "due to injury, to gout, to rheumatism," or it could strike a person because of "diseases of the pancreas, to the liver and possibly to the kidneys."

Otherwise healthy people who get diabetes may not know they have it and then die within a week of experiencing the symptoms. Young women are more likely to get diabetes than young men. Regardless, the disease progresses rapidly in young people. Those who develop the disease need to be careful and avoid injury because "it is dangerous for a diabetic to have wounds of any kind." Dr. Spafford didn't say it, but he implied that it was always a fatal disease.[29]

~

At 6:45 P.M. on June 17, 1909, the fate of Emma Kaufmann was placed in the hands of the jury for the second time. The closing arguments were eloquent and effective and conducted well within the constraints of the law that governed criminal trials. No one wanted another messy appeal, and it was noticed that "the second trial of Mrs. Kaufmann was utterly devoid of the dramatic features of the first one." Translation: no George W. Egan to mess things up.[30]

One unexpected sliver of truth emerged from the second trial: people were tired of the case and wanted it to go away. The lawyers were anxious for relief from the daily stress, and the witnesses had expended more than enough time answering questions that had been asked once or twice before during the long saga. In Flandreau, where folks were working hard to resolve "this dispute for their neighbors in Minnehaha County," it was pointed out that citizens would be "more than rejoiced at the termination of the trial," but only if the jury provides closure.[31]

The defense having rested, it was up to the lawyers to show some power of persuasion. Both Danforth and Orr found they had the intellectual energy to make "straightforward" arguments, summing up the evidence presented by the state. Understanding that a conviction, if there were one, would be based on circumstantial evidence and the credibility of the medical experts, the prosecutors had to convince the jury that the state's witnesses carried more weight.

The state had no smoking gun. While three witnesses, Erickson, Udell, and Bessler, all testified that they observed Mrs. Kaufmann mistreating Agnes, no one saw her deliver what the prosecution believed were death blows to the head, wounds that were only discovered after she was taken to the hospital. The wounds on the shoulders were also a problem because the cuts were on the same place on each shoulder. Nevertheless, to the lay person, the logical inference was that they were caused by external violence rather than disease. The prosecution also argued that the defense medical experts were uncertain and unsure in their testimony, for although the general thrust of their argument was that Agnes died of diabetes, they also suggested other possible causes of death by mentioning "Raynaud's disease" and "anemia and pachymeningitis."

Thomas H. Null made a closing argument that, for clarity and eloquence, was hard to eclipse. His principal targets were Dr. Germain and the defendant. He told the jury that the doctor had failed in every respect. Did he "ask Mrs. Kaufmann what these sores [on Agnes] came from"? Going on, Null said, "Did he ask her how long this girl had been down on her back?" He urged that taking the history of a case is fundamental to making a diagnosis and Dr. Germain had failed in this important element of treatment. Null rather pointedly suggested that "there seemed to be a little mental telepathy between Dr. Germain and this woman. He did not have to ask her any questions. Those fearful wounds told the story."

Moving on to the time Agnes was at the hospital, Null said that Germain "testified that he did not know there were wounds on her head and yet Miss Larson . . . says that Dr. Germain gave directions for dressing those wounds" and stayed in the room while the nurses were following his orders. Null added: "They may talk of disease but it does not matter as to the ultimate result, if this girl had all of these diseases, Mrs. Kaufmann had no right to assault her."

Null essentially dismissed Mrs. Kaufmann's brief testimony as self-serving and misleading. Answering those who questioned the prosecution's decision not to cross-examine her, Null flatly said that, according to his experience in dealing with "adverse witnesses," unless they have produced damaging testimony, "let them go.

Mrs. Kaufmann did not change the status of the case." Commenting on her testimony, Null declared that "if Mrs. Kaufmann was not guilty, she could have told us when those sores began to appear. She might have told us how Agnes fell down stairs and then keeled a double sommersault [sic] and hurt her head on the other side. There was so much that she might have explained but she did not."

Null reminded the jury that they were charged with using common sense when considering the evidence of the case. Then he made reference to something every man could understand: good horse sense. "If you find your horse dead in your pasture with a hole in its head and a Sioux Falls doctor and lawyer argued that the horse died of disease and not by violence you would say that they were either crazy or they thought you were." Null reasoned that if the jury used this analogy, along with the common sense necessary to conduct the affairs of their daily lives, they would not struggle hard in reaching a decision of guilt.[32]

For the defense, George Rice gave a spellbinding closing argument that his friends called his best ever. He carefully read the letters that Agnes had sent to her parents and her friends in the old country, and he viciously attacked the prosecution witnesses, calling the state's medical experts merely hired guns whose purpose was to provide the desired testimony. And Peter Erickson, the worst of them all, whom he likened to a Sioux Indian in the first trial, was now "a man who is worse than a beast."[33] Dehumanized once again for testifying under oath, Erickson could not be faulted if he never again wanted to step inside a courthouse.

Aikens closed out the defense arguments with an emotional appeal that was reminiscent of his spectacle in June 1907. He apparently forgot that during the first trial he told all those present that he could not undertake another stressful trial. Yet he was somehow able to make another great effort. He spoke with energy and "assailed the attorneys for the state and a number of witnesses with unsheathed sarcasm."[34]

As for his client, he characterized her as a humble "daughter of Israel," who had been pursued by a mob and worse yet was constantly harassed by the press that "was profiting by publishing statements of things that never happened." He had words of praise for W. J. Hooper, who turned over the letters Agnes wrote to the defense. Hooper, Aikens said, had "a face as radient [sic] as an angel" and that he promptly did his duty by turning over the letters.

Aikens "paid the highest character to Agnes Polreis" but angrily pounced upon Erickson, whom he said paid a visit to the back room of a Parkston bank and was thereafter ready to "do anything on earth." Next, he attacked Egan, whose conduct at the first trial resulted in a "betrayal of justice." It all happened, Aikens said, because Sanford Cochran used the Kaufmann case "as a fire escape for his degenerate son-in-law" to get him out of a "bad predicament in Iowa." Egan, he said, could "use words but that is the end of his ability."[35] It was an improper closing argument. Flaying Egan in a public forum may have felt good, but in doing so, Aikens was stooping to the same tactics that he accused his foe of using. Ending his argument in tears, he begged the jury to acquit his client and thereby spare her family undue shame and suffering.

The jury went into deliberation and the next day, June 18, at 9 A.M., they filed back into the courtroom like tired soldiers, survivors of fire and cold steel. They had come to a decision. The written verdict was handed to the clerk to be read. At that moment, all eyes were focused on Emma Kaufmann, who showed no emotion nor any greater interest than the spectators. Nor did she jump for joy when the verdict was read: "We the jury find the defendant guilty of battery." The murder case, the two trials that had for so long been the cause of a noisy, national sensation, ended with a quiet, dull thud.

It was not an acquittal, but to someone living under the shadow of the death penalty for three years, it was instant relief. Emma Kaufmann would not hang, nor would she reside for the rest of her life "up on the hill." Agnes Polreis would remain a ghostly victim, her death forever shrouded in mystery. In the stillness following the announcement of the verdict, Moses Kaufmann hung his weary head in disbelief. His beloved wife, whom he had stood by unfailingly, for whom he had invested his fortune while casting aside all worldly ambitions, had not been acquitted as he had hoped.

Mr. Kaufmann needed an acquittal, and not only for his wife. He needed it for himself in order to validate his support for her. He also needed it to provide cover for his own guilty conscience and as a way to escape the harsh judgment of history for having done nothing to stop the cruelty going on under his roof.

Aikens was undoubtedly satisfied with the result. He had come through for his friends, and wearing the banner of a winner, he could ignore the public outcry that the "jury was bought." He knew that the wave of anger and disbelief would subside over time. Besides, he was living in the pre-internet age, when routine death threats were not yet fashionable—or so easy to publish. While Judge Rice could have sentenced Emma to thirty days in jail and a fine up to $100, Aikens pleaded that she had suffered enough over the years. The judge was in accord and Emma was sentenced to pay a $100 fine which was immediately remitted.[36]

Maggie Ross of the *Soo Critic* was present in court when the surprising verdict was announced. She was "among the last half dozen" who left the Flandreau courthouse. As she "turned to go down stairs, she faced Mrs. Kaufmann" standing about six feet away from her. Mrs. Ross had never before "met face to face" with the woman against whom the *Soo Critic* had labored so hard to prove had tortured and killed an innocent girl. As such, she was not all that surprised at the "look of rage and hate that flashed from Mrs. Kaufmann." Ross had often heard that Kaufmann "had the wickedest eye ever seen in a human being, but we never appreciated the force of it until that moment."[37]

After savoring a moment of triumph, and with their heavy burden lifted, the Kaufmanns returned to the Mead house for some relaxation. Not long after, Moses went to the telegraph office and sent a telegram to his son with the good news. A reporter caught up with Mr. Kaufmann and asked him if he was satisfied with the verdict. He responded that he wanted to hear the jury exonerate her completely, but he was just glad the legal process had come to an end. After three years of being shackled to anguish, worry, and stress, Moses and Emma Kaufmann were free to go. The couple made it known that they wanted to take the train to New Haven, Connecticut, and attend their son's graduation ceremony at Yale University.[38]

Some months before, it was reported that Charles Kaufmann had married a divorcée, Mrs. Genevieve Randolph, at one time a distinguished member of the Sioux Falls "Divorce Colony."[39] It was a report with a short life, for it was highly unlikely that he would commit to such a daring, if not scandalous, relationship in view of the suffering his parents were experiencing.

At some point the Kaufmanns returned to Sioux Falls and essentially locked themselves up in their mansion on the 7th Street hill. If Emma Kaufmann had lived in isolation before the death of Agnes Polreis, the unpopular verdict and light sentence left her utterly and completely cut off from a city that believed she got away with murder.

The strange verdict cast a dark shadow over the city because the case ended with more questions than answers. The erratic, violent character of Emma Kaufmann came to light through the testimony of witnesses and newspaper articles. But what was it that really happened at the Kaufmann house? Was it truly a house of horrors? That the lady of the house abused and maltreated Agnes few doubted. But was that abuse the direct cause of death or a contributing factor? Was Agnes suffering from disease? If she were sick, the nature of the malady was not revealed at the trial, for the "expert" testimony of the doctors for defense only raised the level of speculation. And even if she had been sick, a thoughtful, reasonable person would have at the very least contacted her family.

The reclusive, enigmatic Emma Kaufmann was not a reasonable person. She was probably suffering from some type of undiagnosed mental illness or brain injury. She may have been the victim of child abuse. This would explain her paranoid attitude, her violent behavior, and her need to dominate, terrorize, and inflict pain on her victim. Modern research has revealed that many abusive and cruel people were themselves victims of abuse and neglect as children. The unholy triad of abuse, brain damage, and paranoia has produced a large number of violent offenders that have long occupied American prisons.[40] The past is seldom revealed with the desired clarity. However, the record suggests that Emma Kaufmann was as much a victim as Agnes Polreis, albeit of another kind.

Chapter 15

Reaction to the Verdict and the Fate of the Kaufmanns

> *It is inconceivable that men in their right senses can believe that a girl . . . could be made the victim of an assault and battery, without lessening her [life] expectancy, if they thot [sic] the assault was in any way responsible for the pitiful condition of her body when it went into the grave.*
>
> *The Sioux Falls Daily Press*
> July 1, 1909

People in South Dakota, and across America, were utterly baffled by the verdict rendered by the Flandreau jury. For those with a personal connection to the case or who otherwise followed it closely, it was with complete, slack-jacked disbelief that twelve men of reasonable intelligence came to the conclusion that Emma Kaufmann was guilty of battery only. That she struck Agnes Polreis was established by the evidence. But despite this, and in the face of testimony about numerous wounds on her body that medical experts said could not have been caused by disease, the blow or blows, combined with other forms of mistreatment and maltreatment, did not kill the girl nor did they contribute to her death: So sayeth the jury.

Following the announcement of the much-anticipated decision, the South Dakota press erupted in a volcanic outrage of angry articles and editorials that flowed forth like a fiery scourge across the land, as if in one grand swath all the guilty would be reduced to ashes. Leading the chorus of dissent was none other than the *Soo Critic*, under the new editorial hand of Maggie Ross, a tough-minded woman who wept when she heard the verdict. In an even-handed manner, she picked apart the shocking, inexplicable verdict that represented a bizarre turn of events following a conviction of manslaughter at the first trial. Most court watchers were familiar with the facts of the case, all of which pointed toward guilt or at least manslaughter.[1]

Having followed both trials, Ross and other journalists were at a loss to understand how the jury could come to its conclusion. Clearly, they had disregarded Emma Kaufmann's testimony that she never struck the girl because the jurymen concluded that she committed a battery. Therefore, they must have believed the testimony of Peter Erickson and George Bessler, both of whom swore under oath that they saw Mrs. Kaufmann strike and abuse Agnes, and further, that their testimony placed the worst of the bad conduct at the last days of the girl's life. Although no one saw the defendant strike more than one blow, a reasonable person could infer that more were struck because of the battered, weakened, and wounded condition of her body.

When this evidence was considered, along with the judge's charge to the jury that even if they believed Agnes had some terrible disease, "and the defendant by an act of violence, shortened her life by so much as a few minutes, she must be found guilty of murder or manslaughter." But to most observers the jury's use of logic failed and their thinking went awry. To accept the jury's decision, one had to reach "the remarkable conclusion that the woman assaulted the girl and that cuts and bruises all over her body" were evidence of the assault, and yet the blow or blows and the injuries "had nothing whatever to do with her death."[2]

In Parkston, where the people had a deep and abiding interest in the case because the victim was one of their own, the news from Flandreau was greeted with a mixture of anger and pain. Calling it an "outrageous verdict," the *Parkston Advance* attempted to give written expression to the voices of the people it served. In a balanced but searching article that lacked shrill and overkill, the *Advance* made it clear that the verdict met "with general condemnation." The thought process of the soon-to-be infamous twelve men was called into question because it seemed to be an entirely random verdict, "disgusting to all lovers of right and justice." The *Advance* concluded that "the jury felt the woman was guilty, but they were loath to punish her."[3]

The *Mitchell Clarion* was equally baffled and upset over the decision in "the foulest murder case in the history of the state." The puzzling verdict left a "stench" that in every way "is an offense to every self-respecting and justice loving citizen of the state," for the "intelligent reading public will never be convinced that she was not guilty of one of the most heinous crimes on the criminal record of the state."

The *Clarion* blamed the outcome on money and social position. "Had the conditions been reversed and the poor dead girl been the defendant, and the evidence the same, is there any doubt in the mind of any intelligent person what the verdict would have been?" Better had the jury brought in a not-guilty verdict, as it would have been more acceptable to the public. Instead they came up with a verdict that "is a disgrace to the state and a travesty on justice." In a frothy finish to the article, the journalist reminded readers that it was "such verdicts that encourage lynch law and breed anarchy."[4]

The *Arlington Sun* was equally blunt. "In the minds of every man and woman in this state who has followed the two trials, Mrs. Kaufmann stands convicted of the murder of Agnes Polreis, and the jury . . . stands convicted of betraying the charge given into their hands. It was a mockery of justice and a premium upon crime."[5]

Mockery was the charge of the *Plankinton Herald*. It pointed an accusatory finger at the mealy-mouthed jury that seemed to have lost its direction or the ability to think carefully and logically. Laying it on hard and thick, the *Herald* offered a post-verdict tip: "If Mrs. Kaufmann is guilty of battery then she is guilty of murder," and the "twelve tried and true" men should hang their heads in shame for failing to grasp what seemed obvious to the public. "Had this woman been poor she would now be serving time."[6]

The *Lyman County Democrat* chimed in, agreeing with the *Herald* by declaring that had the defendant been poor, "she would have been long ago serving time in the penitentiary." Thoroughly disgusted with the verdict and those responsible for it, the *Democrat* pounded away, insisting that, based on the evidence presented at trial, Emma Kaufmann was guilty of murder. And yet the editor for the *Democrat* was forced to accept that the celebrated case was relegated to history and honest people had no choice but to concede that "truth has turned to falsehood, water is dry, ice is hot and fire is cold."[7] But nothing could be done to change the result; and sadly, there was no justice in it for Agnes.

The condemnation of the verdict continued with an editorial by the *Fort Pierre Fair Play*. This newspaper, like the others, was unable to understand how any verdict other than guilty of manslaughter or murder could have resulted from the jury's deliberation. Considering the light sentence of a $100 fine, for all practical purposes, Kaufmann had been exonerated after "one of the most disgraceful and farcical proceedings ever taken in court in the state of South Dakota." People were left with the eerie feeling that the life of Agnes Polreis was valued at a mere $100.

The Pierre newspaper, along with others, recognized that there was always a dark side to the past. South Dakota had crossed into that realm, having recorded "a foul blot upon the pages . . . of history."[8] Bleeding from a self-inflicted wound, the young state was compelled to stand alone in shame, outside of the sacred perimeter of other honorable jurisdictions where blind justice reigned supreme. Once again, wealth had triumphed over poverty and the result was ugly.

The *Canton Leader* was outraged at the verdict and those responsible for it. The people of Canton called the trial and verdict a "farce." The verdict set such a low standard for judging evidence that no one in Moody County needed to fear the consequences of committing an assault and battery, nor should they be surprised "if people up there try the next murder case with a rope." The verdict in the Kaufmann case "breeds contempt for courts and jury trials."[9]

From the other side of the state, the *Deadwood Lantern* castigated and condemned the entire trial and its participants, even bringing politics into the spectacle: “This re-trial has been a farce from the start. The prosecution has been the most pliant tools of the corrupt republican gang at Sioux Falls with Kittridge [sic] at its head.” Danforth and his crew were hammered because they made “no real attempt to convict the murderess.” The jurymen were called out for their “cowardice” and corruption. They were “selected for the express purpose of making a farce of the case.” The fiery editor ended his tirade by mocking the legal system: “Oh yes, ALL MEN ARE EQUAL BEFORE THE LAW.”[10]

Although dozens of editorials from throughout the state screamed in anger and indignation, surprisingly, there was no hard and fast attempt to bring anti-Semitism into the critique of the case. The *Herrick Press*, in a fury while condemning the failed judicial system, came close. The editor said that “a millionaire in politics cuts a great figure,” while the rights of a poor immigrant girl were easily brushed aside and not allowed to “stand in the way of a Jew brewer with a barrel of boodle.”[11]

In other parts of the country, a similar reaction was expressed in the press. A North Carolina newspaper blithely informed its readers that a “woman murderer [was] released by paying a fine.”[12] An Indiana newspaper slammed the Flandreau jury, calling the verdict, “A Farce on Justice.” The measly $100 fine was a “miscarriage of justice that brings courts into disrepute.”[13]

Of course, the former special prosecuting attorney, George Egan, through the columns of the *American Republic,* got in some good licks too, after having predicted, correctly, that the defendant would walk away when the trial ended. Declaring that the “farcical proceedings ended as a joke,” Egan expected that “there will be a big dance at the Kaufmann home tomorrow night. We heard sweet strains of music coming down Ninth Street.” Egan also slammed the prosecution team for making a weak effort and hinting that they were under the spell of “Foxy Grandpa,” meaning Frank Aikens.[14]

His editorial page lit up, too. He praised the Parkston committee for its unwavering devotion to Agnes and for the steadfast pursuit of justice for the girl, one of their own. The Parkston men were the real heroes, models of decency, holding their heads high, while surrounded by a great indecency. Egan pounced on the jury and the ridiculous verdict that resulted in less than a slap on the wrist. The $100 fine was a joke, a pittance, and an insult to justice and to the people who believed that the law respected everyone, not just the rich. "What does it show? It can show but one thing and that is that the jury was bought and paid for." Egan claimed that the "defendant's man," whom he did not name, pressured other "simple-minded" jurors into voting for battery after convincing them that Kaufman would spend a year in jail and get hit with a $5,000 fine. They bought the false promise and came up with "the ridiculous and absurd verdict."

Post-trial cartoon in the *American Republic*, June 25, 1909. The scene is of a party at the Kaufmann residence on the evening of June 19, when Emma Kaufmann's earlier murder conviction was overturned.

With the controversial matter in the public mind, Egan published another cartoon that featured all the main players in the "farcical proceedings." All but one was celebrating the jury verdict. With Joe Kirby and Maggie Ross furiously at their violins, a smiling Emma Kaufmann danced with the Moody County sheriff while the jury enjoyed a keg of "Old Style Lager." The foreman was offering a toast: "Here's to Emma who did it—Yet she didn't do it!" While Aikens, Kittredge, Dr. Germain, and others were happily reveling in their success, the ethereal form of Agnes Polreis lilted above the celebrants, begging, "Frau Kaufmann, Frau Kaufmann!" It was vintage George Egan.[15]

Egan could pour on the hot oil with the best of them. He never seemed to run out of cartoons or pejoratives. But his sharpest, most cutting line was probably this: "If your hired girl does not catch on, kill her, says the jury, and pay a $100.00 fine."[16]

~

Was the judge partially responsible for the outcome? Maggie Ross spoke to Judge Rice at some length after the trial was over and came away thinking that he "was unmistakably in favor of the defendant." In a cutting critique of the judge's rulings, Ross said, "He either believed in her innocence or he has mistaken his calling and should have been an actor." She could not understand how the judge could see the evidence as something that cleared Kaufmann when so many others were absolute in their belief that she was guilty. Still, the astute editor would leave it alone, for "we are not running a smut mill and do not intend to scream liar at everyone who does not agree with us."[17] Although she was done with Judge Rice, she could not resist taking a little jab at Egan and the "smut mill" that he called a newspaper.

The *Sioux Falls Daily Press* also weighed in on the judge's post-trial comments, focusing on one remark in particular. Although an impartial judge would have kept silent, Judge Rice was heard to say that the two letters from Agnes to Emma that spoke of good treatment and were introduced as evidence in the trial convinced him of the defendant's innocence. This injudicious slip of the tongue explained why he only sentenced her to pay a $100 fine when he could have tacked on thirty days in jail.[18]

The blaze caused by the "strange verdict" would not readily subside. There was not enough muddy water in the Missouri River to put out the fire that had cast a bright and terrible light for all the world to see. There was an assortment of villains to choose from, but throughout the long, dark night of indignant scrutiny, it was the jury, not the defense counsel or any others, that remained the focus of public and press anger and disgust.

Some months after the trial, it was learned that the Flandreau law firm of Rice and Benson "worked like beavers to find out just how every man summoned on the jury . . . stood, upon certain questions . . . in connection with the trial of the case." Members of the firm filtered into the countryside, questioning neighbors "of every man whose name appeared on the jury list" about guilt or innocence of the accused. And in this manner, and because of the diligence of Rice and Benson, Aikens got a favorable jury, for "it was known in advance" whether a juror "ever expressed an opinion detrimental to the interests of Emma Kaufmann."[19]

"We firmly believe they [the jury] were bot [sic]," was the position of the *Soo Critic*. But Maggie Ross was not content merely to make the accusation. She went in search of jurors who were willing to talk. A key member of the jury was Flandreau Mayor Edward Gray. Upon reaching his Flandreau store, Ross was informed by his wife that the mayor was gone. Still she heard enough from the wife to know that Gray "voted for an acquittal on the first ballot and was Mrs. Kaufmann's strongest defender."

Another juror, H. Cavmer of Egan, South Dakota, was interviewed and he was quoted as saying, "That woman was black with guilt!" A third juror, whose name was not given in the article, told Ross that no member of the jury believed the claim by the defense that Agnes died of disease. "Not any of them." A fourth juror, F. B. Newton from Coleman, was said to be "one of the square men on the jury." He voted for battery on the belief that the defendant would receive a sentence of five years imprisonment. It was a mistaken assumption based on an outdated version of state law that was given to the jury.

After her discussions with some members of the jury, Ross was convinced "the jury had clearly been looked after," although she didn't explain the how and who of it. Her otherwise serious article contained one amusing anecdote, a story that she could not resist telling her readers. One of the attorneys for the defense was the father of a little girl. As the little girl listened to her parents talk about the case, she made the following remark, which was overheard by others: "Papa told mamma that she was guilty as Hell."[20]

Newspapers were inundated with correspondence from the public, much of it highly critical of the verdict and Emma Kaufmann. Perhaps one of the most surprising was a letter dated July 6, 1909, from "T. F." to the editor of the *American Republic.* It revealed the stories of two girls from Hutchinson County who shared their horrible experiences as servants in the Kaufmann house. Neither girl testified at the trial. Egan doubtlessly published the letter to stir the pot, so to speak, and thus keep alive in the public mind his hatred of the Kaufmanns and his disappointment over the outcome of the case.

Katy Knobel was sixteen when she was hired, and after serving six months, she managed to escape. Knobel recalled that Emma Kaufmann would pinch her arms and "person" until she was "black and blue." She was also hit with a broomstick and sent tumbling down the stairs to the basement. In the winter, her cruel employer would deny her the use of blankets at night. To keep her from running away, Mrs. Kaufmann would tell her that, should she try, she would be kidnapped by evil men and women and taken to a place "worse than a prison." Stranger yet, Mrs. Kaufmann would force the girl to roam throughout the house in the dead of night, "looking for burglars." Upstairs, downstairs, from room to room in the dark she walked while her tormentor followed behind with a club. Ultimately, Katy was able to get away from the house and thus escape a fate like that of Agnes.

Another teenage girl from Hutchinson County, Mary Ploom, had similar experiences while working at the Kaufmann house for a period of six weeks. To assist her in tormenting Mary, Mrs. Kaufmann had the services of "a colored woman," who delighted in seeing the girl suffer. "With that African she bear on one side, and the female hyena on the other, Mary barely escaped with her life."[21]

Emma Kaufmann never wanted her servants, including Agnes, to die. She desperately needed the dehumanized objects of her wrath to live in order to fulfill her obsession to punish and inflict pain. Conscience, empathy, and good morals are all learned behavior. In all likelihood, Emma was never subjected to the ordinary experiences in life that allow these virtues to develop. Instead, it is likely that during her childhood she learned fear, cruelty, and hate at the hands of some dominating adults.

Another letter to Egan, this one by John Mack of Ramona, South Dakota, took aim at the *Argus-Leader*, blaming Charles M. Day's much-maligned newspaper for Egan's disbarment. Mack believed this was accomplished for the sole purpose of preventing Egan from prosecuting the second Kaufmann trial. He further believed that had Egan been the state's attorney, Dr. Germain and Joe Kirby would have been sent "up the hill" against the wishes of Day and his friends. Mack angrily mocked the *Argus-Leader*, calling it the "Argus-Liar." He claimed to have spoken to an *Argus-Leader* reporter and could expound from a position of authority.[22]

But for pure elegance, laced with sarcasm, the letter from Jacob Olson of Canton rose to the top of the heap. Olson, like many others, believed in a legal system that treated rich and poor alike. That concept, he insisted, was at the heart of the American Constitution and therefore embodied the promise that fairness and justice should prevail though the heavens may fall. But instead of living up to the promise of equal justice, those who were charged with "executing justice in this celebrated case, stand consigned to infamy and branded with dishonor." The great trial, the "tragic farce," the "amazing absurdity . . . has scarcely been equaled and never surpassed." Olson cast the Kaufmann trial into a black hole of ignominy, where it would forever swirl in silence. "No event in the history of American jurisprudence has more deeply astonished and offended the public."[23]

The post-trial fallout produced other forms of reaction, too. Some weeks after the trial, Ira F. Blewitt, state's attorney for Moody County, came under harsh criticism from unnamed persons who accused him of "selling out the case." He was also slammed for having apologized to Mrs. Kaufmann for his conduct in the first trial. An indignant Blewitt—who did not actively participate in the second trial—denied ever talking to the defendant. He then called out the rumor-mongers, declaring that he had deposited $500 in a Moody County Bank and would pay that sum to anyone who came forth and exposed any unlawful act that he committed.

Blewitt then addressed the persistent rumors circulating about the jury being somehow bribed. Again he provided $500 to anyone who was offered a bribe, so long as they could identify the offeror. Blewitt challenged his accusers, insisting that any honest man who had been offered and then refused a bribe would most certainly want to take the next step and expose the briber. While he refused to charge the jury with bad faith, he expressed his disappointment in their verdict.

Minnehaha County State's Attorney George J. Danforth issued his own statement, supporting Blewitt one hundred per cent. "I endorse every word that Mr. Blewitt has said in regard to bribery in the Kaufmann case and I will meet the same conditions even to the last dollar that I own."

Maggie Ross of the *Critic* published the statements of Blewitt and Danforth after she was accused by Egan and his "yellow sheet" of favoring or assisting the "murderess" Kaufmann. She entered the post-trial fray with a fury. Waving her contempt for Egan like the star-spangled banner, she declared that she was willing to turn over all her publishing assets, furniture, printing press, subscription list, and good will to anyone "who will produce proof that we sold out in that case." Do so or "forever hold your peace." As for bribing the jury, she left that door open. Ross wrote, "In our humble opinion [Flandreau Mayor] Ed Gray might explain what happened to his jury."[24]

On so many levels, the long-running Kaufmann case generated volumes of pain, anger, loss, and bitterness. Like a Victor Hugo novel, the celebrated crime drama crept into a thousand dark corners of an endless night illuminated only by screaming and suffering. How long it would take to heal and restore calm to Sioux Falls was an open question.

The general consensus was that it would be wise for Moses Kaufmann, now broken and exhausted, to take his "cruel" wife and leave Sioux Falls for good. Should they stay, their safety would be in jeopardy. The angry mood of the city was such that the slightest provocation could ignite mob violence.[25] Because the ugly past always catches up with someone trying to run from it, the prudent course was to change directions. For the Kaufmanns the logical choice was a change of scenery, a new address.

But they stayed in Sioux Falls, mostly keeping out of sight within the relative safety of their luxurious home, replete with haunting memories. They had become outcasts, social pariahs. Few, if any, wanted to risk widespread condemnation by claiming friendship with, or even associating with, the Kaufmanns. It was firmly and widely believed that Emma tortured Agnes to death and got away with murder.

Moses Kaufmann was sued over legal fees incurred in the defense of his wife. While he believed it was money well-spent, and that he would have spent every penny of his fortune in her defense, the relationship between Kaufmann and his lawyers apparently soured. Aikens and Judge sued the former brewer for $20,000[26] and the Flandreau firm of Rice and Benson took a $5,000 judgment against him.[27] In the process, he lost more friends.

When Egan learned that Aikens was suing Kaufmann for fees, he broke out gleefully with another front-page cartoon entitled "'Stripping' the Kaufmann Cow." In it, Aikens is on a wooden stool, milking the cow while others who profited from the case are engaged in animated posing with milk pails at the ready.[28]

Post-trial cartoon in the *American Republic*, January 14, 1910. "Be careful, Frank [Aikens]. She is awful hard to hold and she's almost dry now," remarks Jordan, standing next to Warren, holding a bucket labeled "Give us $3,000."

Editor Egan, who had petitioned the South Dakota Supreme Court for re-admission to the state bar, and who had entered the political arena again, this time for the office of governor, was still acting like a sore loser. But in actuality he, too, was "stripping" the Kaufmann cow, hoping that the famous case that brought him to great heights in 1907 might once again be useful in his quest to restore his professional standing as a springboard for future achievement.

While Moses' financial losses were substantial, worse yet was the emotional cost. If ever a man were tragically haunted by his past it was Mr. Kaufmann. A once genial and proud man, respected and admired for his success and political acumen, he was reduced to a pitiable figure who sadly walked the streets of Sioux Falls, a bent, faint shadow of his former self, perhaps hoping that on some new day, a glimmer of sunshine might stream back into his miserable life.

On April 18, 1911, Moses Kaufmann rose at 7 o'clock in the morning, went outside to supervise some yard work, and noticed a sizeable patch of dry grass. He announced to the yard worker that he was going downtown to buy grass seed. At about 8:30 that same morning, as he was seen walking back home up the 7th Street hill, he paused to greet Frank Millard, "but words failed him." Instead of saying, "Good morning," he suddenly fell over backwards on the sidewalk at 7th Street and Spring Avenue. He "gasped three or four times and expired."

Two women standing nearby rushed over to assist Millard and placed a pillow under Kaufmann's head. But it was small comfort and to no avail. Doctors, who were not named in the *Daily Press* article, were summoned but could only pronounce life extinct due to "heart failure." There was nothing left to do but take his remains to the "Miller undertaking rooms."[29] Moses Kaufmann was dead at the age of fifty-three.

It was believed in the community that Moses Kaufmann was in fairly good health, although he had been heard to make some complaints. Most Sioux Falls folks, of course, knew about the stress and strain he had endured during his wife's long and tortuous legal saga. The talk in the streets was that it had worn him down considerably until simply walking up the gentle 7th Street hill, carrying a sack of seed along with the heavy burden of bad memories, was too much for his heart.

The *Argus-Leader* was generous in its praise for "one of Sioux Falls' most liberal citizens." He was credited with helping poor families sincerely and with humility, for he was not a man known to engage in self-promotion. "Moses Kaufmann was a man among men." He did not solicit sympathy over his troubles, but rather "he carried his burden in the depths of his heart and there is little question that the experiences of the past five years have shortened the life of this noble man."[30]

Before funeral arrangements could be made, his widow of course had to be notified of his death. Some man, or men, came to the Kaufmann house and told Emma that her husband, the man who had stood by her unflinchingly for the duration of her legal battles, would not be coming home. Sudden, unexpected death usually means sudden shock. True to form, the newly widowed woman fell into a spasm of wailing and moaning upon receiving the sad news. "She appeared crazed with grief" and hysterically "ordered" friends of her late husband, who came to offer sympathy, "to bring him back to life."[31]

Although the grieving widow felt she could not live without him, she had no choice but to bury her dead husband. The well-attended funeral at the Kaufmann residence was conducted in accordance with the Jewish religion, with a rabbi from Sioux City performing the solemn ceremony. Representatives from the Germania Verein, Elks, Eagles, and Masons were present to honor their deceased member. Moses Kaufmann was laid to rest in Mt. Zion Cemetery in Sioux Falls amid reports that Emma was planning to construct a mausoleum in Sioux Falls or Sioux City as a final resting place for her husband and herself.[32]

A Sioux Falls newspaper published a brief memorial for Moses Kaufmann. Entitled "A Man Died," the editorial praised the deceased who, as a result of a tragic twist of fate, and after enduring the loss and respect of his fellow citizens, had been hounded to an early grave. It all happened because he stood by his wife, the woman he loved, who once upon a time was "accused of a great crime." It was as if he had committed a crime himself, for he was widely reviled and accused of bribery. His name, his character, his reputation—all poisonous, even though at no time previous had he ever been thought of as anything but an honorable, decent man. In death, however, Moses Kaufmann could reclaim all lost honors, for death changed everything, according to the memorial.[33]

For those people who believed that Moses Kaufmann knew of the strange and cruel treatment that his wife meted out to her domestics, including Agnes, death changed nothing. Although he had escaped the coils of justice, he stood guilty in the court of many households for allowing his wife to commit terrible acts of violence under his roof when other men would have prevented such activity. He allowed his love and devotion to his wife trump his duty as a citizen. For that he deserved no sympathy or praise.

His widow was consigned to a similar fate. Isolated, unrepentant, unloved, unwanted, but safely cloistered inside her handsome home, Emma was, for all practical purposes, a prisoner under fate's lock and key. She never recovered from the loss of her husband. She fell ill, and month by month, her condition worsened until she was taken to the McKennan Hospital in Sioux Falls where, on November 17, 1913, she died of "pernicious anaemia."[34] She was fifty years old. The malady that caused her death was at the time a fatal disease, characterized by a deficiency of red blood cells, or hemoglobin, in the blood. It was reported that she experienced a "gradual wasting away of the body," going from a large, "robust" woman to a "mere skeleton weighing 65 pounds at the time of her death."[35]

Because she was "almost a walking skeleton,"[36] her death was expected, but there was no attempt by the Sioux Falls and Yankton newspapers to regurgitate the ugly details of the Kaufmann case. Rather they chose to downplay the death of, arguably, the strangest, most notorious woman in the history of South Dakota. The *Argus-Leader* merely mentioned her funeral in its "City Briefs" column, easily missed unless one was reading carefully.

On November 19 the funeral service for Emma Kaufmann was conducted by Rabbi Maurice M. Mazure of Sioux City at the Kaufmann home.[37] In all likelihood, attendance was light, especially when compared to the audience at the Orpheum Theater on Phillips Avenue that same day, where the famous American actress, Lillian Russell, was performing. Burial was at Mt. Zion Cemetery beside her husband. She never got around to building a mausoleum. The only surviving family member was her son, Charles, who was living with her at the time of her death.

And so it came to pass that Emma Kaufmann, who "figured in a world-wide sensation,"[38] was quietly and quickly put in the ground, almost as an afterthought, in hushed tones that belied the loud and tumultuous stories that erupted when she was arrested, when a mob threatened to hang her, and during the two well-publicized, hard-fought trials for her life. No one needed to be reminded of what transpired after the emaciated and damaged body of Agnes Polreis had been exhumed and exposed to the nation via the press.

The death of the sixteen-year-old servant girl had riled the city and state, raising the emotional temperature to a white-hot anger so intense that the constitutional guarantee of due process was almost subverted. No one needed to be reminded of all that.

By November of 1913 all that ugliness was more than seven years in the past. The passage of time and the long judicial grind quieted the bloodlust and wore down the curiosity of even the most avid of Kaufmann followers. But most important, it left unanswered a looming question: Was the death of Agnes Polreis partially or entirely caused by Emma Kaufmann? Now that she, too, was numbered among the dead, her precise role in the dark mystery was lost forever.

The dead keep their secrets, and those who survived the death of the infamous defendant, those who had personal knowledge of the Kaufmann house mystery, who did not testify at the trials, chose not to reveal even a kernel of the truth. Sadly, time failed to loosen tongues or prod a troubled conscience to speak out. Sadder still, there was no justice for Agnes, nor was there closure for her family and friends.

Everyone touched by the terrible event was troubled or haunted by a sense of injustice. And for those people—both sympathetic and guilt-ridden—who were denied relief from the dreadful mystery, there remained in their minds the memory of poor Agnes, lingering in painful silence, unheard but felt. Like a cold breeze, like the soft touch of a silken curtain, or the ethereal caress of a restless spirit.

Endnotes

Chapter 1

[1] Stewart H. Holbrook, *The Golden Age of Quackery* (New York: Collier Books, 1962), 12.

[2] *American Republic* (Sioux Falls, SD), June 11, 1909. At the time, commonly referred to as Austria-Hungary. The family's last name was also spelled "Pollreis."

[3] *Norfolk Weekly News-Journal* (Norfolk, NE), June 4, 1909.

[4] *South Dakota State Forum*, (Sioux Falls, SD), August 16, 1907.

[5] *Soo Critic* (Sioux Falls, SD), July 19, 1906. His name is also spelled "Mueller."

[6] *Daily Argus-Leader* (Sioux Falls, SD), June 21, 1906.

[7] Twelfth Census of the United States, Sioux Falls, SD, 1900, Microfilm.

[8] *Soo Critic*, July 19, 1906.

[9] *Sioux City Journal* (Sioux City, IA), June 16, 1907.

[10] *Daily Argus-Leader*, December 22, 1888.

[11] *American Israelite*, (Cincinnati, OH), December 27, 1906.

[12] *Weekly Cataract* (Sioux Falls, SD), June 12, 1906. Jacob and Rosa Blum are interred at Mt. Zion Cemetery in Sioux Falls, SD.

[13] *Sioux Falls Daily Press* (Sioux Falls, SD), October 25, 1904; Twelfth Census of the United States, Sioux Falls, SD, 1900, Microfilm.

[14] Dana R. Bailey, *History of Minnehaha County, South Dakota* (Sioux Falls, SD: Brown & Saenger, 1899), 584.

[15] Personal interview with Freda Hosen, Sioux Falls, SD, August 7, 1915.

[16] *Sioux Falls Daily Press*, April 17, 1885.

[17] Ibid., March 6, 1886

[18] Bailey, 384.

[19] *Sioux Falls Daily Press*, March 6 and 7, 1886.

[20] *Daily Argus-Leader*, December 22, 1888.

[21] *Evening Argus-Leader*, June 1, 1897.

[22] Bailey, 387-88.

[23] *Daily Argus-Leader*, June 30, 1899.

[24] *Weekly Cataract*, March 28, 1906.

[25] *Daily Argus-Leader*, August 23, 1897. The hospital was incorporated in 1894 to care for the sick and injured "not for private gain but for public good."

[26] *South Dakota State Forum*, October 5, 1906.

[27] *Yankton Press and Dakotan* (Yankton, SD), June 16, 1906. The Minnehaha County Office of Vital Records has no record of a death certificate for Agnes Polreis.

[28] *Parkston Advance* (Parkston, SD), June 15, 1906.

[29] *Yankton Press and Dakotan*, June 9, 1906.

[30] *Parkston Advance*, June 29, 1906.

[31] *Omaha Daily Bee*, June 15, 1906.

[32] *Evening Star* (Washington, DC), June 26, 1906.

[33] *Daily Argus-Leader*, June 21, 1906.

[34] *Mitchell Daily Republican* (Mitchell, SD), June 19, 1906.
[35] *Parkston Advance*, June 15, 1906.
[36] *Yankton Press and Dakotan*, June 9, 1906.
[37] *Sioux Falls Daily Press*, June 10, 1906; *Mitchell Daily Republic*, June 18, 1906.
[38] *Yankton Press and Dakotan*, June 11, 1906; *Daily Argus-Leader*, June 11, 1906.
[39] *Parkston Advance* in the *Sioux Falls Daily Press*, June 19, 1906.
[40] *Daily Argus-Leader*, June 11, 1906.
[41] *Parkston Advance*, June 15, 1906.
[42] Ibid., June 22, 1906.
[43] *Daily Argus-Leader*, July 6, 1926; Bailey, 543-44.
[44] Charles A. Smith, *A Comprehensive History of Minnehaha County, South Dakota* (Mitchell, SD: Educator's Supply Co., 1949, 293-94).
[45] *Omaha Daily Bee*, June 13, 1906.
[46] *Weekly Cataract*, June 12, 1906.
[47] *Sioux Falls Daily Press*, October 25, 1904.
[48] *Mitchell Daily Republican*, June 15, 1906

Chapter 2

[1] *Sioux Falls Daily Press*, June 11, 1906.
[2] Freda Hosen, "The Trials and Tribulations of Emma Kaufmann" (Sioux Falls, SD: Center for Western Studies, Augustana University, 1974), 6. [unpublished]
[3] *Daily Argus-Leader*, June 13, 1906. The Miller Funeral Home in Sioux Falls is in its third century of business, although under different ownership.
[4] Doane Robinson, *History of South Dakota*, Vol. III (Chicago and New York: American Historical Society, 1930), 316.
[5] *Norfolk Weekly News-Journal* (Norfolk, NE), June 4, 1909.
[6] *Mitchell Daily Republican*, June 19, 1906.
[7] *Norfolk Weekly News-Journal*, June 4, 1909.
[8] *Mitchell Daily Republican*, June 19, 1906.
[9] *Parkston Advance*, June 22, 1906.
[10] *Yankton Press and Dakotan*, June 12, 1906.
[11] *Parkston Advance* in the *Sioux Falls Daily Press*, June 19, 1906.
[12] *Sioux Falls Daily Press*, June 12, 1906.
[13] Bailey, 433-34.
[14] *The Weekly Cataract*, November 26, 1906.
[15] Bailey, 591-92.
[16] *Daily Argus-Leader*, October 24, 1888.
[17] Ibid, January 22, 1904.
[18] *Argus-Leader South Dakota 99* (Sioux Falls, SD: Ex Machina Publishing Co., 1989), 121-24.
[19] *Evening Argus-Leader*, June 14, 1897.
[20] Ibid., June 25, 1897.
[21] Ibid., July 12, 1897.
[22] Ibid., July 14, 1897.

[23] *Argus-Leader South Dakota 99*, 121-24.
[24] *Parkston Advance* in the *Sioux Falls Daily Press*, June 19, 1906.
[25] *Sioux Falls Journal*, July 15, 1904.
[26] *Sioux Falls Daily Press*, June 13, 1906.
[27] *Daily Argus-Leader*, June 12, 1906.
[28] *Sioux Falls Daily Press*, June 13, 1906.
[29] *Yankton Press and Dakotan*, June 13, 1906.
[30] *Sioux Falls Daily Press*, June 13, 1906.
[31] *Yankton Press and Dakotan*, June 13, 1906; *Sioux Falls Daily Press*, June 14, 1906.
[32] *Sioux Falls Daily Press*, June 14, 1906.
[33] *Yankton Press and Dakotan*, June 13, 1906.
[34] *Sioux Falls Daily Press*, June 14, 1906.
[35] Ibid., June 14, 1906.
[36] *Daily Argus-Leader*, June 10, 1909.
[37] Ibid., June 13, 1906
[38] *South Dakota State Forum* (Sioux Falls, SD), June 15, 1906.
[39] *Parkston Advance*, June 15, 1906.
[40] *Yankton Press and Dakotan*, June 13, 1906.
[41] *Sioux Falls Daily Press*, June 14, 1906.
[42] *Daily Argus-Leader*, June 13 and 20, 1906.
[43] Ibid., June 20, 1906.
[44] Ibid., June 13, 1906.
[45] *Mitchell Daily Republican*, June 14, 1906.
[46] *Parkston Advance*, June 15, 1906.
[47] *Daily Argus-Leader*, June 13, 1906.
[48] *South Dakota State Forum*, June 15, 1906.
[49] *Daily Argus-Leader*, June 13, 1906.
[50] *Minneapolis Journal*, June 15, 1906
[51] Ibid., June 23, 1906.
[52] *Parkston Advance*, June 15, 1906.
[53] *Yankton Press and Dakotan*, June 15, 1906.
[54] *Parkston Advance*, June 15, 1906.
[55] *Sioux Falls Daily Press*, June 15, 1906.

Chapter 3

[1] Smith, 160.
[2] *Soo Critic* (Sioux Falls, SD), December 18, 1903.
[3] Ibid., June 14, 1906.
[4] *South Dakota State Forum* (Sioux Falls, SD), June 22, 1906.
[5] *Soo Critic*, June 14, 1906.
[6] *Mitchell Clarion* (Mitchell, SD), June 14 and 28, 1906.
[7] *Daily Argus-Leader* (Sioux Falls, SD), June 16, 1906.
[8] *Yankton Press and Dakotan* (Yankton, SD), June 14, 1906.
[9] *Weekly Cataract* (Sioux Falls, SD), June 12, 1906.

[10] *Minneapolis Journal*, June 17, 1906.
[11] *Yankton Press and Dakotan*, June 18, 1906; *Daily Argus-Leader*, June 18, 1906.
[12] *Soo Critic*, June 21, 1906.
[13] *Mitchell Daily Republican* (Mitchell, SD), June 18, 1906.
[14] *Sioux Falls Journal*, June 22, 1906.
[15] *Weekly Cataract*, June 12, 1906.
[16] *Minneapolis Journal*, June 17, 1906; *Mitchell Daily Republican*, June 18, 1906.
[17] *Minneapolis Journal*, June 18, 1906.
[18] *Evening Star* (Washington, DC), June 26, 1906.
[19] *Mitchell Daily Republican* (Mitchell, SD), June 22, 1906.
[20] Ibid.
[21] Ibid., June 19, 1906.
[22] *Parkston Advance* (Parkston, SD), June 22, 1906.
[23] *Evening Times* (Grand Forks, ND), June 3, 1907.
[24] *Evening Star*, June 26, 1906.
[25] *Fort Mill Times* (Fort Mill, SC), July 25, 1907.
[26] *Daily Argus-Leader*, March 21 and 22, 1900.
[27] *Minneapolis Journal*, June 18, 1906.
[28] *Mitchell Clarion* (Mitchell, SD), June 21, 1906.
[29] *Mitchell Daily Republican*, June 22, 1906.
[30] *Diagnostic and Statistical Manual of Mental Disorders*, 4th Edition, Text Revision, DSM-IV-TR (Arlington, VA: American Psychiatric Association, 2000), 702.
[31] Simon Baron-Cohen, *The Science of Evil: On Empathy and the Origins of Cruelty* (New York: Basic Books, 2011), 6.
[32] *Diagnostic and Statistical Manual of Mental Disorders*, 702.
[33] Daniel Goleman, *Emotional Intelligence: Why It Can Matter More Than IQ* (Bantam Books, 1997), 106-108.

Chapter 4

[1] *Yankton Press and Dakotan*, June 15, 1906.
[2] Ibid.
[3] *Daily Argus-Leader*, June 20 1906.
[4] *Yankton Press and Dakotan*, June 19, 1906.
[5] *Weekly Cataract*, June 12, 1906.
[6] *Mitchell Daily Republican*, June 15, 1906.
[7] *Yankton Press and Dakotan*, June 16, 1906; *Sioux Falls Daily Press*, June 17, 1906.
[8] *Daily Argus-Leader*, July 19, 1906.
[9] Wayne Fanebust, *Echoes of November: The Life and Times of Senator R. F. Pettigrew of South Dakota* (Freeman, SD: Pine Hill Press, 1997), 271.
[10] *Mitchell Daily Republican*, June 19, 1906.
[11] *Yankton Press and Dakotan*, June 19, 1906.
[12] *Minneapolis Journal*, June 18, 1906.
[13] *Daily Argus-Leader*, June 18, 1906.

[14] *Minneapolis Journal*, June 18, 1906.
[15] *Sioux Falls Daily Press*, June 21, 1906.
[16] *Daily Argus-Leader*, June 19, 1906.
[17] Ibid., June 10, 1907.
[18] *State of South Dakota vs. Emma Kaufmann*, Case No. 11106, 2nd Circuit, Minnehaha County, Affidavit of John Emmke.
[19] *Minneapolis Journal*, June 20, 1906.
[20] *Parkston Advance*, June 22, 1906.
[21] *South Dakota State Forum* (Sioux Falls, SD), June 22, 1906.
[22] *Sioux Falls Journal*, June 22,1906. The City Auditorium was located at the northeast corner of 9th Street and Dakota Avenue. It was built in 1899 to house the convention of the National Butter Makers Association. W. A. Dow was the architect. See R.E. Bragstad, *Sioux Falls in Retrospect* (Sioux Falls, 1967), 57.
[23] Ibid.
[24] *Minneapolis Journal*, June 20, 1906.
[25] *Yankton Press and Dakotan*, June 21, 1906; *Daily Argus-Leader*, June 20, 1906.
[26] *Sioux Falls Daily Press*, June 21, 1906.
[27] *Minneapolis Journal*, June 20, 1906.
[28] *South Dakota State Forum*, June 22, 1906.
[29] *Mitchell Daily Republican*, June 19, 1906.
[30] *Minneapolis Journal*, June 20, 1906.
[31] *Yankton Press and Dakotan*, June 21, 1906; *Daily Argus-Leader*, June 20, 1906.
[32] *Sioux Falls Daily Press*, June 21, 1906.
[33] *South Dakota State Forum*, June 22, 1906.
[34] *The Minneapolis Journal*, June 20, 1906.
[35] *Yankton Press and Dakotan*, June 21, 1906; *Daily Argus-Leader*, June 20, 1906.
[36] *State of South Dakota vs. Emma Kaufmann*, Case No. 11106, 2nd Circuit, Minnehaha County, Affidavit of Frank R. Aikens.
[37] *Minneapolis Journal*, June 20, 1906.
[38] *Sioux Falls Journal*, June 22, 1906.
[39] *State of South Dakota vs. Emma Kaufmann*, Case No. 11106, 2nd Circuit, Minnehaha County, Affidavit of Frank R. Aikens.
[40] *Yankton Press and Dakotan*, June 21, 1906; *Daily Argus-Leader*, June 20, 1906.
[41] *Sioux Falls Daily Press*, June 21, 1906.
[42] Ibid., June 26, 1906.
[43] *Rock Island Argus* (Rock Island, IL), June 21, 1906.
[44] *Parkston Advance*, June 22, 1906.
[45] *Daily Argus-Leader*, October 21, 1901.
[46] *Yankton Press and Dakotan*, June 21, 1906; *Daily Argus-Leader*, June 20, 1906; *Mitchell Daily Republic*, June 21, 1906.
[47] *Daily Argus-Leader*, June 22, 1906.

Chapter 5

[1] *Daily Argus-Leader*, June 23, 1906.

[2] *Weekly Cataract*, August 21, 1906.
[3] Ibid.
[4] *Soo Critic*, June 28, 1906.
[5] *Minneapolis Journal*, June 23, 1906.
[6] *Sioux Falls Daily Press*, June 22, 1906.
[7] *Yankton Press and Dakotan*, June 20, 1906.
[8] *Daily Argus-Leader*, June 22, 1906.
[9] *Sioux City Journal*, June 22, 1906.
[10] *Daily Argus-Leader*, June 21, 1906.
[11] *Mitchell Daily Republic*, June 23, 1906.
[12] *Sioux Falls Daily Press*, June 22, 1906.
[13] *Sioux City Journal*, June 25, 1906.
[14] *Sioux Falls Daily Press*, June 23, 1906.
[15] *Daily Argus-Leader*, June 27, 1906.
[16] Ibid, June 25, 1906.
[17] *Yankton Press and Dakotan*, June 26, 1906.
[18] *Pioneer Express* (Pembina, ND), June 29, 1906.
[19] *Yankton Press and Dakotan*, June 26, 1906.
[20] *Parkston Advance*, June 29, 1906.
[21] *Soo Critic*, June 28, 1906.
[22] Ibid, July 5, 1906.
[23] *San Francisco Call*, June 14, 1906.
[24] *Sioux Falls Journal*, July 6, 1906.
[25] *Minneapolis Journal*, June 26, 1906.
[26] *Sioux City Journal*, June 23, 1906.
[27] *Daily Argus-Leader*, July 5, 1906.
[28] *Soo Critic*, July 12, 1906.
[29] *Yankton Press and Dakotan*, July 10, 1906.
[30] *Sioux Falls Daily Press*, July 18, 1906.
[31] *Daily Argus-Leader*, July 5, 1906.
[32] *Dakota Farmer's Leader* (Canton, SD), July 6, 1906.
[33] *Parkston Advance*, July 6, 1906; *The Sioux City Journal*, June 8, 1907. A photograph of the handsome gravestone was published in the *Journal*. The large marker was replaced by one much smaller, but the Sacred Heart Church in Parkston has no record of the replacement.
[34] *Parkston Advance*, July 27, 1906.
[35] *Sioux Falls Journal*, July 6, 1906.
[36] *Soo Critic*, July, 19, 1906.
[37] Ibid, July 26, 1906.
[38] *Daily Argus-Leader*, July 11, 1906.
[39] *Milwaukee Sentinel* in the *Sioux Falls Daily Press*, July 19, 1906.
[40] *Soo Critic*, August 16, 1906.
[41] Ibid., September 27, 1906.
[42] *Weekly Cataract*, October 2, 1906.
[43] Ibid.
[44] *Minneapolis Journal*, October 8, 1906.

[45] *State of South Dakota vs. Emma Kaufmann*, Case No. 1106, 2nd Circuit, Minnehaha County, Affidavit of David Ricker.
[46] *Soo Critic*, September 27, 1906.
[47] *Sioux Falls Journal*, November 21, 1913.
[48] *Soo Critic*, October 4, 1906.

Chapter 6

[1] Frederick Lewis Allen, *The Big Change: America Transforms Itself 1900-1950* (New York: Harper & Row, 1952), 107.
[2] *Daily Argus-Leader*, September 15 and 21, 1906.
[3] Ibid., November 23, 1906.
[4] *Sioux Falls Journal*, January 31, 1908.
[5] *Parkston Advance*, September 28, 1906.
[6] Ibid., October 12, 1906.
[7] *Yankton Press and Dakotan*, November 13, 1906.
[8] *Daily Argus-Leader*, November 26, 1906.
[9] *Parkston Advance*, November 30, 1906.
[10] *Daily Argus-Leader*, November 26, 1906.
[11] Ibid., November 28, 1906.
[12] *Soo Critic*, November 29, 1906.
[13] Bailey, 511.
[14] Robinson, 164.
[15] *Daily Argus-Leader*, November 20, 1906.
[16] Ibid., July 6, 1926.
[17] Ibid., December 1, 1906.
[18] *Sioux Falls Journal*, December 14, 1906.
[19] *Daily Argus-Leader*, December 1, 1906.
[20] *Sioux Falls Journal*, December 7, 1906.
[21] Ibid., December 7, 1906.
[22] *Parkston Advance*, November 16, 1906.
[23] *Sioux Falls Journal*, December 14, 1906.
[24] *Daily Argus-Leader*, December 1, 1906.
[25] *American Israelite* (Cincinnati, OH) December 27, 1906.
[26] *Soo Critic*, December 6, 1906.
[27] *Parkston Advance*, December 7, 1906.
[28] *Daily Argus-Leader*, December 10, 1906.
[29] *South Dakota State Forum*, December 14, 1906.
[30] *Nolle prosequi* is a legal term that means the prosecution will no further prosecute the case.
[31] *Soo Critic*, December 14, 1906.
[32] Ibid.
[33] *Daily Argus-Leader*, December 18, 1906.
[34] *Soo Critic*, December 20, 1906.
[35] *Sioux Falls Journal*, December 21, 1906.
[36] *South Dakota State Forum*, December 21, 1906.

[37] *Soo Critic*, January 3, 1907.
[38] Ibid., December 20, 1906.
[39] Ibid., January 3, 1907.
[40] *Parkston Advance*, December 21, 1906.
[41] *Omaha Daily Bee*, January 1, 1907.
[42] *Daily Argus-Leader*, January 1, 1907.
[43] *Soo Critic*, February 14, 1907.
[44] *Parkston Advance*, January 4, 1907.
[45] *Daily Argus-Leader*, January 1, 1907.
[46] Ibid., January 24, 1907.
[47] *Soo Critic*, June 4, 1908.

Chapter 7

[1] *Soo Critic*, April 18, 1907.
[2] Ibid., January 16, 1908.
[3] Lynwood E. Oyos, "George W. Egan: The Demagogue Who Would Be Governor," *South Dakota History*, 36, no. 3 (Fall 2006), 293.
[4] *Soo Critic*, March 7, 1907.
[5] *Saturday News* (Watertown, SD), October 12, 1911.
[6] Andy Van Zanten, *George W. Egan: A Short Biography* (Sioux Falls, SD: Siouxland Heritage Museums, 2002), 1.
[7] *Saturday News* (Watertown, SD), October 12, 1911.
[8] Oyos, 293.
[9] *Soo Critic*, March 7, 1907.
[10] Ibid.
[11] *Sioux Falls Daily Press*, October 23, 1908.
[12] *Daily Argus-Leader*, February 27, 1907.
[13] Ibid., March 7, 1907.
[14] Ibid., February 18, 1907.
[15] *Soo Critic*, May 9, 1907.
[16] *Daily Argus-Leader*, February 6, 1907.
[17] *Soo Critic*, May 9, 1907.
[18] *Sioux Falls Daily Press*, June 11, 1909.
[19] *Daily Argus-Leader*, May 15, 1907.
[20] *Soo Critic*, May 16, 1906.
[21] *Evening Times* (Grand Forks, ND), May 18, 1907.
[22] *Parkston Advance*, May 17, 1907.
[23] *Daily Argus-Leader*, January 10, 1907
[24] Ibid., May 20, 1907.
[25] *Yankton Press and Dakotan*, May 21, 1907.
[26] *Daily Argus-Leader*, May 21, 1907.
[27] *Flandreau Herald*, May 29, 1907.
[28] *Soo Critic*, May 23, 1907.
[29] *Sioux Falls Journal*, June 14, 1907.
[30] *Sioux Falls Daily Press* in *The Parkston Advance*, June 15, 1908.

[31] *Soo Critic*, May 30, 1907.
[32] *Turner County Herald* (Hurley, SD), June 6, 1907.
[33] *Yankton Press and Dakotan*, June 1, 1907.
[34] *Sioux City Journal*, June 1, 1907.
[35] *Parkston Advance*, May 24, 1907.
[36] *Daily Argus-Leader*, June 4, 1907.
[37] Ibid., June 5, 1907.
[38] Ibid.

Chapter 8

[1] *Sioux Falls Journal*, May 17, 1907.
[2] Ibid., May 24, 1907.
[3] Thomas Egan's step-daughter made a death-bed confession to the murder.
[4] *Parkston Advance*, June 14, 1907.
[5] *Flandreau Herald*, June 19, 1907.
[6] *Daily Argus-Leader*, June 8, 1907.
[7] Ibid., June 7, 1907.
[8] *Bismarck Daily Tribune*, June 11, 1907.
[9] *Cairo Bulletin* (Cairo, IL), June 5, 1907.
[10] *Marlboro Democrat* (Bennettsville, SC), July 26, 1907.
[11] *Soo Critic*, June 6, 1907.
[12] *Yankton Press and Dakotan*, June 4, 1907.
[13] Ibid., June 4, 1907.
[14] *Soo Critic*, June 6, 1907.
[15] *Flandreau Herald*, June 12, 1907.
[16] *Daily Argus-Leader*, June 5, 1907.
[17] *Sioux Falls Journal*, May 24, 1907.
[18] *Daily Argus-Leader*, June 8, 1907.
[19] Ibid., June 13, 1907.
[20] *Sioux Falls Daily Press*, June 4, 1907.
[21] Ibid., June 5, 1907.
[22] *Yankton Press and Dakotan*, June 5, 1907.
[23] *Daily Argus-Leader*, June 5, 1907.
[24] Ibid., June 6, 1907. The St. Vincent Hotel was built in 1897 at a cost of $11,000.
[25] *Yankton Press and Dakotan*, June 10, 1907.
[26] *Weekly Cataract*, June 19, 1906.
[27] "A Century of Liquor Legislation," *South Dakota Historical Collections*, Pierre, SD, 12 (1924): 290.
[28] George Martin Smith, ed., *South Dakota: Its History and Its People,* Vol. III (Chicago: S. J. Clarke Publishing Co., 1915), 754.
[29] *Sioux Falls Daily Press*, June 9, 1907.
[30] *Daily Argus-Leader*, June 10, 1907.
[31] *Daily Argus-Leader*, June 6, 1907; *Flandreau Herald*, June 12, 1907.
[32] *Sioux City Journal*, June 8, 1907.
[33] *Yankton Press and Dakotan*, June 8, 1907.

[34] *Sioux City Journal*, June 6, 1907.
[35] Ibid., June 5, 1907.
[36] *Daily Argus-Leader*, June 7, 1907.
[37] *Sioux Falls Journal*, June 7, 1907.
[38] *Daily Argus-Leader*, June 8, 1907.
[39] Ibid.
[40] *Flandreau Herald*, June 19, 1907.
[41] Gold Dust was a popular household cleaning product.
[42] *Daily Argus-Leader*, June 10, 1907.
[43] *Sioux Falls Daily Press*, June 9, 1907.
[44] *Sioux City Journal*, June 9, 1907.
[45] *Daily Argus-Leader*, June 10, 1907.
[46] *Sioux City Journal*, June 9, 1907.
[47] *Daily Argus-Leader*, June 10, 1907.
[48] *Sioux Falls Daily Press*, June 11, 1907.
[49] *Daily Argus-Leader*, June 10, 1907.
[50] *Parkston Advance*, June 14, 1907.
[51] *Sioux Falls Daily Press*, June 11, 1907.
[52] *Parkston Advance*, June 14, 1907.
[53] *Forest City Press* (Forest City, SD), June 20, 1907.
[54] *Daily Argus-Leader*, June 11, 1907.
[55] *Sioux Falls Daily Press*, June 12, 1907.
[56] Ibid., June 13, 1907.
[57] "Turpentine Uses, Benefits and Dosage," www.drugs.com/npp/turpentine.html#ref8, consulted 6/14/15.
[58] *Weekly Cataract*, June 19, 1906.
[59] *Daily Argus-Leader*, June 12, 1907.
[60] Ibid.
[61] *Yankton Press and Dakotan*, June 13, 1907.
[62] *Daily Argus-Leader*, June 12, 1907.
[63] Ibid.
[64] Ibid.
[65] *Sioux Falls Daily Press*, June 12, 1907.
[66] *Soo Critic*, June 13, 1907.
[67] *Daily Argus-Leader*, June 12, 1907.
[68] *Sioux Falls Daily Press*, June 13, 1907.
[69] Ibid.
[70] Ibid., June 11, 1907.
[71] *Daily Argus-Leader*, June 12, 1907.
[72] *Sioux Falls Daily Press*, June 13, 1907.
[73] *Soo Critic*, June 13, 1907.
[74] *Daily Argus-Leader*, June 12, 1907.
[75] Ibid., June 13, 1907.

Chapter 9

[1] *Sioux Falls Daily Press*, June 13, 1907.
[2] *Evening Star* (Washington, DC), June 14, 1907.
[3] *Daily Argus-Leader*, June 13, 1907.
[4] *Yankton Press and Dakotan*, June 14, 1907.
[5] *Daily Argus-Leader*, June 13, 1907.
[6] *Yankton Press and Dakotan*, June 19, 1906.
[7] www.mayoclinic.org/diseases-conditions/diabetes, consulted on 3/21/15.
[8] Edwin A. M. Gale, "The Rise of Childhood Type 1 Diabetes in the 20th Century," www.diabetes.diabetesjournal.org, December 2002, consulted on 3/21/15.
[9] *Daily Argus-Leader*, June 13, 1907.
[10] Ibid.
[11] *Parkston Advance*, June 21, 1907.
[12] *Soo Critic*, June 27, 1907.
[13] Ibid., June 13, 1907.
[14] *Sioux City Journal*, June 16, 1907.
[15] *Daily Argus-Leader*, June 14, 1907.
[16] Ibid., June 15, 1907.
[17] *Sioux City Journal*, June 14, 1907.
[18] *Sioux Falls Daily Press*, June 18, 1907.
[19] *Yankton Press and Dakotan*, October 16, 1907.
[20] *Daily Argus-Leader*, June 17, 1907.
[21] Ibid.
[22] *Sioux Falls Daily Press*, June 18, 1907.
[23] Ibid., June 7, 1907.
[24] *Daily Argus-Leader*, June 17, 1907.
[25] *American Republic* (Sioux Falls, SD), July 9, 1909.
[26] *Daily Argus-Leader*, June 17, 1907.
[27] *American Republic*, February 29, 1909.
[28] *Sioux Falls Daily Press*, June 18, 1907.
[29] *Sioux Falls Journal*, June 21, 1907.
[30] *Daily Argus-Leader*, June 17, 1907.

Chapter 10

[1] *Daily Argus-Leader*, June 17, 1907.
[2] *Parkston Advance*, June 21, 1907.
[3] *Daily Argus-Leader*, June 17, 1907.
[4] *Bismarck Daily Tribune*, June 19, 1907.
[5] *Sioux Falls Daily Press*, June 18, 1907; Smith, 754.
[6] Krust is also spelled "Kraust" and "Krause."
[7] *Daily Argus-Leader*, June 18, 1907.
[8] *Sioux City Journal*, June 19, 1907.
[9] *Daily Argus-Leader*, June 18, 1907.
[10] *Semi-Weekly Dakota Herald* (Yankton, SD), June 21, 1907.
[11] *Daily Argus-Leader*, June 18, 1907.

[12] Ibid., June 18, 1907.
[13] *Sioux Falls Daily Press*, June 19, 1907.
[14] *Daily Argus-Leader*, June 18, 1907.
[15] Ibid., June 19, 1907.
[16] *Sioux Falls Daily Press*, June 19, 1907.
[17] *Soo Critic*, June 20, 1907.
[18] *Daily Argus-Leader*, June 18, 1907.
[19] *Sioux Falls Daily Press*, June 22, 1907.
[20] Gerry Wilkinson, "Broadcast Pioneers of Philadelphia," Official Archives of the Broadcast Pioneers of Philadelphia, www.broadcastpioneers.com, consulted 2/26/16.
[21] *Daily Argus-Leader*, June 19, 1907.
[22] Ibid., June 20, 1907.
[23] Ibid., June 19, 1907.
[24] *Yankton Press and Dakotan*, June 20, 1907.
[25] *Daily Argus-Leader*, June 19, 1907.
[26] Ibid., June 20, 1907.
[27] *Yankton Press and Dakotan*, June 20, 1907.
[28] *Daily Argus-Leader*, June 20, 1907.
[29] *Soo Critic*, June 20, 1907.
[30] *Daily Argus-Leader*, June 20, 1907.
[31] *Sioux Falls Daily Press*, June 21, 1907.
[32] *Daily Argus-Leader*, June 20, 1907.
[33] *Sioux Falls Daily Press*, June 21, 1907.
[34] *Daily Argus-Leader*, June 20, 1907.
[35] *Yankton Press and Dakotan*, June 21, 1907.
[36] *Flandreau Herald*, June 26, 1907.
[37] *Daily Argus-Leader*, June 20, 1907.
[38] Ibid.
[39] *Sioux Falls Journal*, June 28, 1907.
[40] *Parkston Advance*, June 28, 1907.
[41] *Daily Argus-Leader*, June 21, 1907.
[42] *Sioux Falls Daily Press*, June 20 and 22, 1907.
[43] *Daily Argus-Leader*, June 21, 1907.
[44] *Flandreau Herald*, June 26, 1907.
[45] *Sioux Falls Daily Press*, June 21, 1907.

Chapter 11

[1] *Parkston Advance*, June 21, 1907.
[2] *Forest City Press* (Forest City, SD), July 4, 1907.
[3] *Sioux Falls Daily Press*, June 22, 1907.
[4] *Daily Argus-Leader*, June 21, 1907.
[5] *Manning Times* (Clarendon County, SC), July 24, 1907.
[6] *Daily Argus-Leader*, July 1, 1907.
[7] *Soo Critic*, August 15 & 29, 1907.

[8] *South Dakota State Forum*, August 9, 1907.
[9] *Sioux Falls Journal*, August 30, 1907.
[10] *Daily Argus-Leader*, June 22, 1907.
[11] Ibid., June 24, 1907.
[12] *Soo Critic*, August 1, 1907.
[13] Ibid.
[14] *Sioux Falls Journal*, October 4, 1907.
[15] Bailey, 831.
[16] *Daily Argus-Leader*, September 30, 1907.
[17] *Sioux Falls Journal*, October 4, 1907.
[18] Obituary of Julia Ann O'Grady in an unnamed newspaper, www.findagrave.com, consulted 8/18/17.
[19] Bailey, 38.
[20] Ibid., 921.
[21] *South Dakota State Forum* (Sioux Falls, SD), October 4, 1907.
[22] *Sioux Falls Journal*, October 4, 1907.
[23] *Soo Critic*, October 3, 1907.
[24] *Forest City Press* (Forest City, SD), October 10, 1907.
[25] *Sodbusters:Tales of Southeastern South Dakota*, American Guide Series (Mitchell, SD: South Dakota Writer's League/WPA, 1938), 24.
[26] *Flandreau Herald*, September 25, 1907.
[27] *Soo Critic*, October 3, 1907.
[28] *Sioux Falls Journal*, October 11 and December 23, 1907.
[29] *Sioux Falls Daily Press*, October 13, 1907.
[30] Ibid., October 14, 1907.
[31] *Soo Critic*, October 17, 1907.
[32] *Yankton Press and Dakotan*, October 16, 1907.
[33] *Daily Argus-Leader*, October 15, 1907.
[34] *Yankton Press and Dakotan*, October 16, 1907.
[35] *Sioux Falls Journal*, October 18, 1907.
[36] *Daily Argus-Leader*, October 15, 1907.
[37] Ibid., October 16, 1907.
[38] *Sioux Falls Daily Press*, October 17, 1907.
[39] *Daily Argus-Leader*, October 17, 1907.
[40] *Sioux Falls Daily Press*, October 17, 1907.
[41] *Sioux Falls Journal*, October 18, 1907.
[42] *Sioux Falls Daily Press*, October 20, 1907.
[43] *Yankton Press and Dakotan*, October 21, 1907.

Chapter 12

[1] *Sioux Falls Journal*, October 25, 1907.
[2] *Soo Critic*, October 24, 1907.
[3] *Daily Argus-Leader*, November 19, 1907.
[4] *South Dakota State Forum*, October 25, 1907.
[5] *Sioux Falls Journal*, October 25, 1907.

[6] Ibid., November 8, 1907.
[7] *Daily Argus-Leader*, November 12, 1907.
[8] Ibid., November 14, 1907.
[9] Ibid., November 16, 1907.
[10] *Soo Critic*, December 5, 1907.
[11] *Sioux Falls Journal*, December 27, 1907.
[12] *Daily Argus-Leader*, December 20, 1907.
[13] *Soo Critic*, December 19, 1907.
[14] *Sisseton Weekly Standard*, January 24, 1908.
[15] *Daily Argus-Leader*, January 14, 1907.
[16] *Soo Critic*, January 16, 1908.
[17] *Daily Argus-Leader*, January 15, 1908.
[18] *Soo Critic*, February 20, 1908.
[19] *Sioux Falls Journal*, April 3, 1908.
[20] *Dakota Farmer's Leader* (Canton, SD), April 10, 1908.
[21] *Daily Argus-Leader*, March 30, 1908.
[22] Ibid., May 23, 1908.
[23] *South Dakota State Forum*, May 29, 1908.
[24] *Soo Critic*, April 16, 1908.
[25] Ibid., April 30, 1908.
[26] *Yankton Press and Dakotan*, May 9, 1908.
[27] *South Dakota State Forum* (Sioux Falls, SD), January 24, 1908.
[28] O.W. Coursey, *Biography of Senator Kittredge* (Mitchell, SD: Educator's Supply Co., 1915), 202.
[29] *Sioux Falls Journal*, June 12, 1908.
[30] Herbert S. Schell, *History of South Dakota (*Lincoln: University of Nebraska Press, 1961), 262.
[31] Ibid., June 13, 1908.
[32] *South Dakota State Forum*, July 3, 1908.
[33] *Soo Critic*, July 30, 1908.
[34] *Sioux Falls Journal*, August 14, 1908.
[35] *The Daily Argus-Leader*, August 21, 1908.
[36] *Sioux Falls Daily Press*, October 11, 1908.
[37] Ibid., October 15 and 16, 1908.
[38] *Daily Argus-Leader*, October 19, 1908.
[39] Ibid., November 7, 1908. Julia Ann O'Grady died in an Oklahoma insane asylum on November 6, 1908.
[40] Ibid., October 23, 1908.
[41] Ibid., September 23, 1908.
[42] Ibid., September 10 and October 20, 1908.
[43] *Sioux Falls Daily Press*, November 4, 5, 6, and 10, 1908.
[44] *State vs. Kaufmann*, 118 Northwestern Reporter 337, et seq.

Chapter 13

[1] *Daily Argus-Leader*, November 20, 1908.

[2] *Soo Critic*, November 19, 1908.
[3] *Sioux Falls Daily Press*, November 20, 1908.
[4] Ibid., April 22, 1909.
[5] Ibid., December 13, 1908.
[6] Ibid., December 27, 1908.
[7] Ibid., November 10, 1908.
[8] *American Republic* (Sioux Falls, SD), January 1, 1909.
[9] Ibid.
[10] *Parkston Advance*, February 12, 1909.
[11] *Sioux Falls Daily Press*, March 25, 1909.
[12] *Daily Argus-Leader* in *The American Republic*, February 12, 1909.
[13] *American Republic*, March 12, 1909.
[14] *Sioux Falls Daily Press*, March 27, 1909.
[15] Ibid., March 20, 1909.
[16] Ibid., May 9, 1909.
[17] *Miller Gazette* in *The American Republic*, January 8, 1909.
[18] *American Republic*, June 4, 1909.
[19] *Norfolk Weekly News-Journal* (Norfolk, NE), June 4, 1909.
[20] *Sioux Falls Daily Press*, June 3, 1909.
[21] *American Republic*, January 1, 1909.
[22] *Soo Critic*, June 10, 1909.
[23] *Daily Argus-Leader*, June 3, 1909.
[24] *Sioux Falls Daily Press*, June 3, 1909.
[25] Ibid., June 4, 1909.
[26] Ibid., June 5, 1909.
[27] *Daily Argus-Leader*, May 31, 1909.
[28] *Spokane Press*, June 5, 1909.
[29] *Sioux Falls Daily Press*, June 6, 1909.

Chapter 14

[1] *Sioux Falls Daily Press*, June 8, 1909.
[2] *Daily Argus-Leader*, June 8, 1909.
[3] Ibid., June 8, 1909.
[4] *Sioux Falls Daily Press*, June 8, 1909.
[5] Ibid., June 9, 1909.
[6] *Daily Argus-Leader*, June 10, 1909.
[7] *Sioux Falls Daily Press*, June 9, 1909.
[8] Ibid., June 10, 1909.
[9] *Daily Argus-Leader*, June 10, 1909.
[10] Ibid.
[11] *Sioux Falls Daily Press*, June 9, 1909.
[12] Ibid., June 10, 1909.
[13] Ibid., June 11, 1909.
[14] *Daily Argus-Leader*, June 11, 1909.
[15] *Sioux Falls Daily Press*, June 11, 1909.

[16] *Sioux Falls Daily Press*, June 11, 1909; *Daily Argus-Leader*, June 10, 1909.
[17] *Daily Argus-Leader*, June 11, 1909.
[18] *Sioux Falls Daily Press*, June 10, 1909.
[19] Ibid., June 11, 1909.
[20] *Daily Argus-Leader*, June 12, 1909.
[21] *Sioux Falls Daily Press*, June 11, 1909.
[22] *American Republic*, June 11, 1909.
[23] *Sioux Falls Daily Press*, June 12, 1909.
[24] *Daily Argus-Leader*, June 12, 1909.
[25] *Sioux Falls Daily Press*, June 13, 1909.
[26] *Daily Argus-Leader*, June 15, 1909.
[27] *Sioux Falls Daily Press*, June 15, 1909.
[28] Ibid., June 16, 1909.
[29] *Daily Argus-Leader*, June 15, 1909.
[30] *Soo Critic*, June 24, 1909.
[31] *Daily Argus-Leader*, June 16, 1909.
[32] *Soo Critic*, June 24, 1909.
[33] *Norfolk Weekly News-Journal*, June 25, 1909.
[34] *Sioux Falls Daily Press*, June 18, 1909.
[35] *Soo Critic*, June 24, 1909.
[36] Ibid., June 19, 1909.
[37] *Soo Critic*, June 17, 1909.
[38] *Daily Argus-Leader*, June 18, 1909.
[39] *South Dakota State Forum* (Sioux Falls, SD), January 3, 1908.
[40] Jonathan H. Pincus, *Base Instincts: What Makes Killers Kill?* (New York and London: W. W. Norton, 2001), 191.

Chapter 15

[1] *Soo Critic*, July 1, 1909.
[2] *Sioux Falls Daily Press* in the *Soo Critic*, July 1, 1909.
[3] *Parkston Advance*, June 25, 1909.
[4] *Mitchell Clarion* (Mitchell, SD) in the *Soo Critic*, July 1, 1909.
[5] *Arlington Sun* (Arlington, SD) in the *Soo Critic*, July 1, 1909.
[6] *Plankinton Herald* (Plankinton, SD) in the *Soo Critic*, July 1, 1909.
[7] *Lyman County Democrat* (Lyman County, SD) in the *Soo Critic*, July 1, 1909.
[8] *Fort Pierre Fair Play* (Fort Pierre, SD) in the *Soo Critic*, July 1, 1909.
[9] *Canton Leader* (Canton, SD) in the *American Republic*, June 25, 1909.
[10] *Deadwood Lantern*, (Deadwood, SD) in the *American Republic*, June 25, 1909.
[11] *Herrick Press* (Herrick, SD) in the *American Republic*, July 2, 1909.
[12] *Caucasian* (Clinton, NC), July 1, 1909.
[13] *Plymouth Tribune* (Plymouth, IN), June 24, 1909.
[14] *American Republic*, June 18, 1909.
[15] Ibid., June 25, 1909.
[16] Ibid.
[17] *Soo Critic*, June 24, 1909.

[18] *Sioux Falls Daily Press*, July 3, 1909.
[19] *American Republic*, May 13, 1910.
[20] *Soo Critic*, June 24, 1909.
[21] *American Republic*, July 16, 1909.
[22] Ibid., July 2, 1909.
[23] Ibid., July 23, 1909.
[24] *Soo Critic*, August 12, 1909.
[25] Ibid., June 24, 1909.
[26] *Norfolk Weekly News-Journal* (Norfolk, NE), January 14, 1910.
[27] Ibid., May 20, 1910.
[28] *American Republic*, January 14, 1910.
[29] *Sioux Falls Daily Press*, April 19, 1911.
[30] *Daily Argus-Leader*, April 18, 1911.
[31] *Sioux Falls Dispatch* (successor to the *Soo Critic)*, April 20, 1911.
[32] *Daily Argus-Leader*, April 20 and 21, 1911.
[33] *Sioux Falls Dispatch*, April 20, 1911.
[34] *Daily Argus-Leader*, November 17, 1913; *Sioux Falls Daily Press*, November 18, 1913.
[35] *Sioux Falls Journal*, November 21, 1913.
[36] *Yankton Press and Dakotan*, November 18, 1913.
[37] *Daily Argus-Leader*, November 19, 1913; *South Dakota State Forum*, November 21, 1913; *Sioux Falls Daily Press*, November 19, 1913.
[38] *Weekly Times-Record* (Valley City, ND), November 20, 1913.

Bibliography

Books

Allen, Frederick Lewis. *The Big Change, America Transforms Itself 1900-1950*. New York: Harper & Row, 1952.

Argus-Leader South Dakota 99. Sioux Falls, SD: Ex Machina Publishing Co., 1989.

Bailey, Dana R. *History of Minnehaha County, South Dakota*. Sioux Falls, SD: Brown & Saenger, 1899.

Baron-Cohen, Simon. *The Science of Evil: On Empathy and the Origins of Cruelty*. New York: Basic Books, 2011.

Bragstad, R. E. *Sioux Falls in Retrospect*, 1967.

Coursey, O. W. *Biography of Senator Kittredge.* Mitchell, SD: Educator's Supply Co., 1915.

Diagnostic and Statistical Manual of Mental Disorders. 4th Edition. Text Revision. DSM-IV-TR. Arlington, VA: American Psychiatric Association, 2000.

Fanebust, Wayne. *Echoes of November: The Life and Times of Senator R. F. Pettigrew of South Dakota.* Freeman, SD: Pine Hill Press, 1997.

Goleman, Daniel. *Emotional Intelligence: Why It Can Matter More Than IQ*. Bantam Books, 1997.

Holbrook, Stewart H. *The Golden Age of Quackery*. New York: Collier Books, 1962.
Moody County Historical Society. *History of Moody County South Dakota.* Dallas, TX: Taylor Publishing Company, n.d.
Pincus, Jonathan H. *Base Instincts: What Makes Killers Kill?* New York and London: W. W. Norton, 2001.
Robinson, Doane. *History of South Dakota*. Vol. III. Chicago and New York: American Historical Society, 1930.
Schell, Herbert S. *History of South Dakota*. Lincoln: University of Nebraska Press, 1961.
Smith, Charles A. *A Comprehensive History of Minnehaha County, South Dakota.* Mitchell, SD: Educator's Supply Co., 1949.
Smith, George Martin, ed. *South Dakota: Its History and Its People.* Vol. III. Chicago: S. J. Clarke Publishing Co., 1915.
Sioux Falls City Directory. Sioux Falls, SD: Dan Scott, compiler and publisher, 1885.

Articles and Interviews

"A Century of Liquor Legislation," *South Dakota Historical Collections.* Pierre, SD, 12 (1924): 290.
"Diabetes." www.mayoclinic.org/diseases-conditions/diabetes.
Dow, W. L. Interview. I.D. Weeks Library, University of South Dakota, July 11, 1975.
Gale, Edwin A. M. "The Rise of Childhood Type 1 Diabetes in the 20th Century," www.diabetes.diabetesjournal.org. December 2002.
Hosen, Freda. Author Interview. Sioux Falls, SD, August 7, 2015.
Hosen, Freda. "The Trials and Tribulations of Emma Kaufmann." Sioux Falls, SD: Center for Western Studies, Augustana University, 1974. [unpublished]
"O'Grady, Julia Ann." Obituary. www.findagave.com.
Oyos, Lynwood E. "George W. Egan: The Demagogue Who Would Be Governor." *South Dakota History*, 36, no. 3 (Fall 2006): 292-317.
Sodbusters: Tales of Southeastern South Dakota. American Guide Series. Mitchell, SD: South Dakota Writer's League/WPA, 1938.
"Turpentine Uses, Benefits and Dosage," www.drugs.com/npp/turpentine.html#ref8.
Twelfth Census of the United States, Sioux Falls, SD, 1900, Microfilm.
Van Zanten, Andy. "George W. Egan: A Short Biography." Sioux Falls, SD: Siouxland Heritage Museums, 2002.
Wilkinson, Gerry. "Broadcast Pioneers of Philadelphia," Official Archives of the Broadcast Pioneers of Philadelphia, www.broadcastpioneers.com, consulted 2/26/16.

Newspapers

American Israelite (Cincinnati, OH)
American Republic (Sioux Falls, SD)

[Sioux Falls] *Daily Argus-Leader* (Sioux Falls, SD)
Arlington Sun (Arlington, SD)
Bismarck Daily Tribune (Bismarck, ND)
Cairo Bulletin (Cairo, IL)
Canton Leader (Canton, SD)
Caucasian (Clinton, NC)
Dakota Farmer's Leader (Canton, SD)
Deadwood Lantern (Deadwood, SD)
Evening Argus-Leader (Sioux Falls, SD)
Evening Star (Washington, DC)
Evening Times (Grand Forks, ND)
Flandreau Herald (Flandreau, SD)
Forest City Press (Forest City, SD)
Fort Mill Times (Fort Mill, SC)
Fort Pierre Fair Play (Fort Pierre, SD)
Lyman County Democrat (SD)
Manning Times (Clarendon County, SC)
Marlboro Democrat (Bennettsville, SC)
Miller Gazette (Miller, SD)
Milwaukee Sentinel
Minneapolis Journal
Mitchell Clarion (Mitchell, SD)
Mitchell Daily Republican (Mitchell, SD)
Norfolk Weekly News-Journal (Norfolk, NE)
Omaha Daily Bee
Parkston Advance (Parkston, SD)
Pioneer Express (Pembina, ND)
Plankinton Herald (Plankinton, SD)
Plymouth Tribune (Plymouth, IN)
Rock Island Argus (Rock Island, IL)
San Francisco Call
Saturday News (Watertown, SD)
Semi-Weekly Dakota Herald (Yankton, SD)
Sioux City Journal (Sioux City, IA)
Sioux Falls Daily Press (Sioux Falls, SD)
Sioux Falls Dispatch (Sioux Falls, SD)
Sioux Falls Journal (Sioux Falls, SD)
Sisseton Weekly Standard (Sisseton, SD)
Soo Critic (Sioux Falls, SD)

South Dakota State Forum (Sioux Falls, SD)
Spokane Press
Turner County Herald (Hurley, SD)
Weekly Cataract (Sioux Falls, SD)
Weekly Times-Record (Valley City, ND)
Yankton Press and Dakotan (Yankton, SD)

Legal

State of South Dakota v. Emma Kaufmann, Case No. 11106, 2nd Circuit, Minnehaha County.
State vs. Kaufmann, 118 Northwestern Reporter 337, et seq.

Index

P

Q

R

S

T

U

W

Y

Z